REVENGE TRAGEDY AND THE DRAMA OF COMMEMORATION IN REFORMING ENGLAND

Considering major works by Kyd, Shakespeare, Middleton and Webster among others, this book transforms current understanding of early modern revenge tragedy. Examining the genre in light of historical revisions to England's Reformations, and with appropriate regard to the social history of the dead, it shows revenge tragedy is not an anti-Catholic and Reformist genre, but one rooted in, and in dialogue with, traditional Catholic culture. Arguing its tragedies are bound to the age's funerary performances, it provides a new view of the contemporary theatre and especially its role in the religious upheavals of the period.

Thomas Rist, PhD, is Lecturer in English at the University of Aberdeen in Scotland. He has published widely on Renaissance drama and is the author of one previous book: *Shakespeare's Romances and the Politics of Counter-Reformation* (1999).

General Editor's Preface
Helen Ostovich, McMaster University

Performance assumes a string of creative, analytical, and collaborative acts that, in defiance of theatrical ephemerality, live on through records, manuscripts, and printed books. The monographs and essay collections in this series offer original research which addresses theatre histories and performance histories in the context of the sixteenth and seventeenth century life. Of especial interest are studies in which women's activities are a central feature of discussion as financial or technical supporters (patrons, musicians, dancers, seamstresses, wigmakers, or 'gatherers'), if not authors or performers per se. Welcome too are critiques of early modern drama that not only take into account the production values of the plays, but also speculate on how intellectual advances or popular culture affect the theatre.

The series logo, selected by my colleague Mary V. Silcox, derives from Thomas Combe's duodecimo volume, *The Theater of Fine Devices* (London, 1592), Emblem VI, sig. B. The emblem of four masks has a verse which makes claims for the increasing complexity of early modern experience, a complexity that makes interpretation difficult. Hence the corresponding perhaps uneasy rise in sophistication:

> Masks will be more hereafter in request,
> And grow more deare than they did heretofore.

No longer simply signs of performance 'in play and jest', the mask has become the 'double face' worn 'in earnest' even by 'the best' of people, in order to manipulate or profit from the world around them. The books stamped with this design attempt to understand the complications of performance produced on stage and interpreted by the audience, whose experiences outside the theatre may reflect the emblem's argument:

> Most men do use some colour'd shift
> For to conceal their craftie drift.

Centuries after their first presentations, the possible performance choices and meanings they engender still stir the imaginations of actors, audiences, and readers of early plays. The products of scholarly creativity in this series, I hope, will also stir imaginations to new ways of thinking about performance.

*For Anna-Maija
with love*

Revenge Tragedy and the Drama of Commemoration in Reforming England

THOMAS RIST
University of Aberdeen, UK

ASHGATE

© Thomas Rist 2008

All rights reserved. No part of this publication may be reproduced, stored in a retrieval system or transmitted in any form or by any means, electronic, mechanical, photocopying, recording or otherwise without the prior permission of the publisher.

Thomas Rist has asserted his moral right under the Copyright, Designs and Patents Act, 1988, to be identified as the author of this work.

Published by
Ashgate Publishing Limited
Gower House
Croft Road
Aldershot
Hampshire GU11 3HR
England

Ashgate Publishing Company
Suite 420
101 Cherry Street
Burlington, VT 05401-4405
USA

Ashgate website: http://www.ashgate.com

British Library Cataloguing in Publication Data
Rist, Thomas, 1971–
 Revenge tragedy and the drama of commemoration in reforming England. – (Studies in performance and early modern drama)
 1. Revenge in literature 2. English drama – Early modern and Elizabethan, 1500–1600 – History and criticism 3. English drama – 17th century – History and criticism 4. English drama (Tragedy) – History and criticism 5. Death in literature 6. Memorials in literature
 I. Title
 822.3'09353

Library of Congress Cataloging-in-Publication Data
Rist, Thomas, 1971–
 Revenge tragedy and the drama of commemoration in reforming England / Thomas Rist.
  p. cm. – (Studies in performance and early modern drama)
 Includes bibliographical references (p.) and index.
 ISBN 978-0-7546-6152-8 (alk. paper)
 1. Revenge in literature. 2. English drama–Early modern and Elizabethan, 1500–1600– History and criticism. 3. English drama–17th century–History and criticism. 4. English drama (Tragedy)–History and criticism. 5. Death in literature. 6. Memorials in literature. 7. Religion and literature–England–History–16th century. 8. Religion and literature–England–History–17th century. I. Title.

PR658.R45R57 2008
822'.309353–dc22

2007017952

ISBN 978 0 7546 6152 8

Printed and bound in Great Britain by MPG Books Ltd. Bodmin, Cornwall.

Contents

Acknowledgements		ix
Introduction		1
	Revenge Tragedy: Critical Issues	1
	The Dead and Performative Religio-Politics at the 'Change of Religion'	3
	Mourning and its Aesthetics at the 'Change of Religion'	18
1	'Outrage Fits': Revenge and the 'Melodrama' of Mourning in *The Spanish Tragedy*, *Titus Andronicus* and *Hamlet*	27
	The Spanish Tragedy, c.1586–1587	27
	Titus Andronicus, c.1592	44
	Hamlet, c.1600, revised 1600–1604	60
2	Funerary Theatre: Mourning, *Antonio's Revenge* and Paul's Theatre	75
3	Melodrama and Parody: Remembering the Dead in *The Revenger's Tragedy*, *The Atheist's Tragedy*, *The White Devil* and *The Duchess of Malfi*	97
	The Revenger's Tragedy, c.1606	98
	The Atheist's Tragedy, c.1611	107
	The White Devil, c.1613	121
	The Duchess of Malfi, c.1613	134
Conclusion		145
Select Bibliography		149
Index		159

Acknowledgements

For invaluable criticisms of earlier versions of this book, I am especially grateful to Derek Hughes, John Rist, Peter Davidson and the anonymous reader for Ashgate; for comments on sections, I thank Cathy Shrank, Anna Rist, Helen Ostovich and Andrew Gordon, to whom thanks also for much discussion and coffee. For responding to queries and for pointers, I thank Peter Marshall, Eamon Duffy, William Naphy, Lisa Hopkins and David Robertson; and for hours in which ideas in this book were tested, I thank my students on EL40CL.

I am grateful to Ashgate for all the work going into publication and thank Erika Gaffney and Emily Ruskell especially for so much help and patience. I thank *Cahiers Elisabéthains: A Biannual Journal of English Renaissance Studies* for permission to reproduce in Chapter 1 material appearing in the Spring 2007 edition under the heading 'Memorial Revenge at the Reformation(s): Kyd's *The Spanish Tragedy*'; and I thank Special Collections at Aberdeen University for similar permission to use the image (from Holbein) on the dust-jacket.

Finally, I am grateful for the enduring support and faith of my family, English and Finnish. Above all, I thank my wife, Anna-Maija; without her kindness and love this book would not have been possible.

Introduction

Revenge Tragedy: Critical Issues

Complaining there existed 'no systematic study of revenge tragedy's dramatic antecedents in England', and mocking the supposed eruption of the genre 'as if by spontaneous generation' from *The Spanish Tragedy*, in 1973 Ronald Broude influentially argued that revenge tragedy emerged mainly through sensitivity to the age's 'currents in religion and politics'.[1] Describing a victim providentially guided to avenge the 'Babylonian' corruption of England's Catholic enemies, and thus a Protestant outlook, the formula in which he then explained such 'classic' revenges as *The Spanish Tragedy*, *Titus Andronicus*, *Hamlet* and *Antonio's Revenge* has been elaborated (as we shall see) and is now well known.[2] At the centre of Broude's analysis, however, was a view confidently inherited from discussion of *The Spanish Tragedy* by S.F Johnson: 'To Protestant interpreters, the symbolic Babylon was of course Rome, the whore of Babylon, being equated with the Antichrist, in turn equated with the Pope, one of whose agents in Kyd's day was the King of Spain.'[3] Assuming Johnson's reading of Reformed England was correct 'of course', Broude reasonably inferred that what was true of the King of Spain applied also to England's other Catholic enemies. A systematic and 'classic' theory of revenge tragedy was born.

Since 1973, however, the face of England's Reformation (or 'Reformations', as Christopher Haigh suggests[4]) has changed. Long after Elizabeth came to the throne, we now know, Roman Catholic habits survived even among England's more consciously Reformed: today, the stark Protestant–Catholic dichotomy of Broude's formula for revenge tragedy seems simplistic. Responding to this development, critics have tried to refine the formula by collapsing the dichotomy. Noticing, for example, that Protestants defined their 'true church' against (and so in terms of) the alleged Babylon of Catholicism, Alison Shell has argued for the unwitting entwinement of Protestantism within Catholicism, and thus for the simultaneous

---

[1] Ronald Broude, '*Vindicta Filia Temporis*: Three English Forerunners of the Elizabethan Revenge Play', in *Journal of English and Germanic Philology* 72 (1973), pp. 489–502 (489).

[2] For Broude's list of these 'classic' revenge tragedies, see Broude, '*Vindicta Filia Temporis*', p. 500.

[3] For Broude's dependence on Johnson for this view, see Broude, '*Vindicta Filia Temporis*', p. 497. For Johnson's original argument and claim, see S.F. Johnson, '*The Spanish Tragedy*, or Babylon Revisited', in *Essays on Shakespeare and Elizabethan Drama in Honour of Hardin Craig*, ed. by Richard Hosley (London: Routledge & Kegan Paul, 1963), pp. 23–36 (24–5).

[4] See Christopher Haigh, *English Reformations: Religion, Politics and Society under the Tudors* (Oxford: Clarendon Press, 1993).

abhorrence *and* attraction of things Catholic in revenge tragedy among Protestant audiences.[5] Following the revisions of the concept of the Reformation(s), however, Shell acknowledges that only 'a certain cast of Protestant' viewed Catholicism through an absolutely 'Babylonian' lens,[6] not noticing that this begs the following question: how did Protestants who were *not* of that cast – not to mention Roman Catholics – perceive the plays? Indeed, for what good reason should we prioritize Broude's or any other Babylonian paradigm in interpretation of the genre? Since *only* a cast of Protestant prioritized it, there is no historical reason: a search for other interpretative paradigms, and a thorough revision of the genre complementing that of the history, is necessary.[7] Arguing that occasional allusions to 'Babylon' are far outweighed by remembrances of the dead, and that revenge tragedy is thus a far less Reformed genre than Broude supposed, this study presents that systematic revision.

Being systematic, the method of the study will be to demonstrate the textual pervasiveness of such remembrance by illustrating it in a range of plays including Broude's classic revenges. The study will also offer a historical method of interpreting such remembrance in each play, and hence an analysis of how each play interprets it. Presenting also a development of dramatic attitudes towards remembrance of the dead, it will follow from such textual demonstration and interpretation that the principal religious context for the genre is that of the remembrance.[8] To establish the

---

[5] See Alison Shell, 'The Livid Flash: Decadence, Anti-Catholic Revenge Tragedy and the Dehistoricised Critic', in *Catholicism, Controversy and the English Literary Imagination, 1558–1660* (Cambridge: Cambridge University Press, 1999), pp. 23–54. For specific discussion of the 'closeness' of Protestant and Catholic, see p. 26.

[6] See Shell, p. 31. The point is also brought out by Young, who notes that recent efforts by historians 'to describe the persistence of pre-Reformation custom and belief in the face of persecution by successive Tudor regimes have described a rich cultural context in which Catholic habits of mind would have been available to the developing dramatist [of the period]'. See R.V. Young, 'Shakespeare's History Play and the Erasmian Catholic Prince', in *The Ben Jonson Journal* 7 (2000), pp. 89–114 (89).

[7] Observing that the Catholic presence in early modern England is at odds with the way it was represented in Protestant polemic, Paul Voss cautions scholars 'against too readily accepting any monolithic assessment of the period, including the largely dominant Protestant ideology, as the only set of viable beliefs and practices available to thoughtful Elizabethans'. In addressing anti-Catholic representation, therefore, we must filter 'the substantial from the insubstantial, the essential from the accidental, the sincere from the bombastic'. Sadly, 'Broudian' criticism has too rarely performed such a filter. See Paul Voss, 'The Catholic Presence in English Renaissance Literature', in *The Ben Jonson Journal* 7 (2000), pp. 1–26 (3). For further, relevant literary revision, see especially Peter Lake, *The Antichrist's Lewd Hat: Protestants, Papists and Players in Post-Reformation England* (New Haven, CT, and London: Yale University Press, 2002); Richard Wilson, *Secret Shakespeare: Studies in Theatre, Religion and Resistance* (Manchester and New York: Manchester University Press, 2004); Claire Asquith, *Shadowplay: The Hidden Beliefs and Coded Politics of William Shakespeare* (New York: Public Affairs, 2005); Gerard Kilroy, *Edmund Campion: Memory and Transcription* (Aldershot and Burlington, VT: Ashgate, 2005).

[8] Notice: the claim is *not* that other cultural contexts such as are noted in the study – for example, the Armada of 1588, the accession of James I to the throne or the Siege of Ostend (1601–1604) – are unimportant to the plays as religio-political contexts; but that –

focal religious context, I begin with the historical controversy over remembrance of the dead and the place of performance in that controversy.

The Dead and Performative Religio-Politics at the 'Change of Religion'

In the development of a Church calendar commemorating Christ's life and death and the lives of His saints, and particularly in the re-presentation of Christ's death in the mass, death and commemoration have been 'at the very core of Christianity'.[9] However, a central debate between early modern traditionalists and Reformers was over the interpretation of such 'remembrance'. In the original Greek, the word is *anamnêsis*, translated in the Latin Bible of Jerome as *memoria*, but both these words imply that 'memory' is present among us, thus 'living'.[10] The paradigm enactment of such Christian 'memoria' is the Roman church of San Sebastian on the Appian Way; the apostles having been buried at its altar, it is still traditionally the 'Memoria Apostolorum': the alleged place the apostles *are*. Though early modern Lutherans continued to understand Christian memorials as living, Calvinism – by 1600 the 'characteristic theology' of the English Church[11] – did not. For Calvinists, Christian memory was of the past: neither 'present' nor 'alive'. But in memorials of Christ (and thus of 'Christianity') these differences were urgent. In debating the status of the Eucharist, Reformers and traditionalists argued over the meaning of Christ's instruction to re-enact the Last Supper 'in remembrance of me' (Luke 22:19; 1 Cor. 11:25). Was the memorial of Christ successively re-presented at the altar (or as Calvinists preferred, at the communion table) to imply a 'real presence', or were these re-enactments 'bloodless'? Did 'memory' invest the material world with the spiritual, or only provide illusions of such investment? What claim on reality had 'enactment', 'vestiture' and other such 'theatre'? In what sense was such performance re-presentative? Was it illusory or truthful?

---

because these contexts have occasional rather than persistent bearing on the genre – they are of subordinate significance to its 'principal religious context' of remembrance.

[9] The phrase is Clive Burgess's. For discussion, see Burgess, '"Longing to be Prayed for": Death and Commemoration in an English Parish in the Later Middle Ages', in *The Place of the Dead: Death and Remembrance in Late Medieval and Early Modern Europe*, ed. by Bruce Gordon and Peter Marshall (Cambridge: Cambridge University Press, 2000), pp. 44–65 (44).

[10] Illustrating that *anamnêsis* is stronger than our 'memory', Plato uses the term in his theme that knowledge is 'recollection', i.e. the bringing back into lived reality of the experience of the Form seen before birth.

[11] 'The characteristic theology of English Protestant sainthood' in 1600 'was Calvinism, centering on the belief in divine predestination, both double and absolute, whereby man's destiny, either election to Heaven or reprobation to Hell, is not conditioned by faith but depends on the will of God.' See Nicholas Tyacke, *Anti-Calvinists: The Rise of English Arminianism c.1590–1640* (Oxford: Clarendon Press, 1990), p. 1. Notice also that 'before 1604 the challenge to Calvinism never fully escaped from the university [of Cambridge] confines' (Tyacke, p. 9): in the opening years of the seventeenth century, the challenge to English Calvinism was negligible.

For the immediate reason that traditional funerals for the dead included a requiem mass, by 1558 these loaded questions had transmitted from the Eucharist to other commemorated members of the Christian body.[12] Death and dying being fraught with ritual and 'social performance',[13] traditional, Christian remembrance of the dead entailed repeated performances of prayerful memory, themselves considered effective aids to the dead in Purgatory. Thus, in the parishes of pre-Elizabethan (though not Edwardine) England, individuals made provision to ensure their names were remembered in chorus-like recitations of prayers after their decease. In 1405, for example, one Robert Crossman promised the vicar of All Saints, Bristol, 3s. 4d. to put his and his wife's names, and also those of their parents, on the *tabula memoriae* for rehearsal each Sunday. In 1492, Thomas Baker paid the larger sum of 20s. so that 'every Sunday he shall specially exhort parishioners to pray for my soul'. In the same year the Mayor of Bristol, Clement Wiltshire, bequeathed a robe 'to pray for my soul and my first wife's soul, and for the souls of parents, brothers, sisters, kin and friends on every Sunday among the dead of the parish of All Saints' according to the usage there'.[14] Such 'usage' was institutional: as a reminder to pray for the dead, a bede-role of the list of benefactors was read during performances of high mass and at the annual General Mind. Even in the transitional year of 1558–1559, in the very moment Elizabeth Tudor succeeded Mary and Protestantism succeeded Catholicism as England's official religion, accounts of the parish of Morebath note donation for the dead: 'bestowyd a pon the hye auter [alter] and a pon the syd autur for a remembrans for them to be prayed for'.[15]

To a culture owing oratory, literature, painting, architecture, even churches and theatres to the 'social habit' of the art of memory, especially to one in which death was remembrance's 'animating impulse',[16] England's Reformed challenge

---

[12] As Peter Marshall notes, the 'perception that a funereal performance of even the most reformed Eucharistic rite represented an open invitation to pray for the dead was widely shared by Elizabethan bishops'. See *Beliefs and the Dead in Reformation England* (Oxford and New York: Oxford University Press, 2002), p. 149.

[13] David Cressy, *Birth, Marriage and Death: Ritual, Religion and the Life-Cycle in Tudor and Stuart England* (Oxford: Oxford University Press, 1997), p. 391. Performativity suffuses Cressy's view of death; the deathbed, for example, is 'the centre of a moral theatre' (p. 392). For parallel discussion, see Edward Muir on the 'performance' of 'the final scene' of Martin Luther's death in *Ritual in Early Modern Europe: New Approaches to European History* (Cambridge: Cambridge University Press, 1997), p. 44. Muir's opening chapter, asking 'What is a ritual?', presents performativity as vital to all rituals, noting that 'enactment' and 'performance' are central to two of the three main scholarly approaches to the topic, story-telling being central to the third. See Muir, pp. 1–13, especially p. 6. Since this study will make much of the role of emotion in performed memorials, notice also Muir's especial association of ritual with emotion: 'The repetition of everyday gestures within the confines of a special place and time rouses emotional responses' (Muir, p. 2).

[14] Examples from Burgess, pp. 53–4.

[15] Cited in Eamon Duffy's *The Voices of Morebath: Reformation and Rebellion in an English Village* (New Haven, CT, and London: Yale University Press, 2001), p. 171.

[16] For original discussion of the 'art of memory' in its many cultural forms including, substantially, the early modern, see Frances Yates, *The Art of Memory* (Harmondsworth: Penguin, 1966); the phrase 'social habit' derives from p. 24, in which she explains her study's

to Christian 'memoria' was an earthquake. As Clive Burgess observes, prayerful memory considered effective for the dead was part of traditional Christianity's *fabric*:[17] decked with endowments for such prayers, English parish churches and, even more, English cathedrals, were themselves aides-mémoires.[18] To enter such religious theatres (so Reformers would term them) was to be visually reminded of the dead and their need of prayer: prompted to act. Indeed, 'the stripping of the altars'[19] can be understood as anti-theatricality, from which closing the public theatres in 1642 was a logical, if not inevitable, result.[20]

One cannot underestimate the performativity of early modern religion. For Reformers, the claim that Purgatory was unbiblical, and Calvinism's theological view that the dead were predestined to Heaven or Hell,[21] made *enactments* of prayer benefiting the dead redundant. Such enactments, and their meanings, therefore changed. Strict Elizabethan and Jacobean Protestants did pray over their dead, but they ceased to consider the rehearsals helpful *for* the dead. Instead, their actions

---

aim to summon 'a vision of a forgotten social habit'. For mortality as a 'focal purpose and animating impulse' of memorial art in the early modern, see William E. Engel, *Mapping Mortality: The Persistence of Memory and Melancholy in Early Modern England* (Amherst, MA: University of Massachusetts Press, 1995), especially p. 3; for the art of memory's animation of *theatre*, see William E. Engel, *Death and Drama in Renaissance England* (Oxford: Oxford University Press, 2002). For the early modern 'cultivation' of an *Ars Moriendi*, see Cressy, pp. 389–93.

[17] Though such emphasis is also implicit in Engel's discussion of the memorial construction of the Scrovegni Chapel in the Arena of Padua (Engel, *Mapping Mortality*, pp. 13–21), as more holistically in Yates.

[18] For discussion of such aides-mémoires, and of their prayerful effect, see Burgess, especially pp. 46–8; for a similar, though less detailed, perspective see also *Records of Early English Drama: Norwich, 1540–1642*, ed. by David Galloway (Toronto, Buffalo, London: University of Toronto Press, 1984), pp. xv–xvi.

[19] From Eamon Duffy's *The Stripping of the Altars: Traditional Religion in England, 1400–1580* (New Haven, CT, and London: Yale University Press, 1992); *Altars* also contains many further examples of the provisions of medievals to ensure they were remembered in parish-recitations of the names of the dead.

[20] For detailed discussion, see Christopher Hodgkins, 'Plays out of Season: Puritanism, Antitheatricalism and Parliament's 1642 Closing of the Theaters', in *Centered on the Word: Literature, Scripture, and the Tudor-Stuart Middle Way*, ed. by Daniel W. Doerksen and Christopher Hodgkins (Newark, DE: Delaware University Press, 2005), pp. 298–318.

[21] Historians regularly note this point, but for further, recent discussion of this theological 'hub' of difference between Catholic and Calvinist see Marshall, pp. 147–8. Since (in my experience) literary scholars are often uneasy with the notion that the distinctions of 'theology' might be relevant to the 'political' outlooks even of grass-roots early moderns, it is worth noting that all the historians I cite in this section recognize that relevance more or less explicitly. Duffy gives clear illustration of the direct impact of 'theology' on legal institutions and so on popular religious practice: 'in case anyone was in doubt about the doctrinal revolution which underlay all this [popular cultural upheaval], in December 1547 Somerset pushed a new Chantry Act through parliament' (*Morebath*, p. 118). In Cressy's stark and more general phrase, 'the new theology provided both moderate and zealous protestants with a standard against which local practices [of remembering the dead] could be judged' (Cressy, *Birth, Marriage and Death*, p. 396).

emphasized thanksgiving and praise of God for the deceased, commemorations being therapeutic and a sign of love. For example, in his anti-Catholic *The Survey of Popery* (1596), Thomas Bell claimed the Church Fathers had only 'praied for the dead, to insinuate their hope in the resurrection, to mitigate their sorrow, and to declare their affection toward the dead'.[22] Similarly, William Guild claimed a correct remembrance was 'for declaration of their [the people's] love' of the dead, 'not doubting that the soules notwithstanding were in bliss already'.[23] For George Puttenham, as we shall see, 'teaching the people good learning, and also saying well of the departed' was the English reason for remembering the dead. After the accession of Elizabeth, commemoration of the dead would continue, but its 'correct', Reformed meaning had changed.

Revenge tragedy regularly enacts remembrances of the dead, drawing attention to the period's change in religious practices and deriving significance from them thereby. Yet the historical development was 'uncomfortable'.[24] Although the meanings of remembrance – though not entirely its enactments, as we shall see – were settled among the strictly Reformed, un-Reformed habits died hard in the country at large, the historical development remaining – critically for this study – actively contentious well into the seventeenth century.[25] Thus, in John Aubrey's *Remaines of Gentilisme and Judaisme*, we find the popular survival in seventeenth-century England of a host of religious and funerary practices through what he termed the 'Change of Religion',[26] including the survival of funeral songs referring to 'Purgatory'[27] and half-understood 'Diriges or Masses for the Dead'.[28]

Such English practices were noted keenly by 'protestant activists'.[29] Addressing funerals in the *View of Popish [sic] Abuses* accompanying the 1572 *Admonition to the Parliament*, and highlighting especially the styles of their performance, the violently

---

[22] Quoted by Marshall, p. 142.

[23] Quoted (from his *Ignis Fatuus*) by Marshall, p. 142.

[24] See Cressy, *Birth, Marriage and Death*, p. 400.

[25] As noted at the outset, historical revisions have altered our view of 'the Reformations'. It is this point which traditional histories of English theatre – as also the implicitly Reformist interpretations of it by Greenblatt, Diehl and Zimmerman, which I consider further below – fail to take on board. Once we recognize that the period's understanding of memorial for the dead was 'contentiously un-concluded', it follows that such performative memorials presented in the theatre are also controversial.

[26] Hence the title of this sub-section. See John Aubrey, *Remaines of Gentilisme and Judaisme*, ed. by James Britten, Publications of the Folklore Society (London: W. Satchell, Peyton and Co., 1881), p. 40.

[27] Aubrey, p. 30. Pertinently, Aubrey cites '1616' or '1624' as the date at which these songs were sung.

[28] For examples of these 'masses' see Aubrey, pp. 18, 78 and 88. The precise form the masses took, however, is not clear – partly because Aubrey's notes are incomplete and partly because the extent to which his views colour his documentation is unclear. Aubrey's fullest description of such a 'mass', however, is on p. 88, where he calls them 'Sacrifices donne to ye infernall Gods for them that be dead: a Dirige, or Masse for the dead'.

[29] I borrow this useful description of an active social group from Cressy, *Birth, Marriage and Death*, p. 403.

anti-Roman authors complained of the official *English* Church's commemorative rite:

> They appoint a prescript kind of service to bury the dead, and that which is the duty of every Christian they tie alone to the minister, whereby prayer for the dead is maintained ... We say nothing of the threefold peale, bicause that is rather licensed by Injunction than commaunded in their book [of Common Prayer]; nor of their straunge mourning by chaunging theyr garments, which, if it be not hipocritical, yet it is superstitious and heathenish, bicause it is used onely of custome, nor of buriall sermons, whiche are put in place of trentalles, wherout spring many abuses, and therfore in the best reformede churches, are removed. As for the superstitions used bothe in Countrey and Citie for the place of buryall, which way they must lie, how they must be fetched to churche, the minister meeting them at churche stile with surplesse, with a companye of greedie clarks, that a crosse, white or blacke, must be set upon the deade corpes, that breade muste be given to the poore, and offrings in buryall time used, and cakes sent abrode to friendes, bycause these are rather used for custome and superstition than by the authoritie of the boke ... But great charge will hardly bring the least good thing to pass, and therefore all is let alone, and the people as blinde and as ignorante as ever they were.[30]

Though its view of late-sixteenth-century funeral in England is probably exaggerated, the detailed consciousness in the *Abuses* of a 'Countrey and Citie ... as blind and as ignorant as ever they were' implies the contemporary sensitivity to performances of remembrance.

That this view of funerary performance or 'style' was not *wholly* exaggerated is attested elsewhere. Also emphasizing the manner of performance in 1590, Henry Barrow similarly mocked 'popish' funeral within England's Church:

> the priest meeting the corpse at the church style in white array, his ministering vesture with solemn song, or else reading aloud certain of their fragments of Scripture, and so [they] carry the corpse either to the grave, made in their holy cemetery and hallowed churchyard, or else, if he be a rich man, carry his body into the church; each where his dirge and trental is read over him after they have taken off the holy covering cloth, and the linen crosses wherewhith the corpse is dressed, until it come into the churchyard or church into that holy ground, lest sprights in the mean time should carry it away ... If he be a man of wealth, that he make his grave with the rich in the church, he shall then pay accordingly; for that ground is much more precious and holy than the churchyard, having been consecrate and all to be sprinkled with holy water ... Then may they boldly proceed to cover him, whiles the priest also proceedeth to read over his holy gear and say his Paternoster (which fitteth all assaies) and his other prayers over the corpse.[31]

Barrow's ironic reference to the 'trental' – a series of thirty commissioned masses for the dead – was an especially 'unflattering'[32] swipe at the 'popery' inside England's Church. But attempts to halt such scenes of 'superstition' continued well into the

---

[30] Quoted by Judith Maltby in *Prayer Book and People in Elizabethan and Early Stuart England*, Cambridge Studies in Early Modern British History (Cambridge: Cambridge University Press, 1998), p. 62, and by Cressy, *Birth, Marriage and Death*, p. 403.

[31] Cited in Maltby, pp. 61–2, and Cressy, *Birth, Marriage and Death*, p. 404.

[32] Maltby, p. 62.

seventeenth century. In 1629, for example, the Bishop of Carlisle was still trying to eradicate 'praying for the dead at crosses ... or any other superstitious use of crosses, with towels, palms ... or other memories of idolatry at burials'.[33] And in 1639, the suspected Lancashire recusant Robert Abbot was disciplined for accompanying a woman's corpse 'in a superstitious manner', as his accusers made clear:

> there was a cross towel laid over her corpse upon the bier, and she was set down at stone and wooden crosses by the way; and you did at the same cross in a superstitious manner take off your hat and kneeled down and prayed. And many people which saw you do think that you did worship and pray unto crosses.[34]

As a study of English theatre has cause to notice, fundamental in each of these objections was the style, enactment or in this case 'manner' – terms all denoting the performative – of the enacted devotions to the dead; moreover, in each of these cases the style of the performance was a deciding sign of traditional as opposed to Reformed outlook. That the performative habits signalling such 'popery' died hard in England is also clear in each case. As Aubrey would lyrically put it, 'the Ploughboies, and also the Schooleboies will keep up and retain their old Ceremonies and Customes'.[35]

The difficulty of remembering the dead in the old style becomes tangible in individual cases. In 1569 John Stow was officially investigated under suspicion of 'closet Catholicism', thereafter undergoing what Patrick Collinson calls 'conversion by conformity'[36] and censoring the Catholic leanings of his writings: his style – personal and literary – was 'Re-formed'. His anxiety, however, emerges in his self-censorship: 'When Stow quotes the epitaphs inscribed on pre-Reformation tombs [in his *Survey of London*], he turns them into theologically innocuous statements, mere monuments, omitting the lines which invite prayers for the dead or refer to the doctrine of purgatory.'[37]

Similar self-censorship and anxiety is visible in Thomas Browne. In 1642, he recalled a heresy 'which I did never positively maintain or practice, but have often wished ... had been consonant with truth, and not offensive to my religion, and that is the Prayer for the dead'. However, having equivocated on how 'positively' he practiced the forbidden prayer, he then remembers how he could 'scarce contain my prayers for a friend at the ringing of a bell' or barely 'behold a corpse without an orison

---

[33] Quoted by Clare Gittings in 'Sacred and Secular: 1558–1660', in *Death in England: An Illustrated History*, ed. by Peter C. Jupp and Clare Gittings (Manchester: Manchester University Press, 1999), pp. 147–73 (153).
[34] Cited by Cressy, *Birth, Marriage and Death*, p. 402.
[35] Aubrey, p. 40.
[36] Quotations from Collinson, 'John Stow and Nostalgic Antiquarianism', in *Imagining Early Modern London: Perceptions and Portrayals of the City from Stow to Strype, 1598–1720*, ed. by J.F. Merritt (Cambridge: Cambridge University Press, 2001), pp. 27–51 (pp. 42 and 46). But Collinson is not quite unequivocal on Stow's confessional identity: he also notes that 'if Stow did not become a Protestant, he learned to be discreet' (p. 45).
[37] Collinson, p. 46; for a complete account of such self-censorship, including the controversial tomb-inscriptions which Stow self-censored, see pp. 45–6.

for his soul'.[38] Like Stow, Browne's prayer for the dead was repressed, suggesting anxiety and an underlying but disguised desire for the Catholic performance. Notably, something similar happens in the famously elusive *The Phoenix and the Turtle*: in treating 'mourners', 'priest', strict 'obsequy' and 'requiem' in its ambiguous 'session interdict', Shakespeare evokes the era's half-obscured rite of the dead.[39]

Various forms of evidence imply the theatre's exploitation of this anxiety and performative controversy. Michael Neill has observed how in seeking to distinguish comic from tragic in *The Defense of Poesy*, Sir Philip Sidney passingly makes 'funerals' synonymous with 'right tragedies';[40] similarly, Duke Theseus's initiation of comedy's 'merriments' and nuptial with the banishment of 'melancholy forth to funerals' (*A Midsummer Night's Dream*, I.i.12; 14) implies, in a generically self-conscious play, that melancholy and funerals befit tragedy. Brief and elusive these associations are, but they are far from alone: much more sustained and clear theatre-as-remembrance, for example, emerges in 1592 in Thomas Nashe's well-known response to Shakespeare's *I Henry VI*:

> How would it have joyed brave *Talbot* (the terror of the French) to thinke that after he had lyne two hundred yeares in his Tombe, hee should triumphe againe on the Stage, and have his bones new embalmed with the teares of ten thousand spectators at least (at severall times), who, in the Tragedian that represents his person, imagine they behold him fresh bleeding.[41]

Despite being aware that the actor in question 'represents' Talbot, Nashe, considering the actor a 'Tragedian', describes the overwhelming dramatic experience in terms of a conflation of dramatic actor and historical person: Talbot comes to 'triumph againe', evoking 'the teares of ten thousand spectators'. Moreover, the 'triumph' emerges in strikingly funerary terms: the person of Talbot has 'lyne two hundred yeares in his Tombe', his bones are 'new embalmed', his body 'fresh bleeding', and with 'teares'

---

[38] Sir Thomas Browne, *Religio Medici and Other Writings* (London: Dent, 1965), p. 9.

[39] Textual quotations from lines 9, 12, 15, 20. Enjoining that in 'this session interdict' the 'priest in surplus white' should 'Keep the obsequy so strict / ... Lest the requiem lack his right', stanzas three and four are particularly controversial and 'popish' amid this 'tragic scene' (52). For the latest, relevant contribution to this 'famously elusive' poem, see John Finnis and Patrick Martin's 'Another Turn for the Turtle: Shakespeare's Intercession for Love's Martyr', in *The Times Literary Supplement* (18 April 2003), pp. 12–14.

[40] See Michael Neill, 'Feasts Put Down as Funeral', in *True Rites and Maimed Rites: Ritual and Anti-Ritual in Shakespeare and his Age*, ed. by Linda Woodbridge and Edward Berry (Urbana, IL, and Chicago: University of Illinois Press, 1992), pp. 47–74 (48). I shall turn to Neill's *Issues of Death* below. For Sidney's original, if passing mention of the relation of 'funerals' to 'right tragedy' see 'The Defense of Poesy', in *Renaissance Literature: An Anthology*, ed. by Michael Payne and John Hunter (Oxford: Blackwell, 2003), pp. 501–27 (524).

[41] Cited in 'Documents', in *The Norton Shakespeare*, ed. by Stephen Greenblatt *et al.* (New York and London: Norton, 1997), p. 3322.

he is mourned copiously. Substantially, in this contemporary account, drama – in this case historical tragedy – is a commemorative and funerary experience.[42]

Dramatic scenes depicting mourners, the bearing of corpses, funeral processions or all these features (as we find in act I, scene ii of Shakespeare's *Richard III*), all similarly testify to a theatre of funerals – as do the tombs appearing in plays such as *A Midsummer Night's Dream* (in the artisans's 'tragedy') or in Philip Henslowe's 1598 list of stage-properties.[43] And the same is true of the skulls scrutinized as memento mori by such figures as Hamlet or, in *The Revenger's Tragedy*, Vindice. Indeed, assuming with recent discussions of these last properties that they were not imitations,[44] theatrical skulls present material links – or at least undecipherable illusions of them[45] – not just to dead persons, but also to the places of burial from which their remains were removed. Highlighting such materiality in the 'graveyard scene', Hamlet's examination of his stage-property and question 'Why, might not that be the skull of a lawyer?' (*Hamlet*, V.i.) challenges spectators to identify skulls with persons.

Such links with the dead invite other theatrical considerations, the first being the period's anecdotal familiarity with the actor Polos (4BC), popularly supposed in the period to have conjured an overwhelming and tragic pathos by meditating on-stage on his dead son's urn.[46] However exaggerated, the previously noted evocation of Talbot's bones 'conjuring the teares of ten thousand spectators' by Nashe suggests

---

[42] Though emphasizing the funerary and 'tragic' aspects of the passage, my reading here develops Philip Schwyzer's view of it as 'history': 'Thomas Nashe, who may have collaborated with Shakespeare on *1 Henry VI*, understood the nature of what happens in history plays, and the nature of their appeal ... Historical drama fulfills the wish of the living to see the dead again.' See *Literature, Nationalism and Memory in Early Modern England and Wales* (Cambridge: Cambridge University Press, 2004), p. 147.

[43] As well as mentioning skulls, Henslowe's list includes 'i tombe of Guido' and 'i tombe of Dido'. See Andrew Gurr, *The Shakespearean Stage, 1547–1642*, 2nd edn (Cambridge: Cambridge University Press, 1980), p. 171. Although, as noted, Henslowe's description does not pertain to completeness, observe that Henslowe nowhere suggests his skulls and tombs were imitations. In *A Midsummer Night's Dream*, Ninus's tomb stands out among the larger stage-properties ('wall', 'the man in the moon') required by the inept actors of act V, scene i: it is the only one *not* implied to be performed by a person. Other tombs from other plays will figure in this study.

[44] For standard discussion see Gurr, *The Shakespearean Stage*, especially p. 171. For more recent discussion see especially Lena Cowen Orlin, 'Things with Little Social Life: Henslowe's Properties', in *Staged Properties in Early Modern English Drama*, ed. by Jonathan Gil Harris and Natasha Korda (Cambridge: Cambridge University Press, 2002), pp. 99–128.

[45] Skulls are such small objects that – except, perhaps, for those nearest to the actors – an audience could never tell a real one from a fake. What evidence we have, moreover, suggests that theatricalists went to great lengths to make stage-properties representing the dead resemble them. Philip Henslowe's 1598 list of stage-properties, for example, implies that 'the limes dead' of a heifer represented 'Faustus limbs, All torn assunder' at the close of *Dr Faustus*. See Orlin, pp. 99–100.

[46] See Edith Hall, 'The Ancient Actor's Presence since the Renaissance', in *Greek and Roman Actors: Aspects of an Ancient Profession*, ed. by Pat Easterling and Edith Hall (Cambridge: Cambridge University Press, 2003), pp. 419–34, especially pp. 419–20. Notice

this popular ideal, as do the many revengers we shall notice self-consciously seeking (or parodying) histrionics in memory of the dead. Moreover, the precedent of classical theatre provides further reason for considering memorials of the dead as stimuli for vengeful emotion: as early moderns knew, *The Libation Bearers* opens with Orestes grieving by his father's tomb having missed his funeral; but then 'retrospective modulates into a cry for revenge:

> Zeus, Zeus, grant me vengeance for my father's murder. Stand and fight beside me, of your grace.'[47]

In Aeschylus, moreover, the memorial stimulus is focal:

> Exactly the same movement of feeling is experienced by Electra when she, in turn, comes to the tomb with the chorus of libation bearers. Recalling the circumstances of Agamemnon's murder, she shifts abruptly to revenge: 'father, I pray that your avenger come that they / who killed you shall be killed in turn'.[48]

Links with the dead also affirm the religio-politics of theatrical remembrancing. Like their Edwardine predecessors, Elizabethan Reformers programmatically burnt relics of the dead in bonfires, recognizing with the Queen's officials at the Northern Rebellion (1569) that 'the material instruments of Catholic piety were dangerous in themselves, encoded memories, which might erupt and disrupt at any time'.[49] Especially amid the stage-properties looted from monasteries and churches in the sixteenth century, thus, theatrical skulls would seem disruptive in themselves.[50] Nor should such material be considered the only Catholic fabric of the contemporary theatre. As I have already observed, traditional churches had been aides-mémoires for the dead, but what if these buildings – including the Blackfriars and the Whitefriars

---

that I consider the popular *anecdotal* view of Polos in the *Renaissance*; the fact that in the plot of Sophocles' *Electra* (lines 1126 and following) the urn is said to be empty is not relevant.

[47] Quotation and translation from John Kerrigan, '"Remember Me!": Horestes, Hieronimo, and Hamlet', in *Revenge Tragedy: Aeschylus to Armageddon* (Oxford: Clarendon Press, 1996), pp. 170–92 (p. 170), lines 17–18.

[48] Kerrigan, '"Remember Me!"', p. 170.

[49] Duffy, *Morebath*, p. 170; pp. 177–8.

[50] For discussion of such plundered stage-properties, see Glynn Wickham, *Early English Stages, 1300–1660*, vol. 2.1 (Routledge & Kegan Paul, 1963), pp. 38–9. In *Shakespearean Negotiations: The Circulation of Social Energy in Renaissance England* (Oxford: Clarendon Press; Berkeley, CA, and Los Angeles: University of California Press, 1988), Stephen Greenblatt argues that the 'transmigration of a single ecclesiastical cloak from the vestry to the [theatrical] wardrobe' entails 'a sacred sign' being 'emptied' of religious significance (p. 112), but this appears to be false. As Erica Veevers notes in *Images of Love and Religion: Queen Henrietta and Court Entertainments* (Cambridge: Cambridge University Press, 1989), observers of a 'Musician' in 'priest-like habit' in Jonson's *Pleasure Reconciled to Virtue* reported their *priestliness*; see Veevers, pp. 153–5. Consider also the report of the contemporary spectator Orazio Busino of seeing 'priests' at 'the altar' in *The Duchess of Malfi* which I discuss in Chapter 3: clearly the religious significance of the garments of the actors had *not* disappeared. I explore the wider shortcomings in Greenblatt's influential view of theatrical 'emptying' further below.

– were put to theatrical use? The controversial potential of such buildings was immense, as I argue in reading *Antonio's Revenge* as a play for Paul's Theatre in Chapter 2, and it cannot have left even the purpose-built playhouses unaffected.

As final evidence of the involvement of the playhouses not just in styles of memorial but also in their religio-politics, I consider two commentaries of different kinds. The first is a response to Massinger's *Roman Actor*, probably first performed in 1626, thus not quite 'Jacobean'. Recalling Nashe on *I Henry VI*, several responses praise the play's funerary and 'revival' of dead persons,[51] but one such response, by an anonymous *T.I.*, asks of Caesar, 'thus reviv'd, who can affirm him dead?' before adding:

> I am no great admirer of the Plays
> Poets, or Actors, that are nowadays:
> Yet in this Worke of thine me thinks I see
> Sufficient reason for Idolatry.[52]

T.I. thus links his theatrical experience to the revival of a buried man before linking these to the divisive question of 'idolatry' (itself linked to the dead as we shall see). His paradoxical claim that there might be 'sufficient reason' for such idolatry, however, suggests he was simultaneously won over to a theatre *and* religious outlook he had previously condemned.

My second example of theatre, funeral and religio-politics converging is from George Puttenham's *The Art of English Poesie*. Considering theatre a sub-species of 'poesie' in the Aristotelian manner, Puttenham presents the first 'causes of man's sorrowes' and so of all 'Poetical lamentations' as 'the death of his friends, allies, and children', thereafter evoking 'the very burials of the dead' and the 'monethes mindes' as 'chief' sources of such sorrow.[53] Defining epitaphs – which he understands almost as inclusively as 'poesie' – he also titles a sub-section 'Of the poem called Epitaph used for memorial of the dead', thereafter evoking an England in which such literary memorials are 'hanged up in Churches and chauncells over the tombes of great men and others'.[54] Emphasizing a religio-politic already suggested by the 'month's mind'

---

[51] Thus, Robert Harvey claims that in the play Caesar did 'yet out-live his tragic Funeral'; Thomas May claims that in it 'Paris, the best of Actors in his age / Acts yet' as if his soul 'Could into any of our Actors pass', linking a 'history' again come to 'life' with his 'lasting epitaph'; John Ford claims the 'soul' of Domitian was revived by the author's pen. For details, see *Massinger, Thomas: The Roman Actor*, ed. by William Lee Sandidge Jr., Princeton Studies in English (Princeton, NJ: Princeton University Press, 1929), pp. 48–9. I have modernized spelling in these quotations.

[52] *Roman Actor*, p. 47; again, I have modernized spelling.

[53] This and all subsequent references to Puttenham are from *The Arte of English Poesie*, Electronic Text Center, University of Virginia, http://etext.lib.virginia.edu/toc/modeng/public/PutPoes.html, last accessed 30 October 2007. The text was originally published in 1589. The present quotation derives from Chapter 1.24: 'The form of Poeticall Lamentations'.

[54] See *The Art of English Poesie*, Chapter 1.28. Joshua Scodel demonstrates the age's pervasive literary debt to the funerary epitaph, especially in the development and use of epigrams, in *The English Poetic Epitaph: Commemoration and Conflict from Jonson to Wordsworth* (Ithaca, NY, and London: Cornell University Press, 1991). Anticipating my

– a Catholic ritual for the dead – he claims that 'Epicedia' and 'Monodia' are aspects of funeral ceremonies performed differently 'at this day' in England and Rome:

> In Rome they accustomed to make orations funeral and commendatory of the dead parties in the publique place called Prorostris: and our Theologians, instead use to make sermons, both teaching the people some good learning, and also saying well of the departed.

The distinction between the 'theological' practice of English funeral, carefully delineated as 'teaching the people ... good learning' and 'saying well of the departed' (but certainly *not* including prayer for the dead) and the Roman 'commendatory of the dead parties' (suggesting aid for them[55]) re-implicates the 'poetical' (including, for Puttenham, the theatrical) in the religio-political. Observe, therefore, that the broad-brush claim that the contemporary theatre killed 'the credibility of the supernatural' by presenting it as illusory is mistaken.[56] None of the evidence here considered – not the period's pervasively memorial arts, nor the contemporary perceptions of the theatricality of funerals, nor even the contemporary associations of drama with funerals and their religious-politic – suggests playhouses of exclusively or even primarily ironic, distanced or 'demystified' perspective.

Contemporaries being acculturated to theatrical remembrance of the dead as controversial well into the seventeenth-century, it is nevertheless hard to distinguish Protestant from Catholic memorials in the theatre. Thus, though revenge tragedy repeatedly presents acts in remembrance of the dead, it only occasionally makes strong claims about the controversial matter of their effects. Even in the performing of memorials thus ambiguously, however, notice that the drama invites a substantial

---

following discussion of religio-politics, he also discusses issues of *lengthy* mourning on pp. 50–85.

[55] 'Commendatory' has the sense of 'commending a person to favourable notice or reception' – see the *O.E.D.* definition 1b; thus, commending a dead man entails helping him.

[56] The claim derives from Greenblatt's 'Shakespeare and the Exorcists', in *Shakespearean Negotiations*, p. 109. Its interpretative view underpins Huston Diehl's *Staging Reform, Reforming the Stage: Protestantism and Popular Theatre in Early Modern England* (Ithaca, NY: Cornell University Press, 1997) and also Susan Zimmerman's *The Early Modern Corpse and Shakespeare's Theatre* (Edinburgh: Edinburgh University Press, 2005). However, the claim is increasingly disputed. See John Cox's *The Devil and the Sacred in English Drama, 1350–1642* (Cambridge: Cambridge University Press, 2000), especially pp. 150–65; also Gerard Kilroy's reassessment of the Hackney Exorcisms (which underpin Greenblatt's view of the theatre) in *Edmund Campion: Memory and Transcription*, especially p. 27; also Jean-Christophe Mayer, *Shakespeare's Hybrid Faith: History, Religion and the Stage*, Early Modern Literature in History (Basingstoke: Palgrave Macmillan, 2006), especially pp. 9–11. Tom McAlindon casts doubt on Greenblatt's more general view of Shakespeare as a 'relentless demystifier' on p. 32 of *Shakespeare minus 'Theory'* (Aldershot and Burlington, VT: Ashgate, 2004), also casting doubt on his 'theatricality' on pp. 151–2. Greenblatt modifies his original claim in *Hamlet in Purgatory* (Princeton, NJ, and Oxford: Princeton University Press, 2001). For discussion, see my 'Shakespeare Now and Then: Communities, Religion, Reception', in *Religion and Writing in England, 1558–1689: Studies in Community-Making and Cultural Memory*, ed. by Roger Sell and Anthony Johnson (Aldershot and Burlington, VT: Ashgate, 2008).

religious speculation. Notice too, however, that having invited such speculation, dramatists would normally want to proceed cautiously, avoiding overtly polemic claims: the legal demand of the theatre in 1559 that 'matters of religion or of the governance of the estate of the commonweal' be treated only 'by men of authority, learning and wisdom' meant caution was necessary.[57]

But if revenge tragedy does not and – bearing in mind Hume on cause-and-effect – could not demonstrate the true purpose of post-mortem memorial, it regularly surrounds its remembrances of the dead with controversial features of five kinds. First, and irrespective of any eventual interpretation of their falsehood or truthfulness, it famously invokes 'ghosts' in its dramatic worlds, challenging Reformed rationalizations of ghosts as demons.[58] Second, it repeatedly blends dramatic remembrance of the dead with these ghosts, suggesting – though not demonstrating – that remembrance *effects* the dead: presenting post-mortem memorials with active 'ghosts' invites questions of connection. Third, the ghosts of revenge tragedy repeatedly fear being forgotten, reflecting the anxiety of Catholics and religious waverers that without due memorial the dead in Purgatory would languish in torment. Fourth, the Latinate surroundings of the dramatic memorials – including an Italian or Spanish setting – suggest Catholic focus (though not, as yet, Catholic sympathy).[59] Each one of these dramatic features evokes moments of

---

[57] Citation from *The Norton Shakespeare*, p. 37. All citations of Shakespeare will be from this edition. For further discussion of censorship, see especially Janet Claire, *'Art Made Tongue-Tied by Authority': Elizabethan and Jacobean Censorship* (Manchester and New York: Manchester University Press, 1990); Richard Dutton, *Mastering the Revels: The Regulation and Censorship of English Renaissance Drama* (Basingstoke and London: Macmillan, 1991); and Dutton, *Licensing, Censorship, and Authorship in Early Modern England* (Basingstoke and New York: Palgrave, 2000).

[58] Controversy over the status of ghosts in the drama has been most explored in reference to *Hamlet*. See Roy Battenhouse, 'The Ghost in *Hamlet*: A Catholic "Linchpin"?', *Studies in Philology* 68 (1951), pp. 161–92; Miriam Joseph, 'Discerning the Ghost in *Hamlet*', *Publications of the Modern Language Association of America* 76/5 (1961), pp. 493–502; Christopher Devlin, *Hamlet's Divinity* (Carbondale, IL: Southern Illinois University Press, 1963); Miriam Joseph, '*Hamlet*: A Christian Tragedy', *Studies in Philology* 59 (1962), pp. 119–40; Eleanor Prosseur, *Hamlet and Revenge* (Stanford, CA: Stanford University Press, 1967); Rowland Mushat Frye, *The Renaissance 'Hamlet': Issues and Responses in 1600* (Princeton, NJ: Princeton University Press, 1984), pp. 11–24; Greenblatt, *Hamlet in Purgatory*; Thomas Rist, 'Religion, Politics, Revenge: The Dead in Renaissance Drama', in *Early Modern Literary Studies* 9/1 (May 2003), at http://www.shu.ac.uk/emls/09-1/ristdead.html, last accessed 30 October 2007.

[59] Janette Dillon observes: '[Latin] was also, despite Protestant insistence on an English Bible, and an English Prayer Book, the language most directly linked in the popular consciousness with the supreme and sacramental authority of the Word. Latin had after all been reinstated as the language of the English Church during the reign of Queen Mary in the 1550s, and the political aura that encircled English in a religious context was to last beyond the end of the century. The English Bible, contested in different translations with different doctrinal shadings, had not yet achieved the ring of unitary authority that the sound of the Authorized Version came to have for later centuries; whereas the Latin Bible, despite its potential evocation of the hated subjection to Rome, had not fully lost its sacramental ring.'

Introduction

controversy repeated within and across the genre, but in regard to religio-politics it is the fifth feature, which I call the 'aesthetics of mourning', that determines pervasively the genre of revenge tragedy. For being performative, as we have seen, funerary mourning entailed 'aesthetics': a code of action in which – like a theatre – some kinds of act were laudable, others not; a code, moreover, which, taking its bearings from the religions of the day, signalled those religions. Enacting such funerary remembrance pervasively, as we shall see, revenge tragedy asks to be judged on the terms of this aesthetic; spelling out the rationales of its performative remembrances, the genre judges itself on those terms. Before turning fully to this important and last introductory matter, however, a word more on funerary history.

Funerals, as previously observed, were sites not only of memorials but of memorial controversy; but as the late sixteenth- progressed into the seventeenth-century, the rituals of funeral – those performative elements of a burial – were systematically reduced, Reformers seeking to remove the residual 'superstitions' of popery from 'Christian religion'. Accounts such as that noted previously of the Bishop of Carlisle, in 1629, exemplify the performance of 'superstition' being suppressed at funerals by protestant activists.

A decisive historical moment in the process, as historians repeatedly note, lies between the official service for the dead prescribed by the Book of Common Prayer of 1549 and that of 1552. In the rite of 1549, one still finds memorial prayer for the dead, albeit attenuated. As Eamon Duffy originally observed, however, 'There is nothing that could even be mistaken for a prayer *for* the dead in the 1552 rite.'[60] Although the Marian interval presented a brief reversal of such trend, the 'Order for the Burial of the Dead' in the Elizabethan Prayer Book of 1559 re-imposed the 1552 rite.[61] Thus, from 1559 onwards, the authorized definition of remembrance for the dead excluded prayers *for* them, the rite being accordingly reduced.

The reductive trend would continue. In 1644, the *Directory for the Public Worship of God* prescribed what Clare Gittings has called 'tantamount to secular burial rites',[62] in which funeral performativity had all but disappeared. Notably, the *Directory* stipulates that ministers of the church were unnecessary at funerals; if such a minister was present, however, his role was categorically only to put mourners 'in remembrance of their duty' and, notably, to see the corpse 'immediately interred without any ceremony'.[63] The rationale for this drastic reduction was unambiguously Reformed:

Whether the associations were divided or simultaneous, therefore, Latin continued to have Roman Catholic and 'sacramental' association in our period. See Dillon, '*The Spanish Tragedy* and Staging Languages in Renaissance Drama', *Research Opportunities in Renaissance Drama* 34 (1995), pp. 15–40 (21). Notice also Dillon's observation on p. 23 of this article that 'The transition of Latin in no way depended on an audience's understanding of the semantic content of the Latin, but on a response to it as the language of divine authority, embodying a truth rendered distinct from the linguistic abuses of earthly sinners.'

[60] Duffy, *Altars*, p. 475; my emphasis.
[61] Marshall, p. 151.
[62] Gittings, 'Sacred and Secular', p. 153.
[63] Quoted from Gittings, 'Sacred and Secular', p. 153; Geoffrey Rowell goes further, calling the rite 'entirely secular'. See Rowell, *The Liturgy of Christian Burial: An Introductory*

Because the customs of kneeling down and praying by or towards the dead corpse, and other usages in the place where it lies before it be carried to burial, are superstitious; and for that praying, reading and singing, both in going to and at the grave have been grossly abused [and] are in no way beneficial to the dead [*sic*] ... let all such things be set aside.[64]

The baldness of the claim that prayer for the dead is 'in no way beneficial' for them is striking, but the sentiment itself is unsurprising. What is remarkable is that, by mere association with 'superstitious' religion, even such non-specific activity as praying 'by or towards' a corpse has been ruled out. To the Reformed authors of this eventual law of the land, even the smallest acts of funeral remembrance signified popery. Performing such acts, therefore, was 'set aside'.[65]

1559 is not, of course, 1644: Elizabeth's Reformation was neither as uncompromising nor as overt as the *Directory*'s.[66] However, the direct inspiration of the *Directory* is Elizabethan: the document is 'a translation of a book of discipline compiled by the English Puritan divine, Walter Travers, in about 1586'.[67] Nor can we dismiss this Elizabethan version as the work of an extremist. As Gittings observes, the 'logic of the theology' of 1644 was already in place in the Prayer Book of 1559.[68] Thus, though the fullest, practical consequences of 1559 were not developed until 1586, and though these practices would not become law until 1644, under Elizabeth the theology and 'theory' of a Protestant England was anti-memorial from the start.

I end this discussion with a general thought about Elizabethan Reform, a final example of Elizabethan anti-memorialism, and an opening view of our revenge tragedy. In regard to the Reform, it is not entirely reductive to consider the active Protestantism that re-emerged under Elizabeth a movement first and foremost against the traditional performances of post-mortem memory. Collinson, who considers John Stow 'invaluable' on the topic, notes how Stow's account of 'the vestiary disturbances of 1566 which launched the Elizabethan puritan movement' begins with 'Robert Crawley barring the entry of a funeral in St Giles Cripplegate' and (in Stow's words) 'saynge the church was his ... wherof he would rule that place and wold not soffer eny suche superstycious rages of Rome ther to enter'.[69] Crawley barring a 'popish' funeral rite initiates the Elizabethan vestiary controversy.

Further support for the proposition that 'active Protestantism' under Elizabeth was firstly against the traditional rituals for the dead is found elsewhere. For though Elizabeth's bishops defended vestiture, in the *Second Tome of Homilies*, 'issued in 1563 and read in every church during the late sixteenth and seventeenth centuries',

---

Survey of the Historical Development of Christian Burial Rites, Alcuin Club Collections 59 (London: William Clowes & Sons, 1977), p. 83.

[64] Quoted from Cressy, *Birth, Marriage and Death*, p. 416.

[65] In practice, and at least partly because it lacked the necessary 'disciplinary machinery', the dictate of the *Directory* was never fully implemented (Cressy, *Birth, Marriage and Death*, p. 416). This in no way detracts, however, from what is here my only concern: to illustrate the historical rise to official power of the theological ritual of the Reformed.

[66] See Cressy, *Birth, Marriage and Death*, pp. 403–12.

[67] See Rowell, p. 83.

[68] Quotations from Gittings, 'Sacred and Secular', p. 153.

[69] See Collinson, p. 44.

a homily against idolatry – that most Reformed of bugbears – presents it as the worship of 'dead things' instead of 'the living God', explaining and consolidating that definition as follows:

> For ... the origine of images, and worshipping of them, as it is recorded in the eight [*sic*] Chapter of the booke of Wisdome, began of a blinde love of a fond father, framing for his comfort an Image of his sonne, being dead, and so at the last men fell to the worshipping of the Image of him whom they did know to be dead.[70]

Illustrating both Elizabethan and Elizabeth's formation of English anti-memorialism, in the officially sanctioned definition of the second *Homilies*, disseminated throughout the country, idolatry is nothing other than the over-representation of the dead.

A final example illustrates that the aim of reducing memorial action for the dead was a distinctive feature of active Protestantism from Elizabeth's coronation onwards. For the following epistolary condemnation by Edmund Grindal of funerary practices in London in 1570 anticipates the Bishop of Carlisle in 1629, and indeed *The Directory for the Public Worship of God* of 1644, with 'logical' precision:

> I am informed that the greatest part of our gentlemen are not well affected to godly religion, and that among the people there are many remnants of the old. They keep holy days and fasts abrogated, they offer money, eggs, etc. at the burial of their dead: they pray on beads, etc.: so as this seemeth to be, as it were, another church, rather than a member of the rest.[71]

Thus in each commentary, and over the span of more than fifty years, one finds the same Reformist ambition to reduce performed remembrances for the dead. Elizabeth may have tolerated (a diminished number of) such memorials, but the Reformation she actively encouraged, and which flourished around and after her, did not.

This bears crucially on the interpretation of our genre. For especially in its earlier presentations, one of the recurring features of revenge tragedy is the emphatic *value* it attaches to extensive funerary performance, the genre thus defying the reductions of that performance by the Reformers as, indeed, their counter-valuation of its ritual as idolatry. In defiance of the Reform as we shall see, thus, in revenge tragedy corpses are repeatedly viewed as dishonoured and thus devalued if *deprived* of their funeral's ritual, ritually performed funeral being thus positively evaluated; or else dramatic persons are *punished* by a funerary deprivation, rites of funeral being thus again valued positively in defiance of the active Reform.

And thus, revenge tragedy is very different from the Broudian picture of it: though eventually coming to an extent to subvert them, it is a genre rooted in the culture of traditional memorials. As such, however, it seems substantially what Grindal and those like him deemed 'of the old ... another church, rather than a

---

[70] See Scodel, p. 24.

[71] Quoted by Clare Gittings in 'Urban Funerals in Late Medieval and Reformation England', in *Death in Towns: Urban Responses to the Dying and the Dead, 100–1600*, ed. by Steven Bassett (Leicester and New York: Leicester University Press; St Martin's Press, 1992), p. 174. In this essay, Gittings also discusses geographical differences regarding funeral practices in England.

member of the rest': a surviving expression of Catholic culture in the officially, but as yet not completely, Reformed England. Before the demonstration of this claim, however, I at last turn to mourning and the aesthetics of its action. For performances of mourning figure largely in the actions of revengers, making this aspect of funerary memorial require special attention.

Mourning and its Aesthetics at the 'Change of Religion'

Having presented versions of it in 1914 and 1915, in 1917 Freud published 'Mourning and Melancholia', thus presenting Hamlet in what would become to students of Renaissance drama the familiar guise of the melancholic.[72] Criticism of the drama, however, has said much less about mourning – surprisingly as Freud insists there is 'an essential analogy between the work of melancholia and of mourning',[73] and surprisingly too because he associated *both* conditions with such key themes as 'fury', 'mania' and 'revenge'.[74] As Ralph Houlbrooke has observed, even Michael Neill's *Issues of Death* (which illustrates the pervasiveness of mournful funeral in Renaissance drama and with which this study is therefore contiguous) says next to nothing of the substantial religious dimensions of mourning in the period,[75] and

---

[72] On p. 23 of '*Hamlet* Then till Now' (in *Aspects of Hamlet: Articles Reprinted from 'Shakespeare Survey'*, ed. by Kenneth Muir and Stanley Wells, [Cambridge: Cambridge University Press, 1979], pp. 16–27), Harold Jenkins identifies Schückling's *Die Charakterproblem bei Shakespeare* (published 1919, translated 1922) as the first dramatic study of the melancholic, but this is *after* Freud's focus on the topic of melancholy *and* his specific observation of *Hamlet* within it; it also post-dates A.C. Bradley's paragraphs on Hamlet's melancholy in *Shakespearean Tragedy: Lectures on 'Hamlet', 'Othello', 'King Lear' and 'Macbeth'*, which was originally published in 1904. For details of the composition and publication of Freud's essay, see the 'Editor's Note' to 'Mourning and Melancholy', in *The Standard Edition of The Complete Psychological Works of Sigmund Freud*, vol. 14, trans. by James Strachey, ed. by Anna Freud, Alix Strachey and Alan Tyson (London: The Hogarth Press, 1957; repr. 1962; 1964), p. 239; for Freud's citation of Hamlet as exemplary melancholic, see p. 246.

[73] Freud, p. 257.

[74] See Freud, pp. 257, 253 and following and 251 respectively. Notice that one need not rely on the 'anachronism' of Freud to pursue this reading: repression of emotion, which leads to vengeance, is already visible in Seneca. See Gordon Braden, *Renaissance Tragedy and the Senecan Tradition: Anger's Privilege* (New Haven, CT: Yale University Press, 1985).

[75] For Neill's study, see *Issues of Death: Mortality and Identity in English Renaissance Tragedy* (Oxford: Clarendon Press, 1997). A study such as mine cannot overstate its broad debt to Neill for demonstrating the pervasive impact of the contemporary funerary culture on the drama. However, as historian Ralph Houlbrooke observes generally, the 'religious context' is notably underplayed in Neill's book, 'especially … the tension between Catholic and Protestant doctrines of the hereafter'. A more specific difference between Neill's approach and my own is that Neill pays little attention to the official *differences* between contemporary Christian outlooks regarding burial. Thus, following Philippe Ariès, he simply observes that 'the Renaissance [*sic*] continued to preserve the ancient pagan superstition that happiness beyond the grave was somehow contingent upon proper disposal and preservation of one's mortal remains' (Neill, *Issues of Death*, p. 256). For Houlbrooke's criticism, see his review

so there remain calls for further investigation.[76] In addressing mourning *and* its contemporary religious aesthetics, then, I redress a further critical imbalance to that instigated by Broude.[77]

According to the *O.E.D.*, 'mourning' denotes a feeling ('Anxiety, sorrow etc.'), but also 'The action of feeling or expressing' that feeling. The distinction reminds us that mournful feeling can take a form not intrinsic to the feeling itself: that its performance is adaptable.[78] That realisation was central to the Reformed programme for remembering the dead, which attempted (among such reductions of ritual as I have documented) to reduce the performance of emotion. Opposing what he considered the extravagance of popish funerals, thus, the Marian martyr John Bradford argued that 'we [the Reformed] bury the dead in a convenient place, and mourn *in measure*'.[79] Implying behaviour emotionally restrained, such 'measured' mourning presents the standard understanding by active Protestants of appropriate affect in memory of the dead. In his 1595 sermon entitled *The Meane in Mourning*, thus, Thomas Playfere

---

of *Issues of Death* in *Renaissance Forum* 4/1 (1999), http://www.hull.ac.uk/renforum/v4no1/houlbroo.htm, last accessed 30 October 2007.

[76] See, for example, David Cressy's call for studies of death in the drama to match Peter Marshall's historical work, in Cressy's review of Peter Marshall's *Beliefs and the Dead in Reformation England*, in *Renaissance Quarterly* 57 (Spring 2004), p. 358.

[77] Especially in her emphasis on 'Our Lady of Sorrows', this imbalance has gained an opening redress in Katharine Goodland's *Female Mourning in Medieval and Renaissance English Drama: From the Raising of Lazarus to 'King Lear'*, Studies in Performance and Early Modern Drama (Aldershot: Ashgate, 2005), but the general thesis that 'female mourning in early modern drama is a spectral force, often threatening, that shapes the unfolding action and seems to vanish as soon as it is perceived' (p. 2) is reductive: mourning is far from an exclusively female occupation in such drama, thus far more generic than Goodland allows; thus, though in revenge tragedy 'mourning women' are often 'dangerous instigators of revenge' (Goodland, p. 155), mourning *men* are normally the enactors – and thus also instigators – of revenge. Theatrical mourning has also lately received attention from Tobias Döring's *Performances of Mourning in Shakespearean Theatre and Early Modern Culture*, Early Modern Literature in History (Basingstoke and New York: Palgrave Macmillan, 2006), though despite acknowledging that it 'perhaps retrieved some of the emotions associated with the outlawed [Roman Catholic] faith' (Döring, p. 10), Döring presents a 'sceptical and cautious view' of religion in the theatre (Döring, p. 20): his 'performative approach' emphasizes 'recent theoretical debates in cultural and literary studies' (Döring, pp. 20 and 13) at the expense of emphasis on how in the period religion and theatre simultaneously *meant* performance – as I especially argue in this Introduction and in Chapter 2, as more generally in this study. Implying moral and theatrical distinctions which I argue (in Chapter 1) neither the plays nor the era maintain, but which bear crucially on how the genre's mournings are ultimately valued, Döring's further view that the mournings of revengers 'go wrong' so that they 'turn into mad revengers' (Döring, p. 73) presents another substantial difference between us.

[78] 'Grief was both a natural and a cultural phenomenon. It was something people felt, but also something they performed' (Cressy, *Birth, Marriage and Death*, p. 393). For detailed discussion of such adaptable 'performance' in our period, see also Jennifer Woodward, *The Theatre of Death: The Ritual Management of Royal Funerals in Renaissance England, 1570–1625* (Woodbridge: The Boydell Press, 1997), especially pp. 37–61 on 'Funeral Ritual and the Reformation'.

[79] Marshall, p. 113; my emphasis.

allowed mourners to weep 'so long as it was not immoderate':[80] the purportedly Aristotelian 'mean' he advocated was to be 'balanced' rather than 'excessive'. Similarly, in the 1620s, Bishop Gervase Babington and Samuel Gardiner reiterate how 'fit and allowable' duties toward the dead included moderate, but only moderate, mourning.[81] The prescription of the 1644 *Directory* that those 'Christian friends' (significantly not, notice, 'mourners') 'which accompany the dead body to the place appointed for public burial' must 'apply themselves to meditations and conferences suitable to the occasion' ruled out extravagant displays of funerary emotion.[82]

This aesthetic of behaviour was not legally achieved without resistance. As the English Church of the early 1600s began to imagine a future 'Via Media', Protestants also imagined a 'new generation of "affective" relations' with the dead,[83] which in the 1630s became, however relatively, 'more pronounced'.[84] Yet the gradualness of this development is telling: the Reformed emphasis on 'moderate' mourning was deep-seated and widespread.[85] Reformed exhortations for such mourning in England echoed views expressed by John Foxe in his massively popular *Acts and Monuments*, which themselves echoed Calvin's *Institutes*. Commenting on the father who keeps an image of his dead son in *The Book of Wisdom*, a favourite text for Reformers, Calvin had argued that the father 'conferred ... honor on the dead, and thus superstitiously worshipped [his son's] memory', presenting a rhetoric of 'honour' (though not always its condemnation) recalled in successive revenge tragedies. Recalling Calvin's admonition, however, Foxe warned his readers against excessive grief: the mourner must not 'let the remembrance of your children keep

---

[80] Cressy, *Birth, Marriage and Death*, p. 393.

[81] Marshall, p. 266.

[82] Citation from Rowell, p. 83. Recall, too, that the minister was to put such 'friends' in 'remembrance of their duty'.

[83] Nigel Llewellyn, *Funeral Monuments in Post-Reformation England* (Cambridge: Cambridge University Press, 2001), p. 356.

[84] Llewellyn, p. 51. Although an exceptional moment, the death of Prince Henry in 1612 is of note in this development: it elicited a host of English funeral elegies openly calling for floods of tears. Yet even these texts present mourning as problematic. Emphasizing funerary ritual and calling for the tears of its readers as the response of 'faithful subjects', for example, the anonymous collection of verse *Great Britans Mourning Garment Given to all faithfull subjects at the funeral of Prince Henry* (1612) presents itself as an extended lamentation. Appealing to higher powers to aid in this funerary project, however, the second sonnet in the sequence emphasizes that for the poet to succeed in inducing tears, a 'refounding' of funerary ritual will be necessary: 'You that have fill'd your veins with heavenly foode, / And scorn to pray upon the barraine ground, / Help me these Funerall Anthems to refound.' Here as elsewhere, the collection implies that the extensive grief it advocates is no longer integral in funerals, suggesting the death of Henry presented an opportunity to protest at restrictions over commemorative emotion. See *Great Britans Mourning Garment Given to all faithful subjects at the funeral of Prince Henry* (London, 1612) in the Henry E. Huntington Library and Art Gallery, http://eebo.chadwyck.com/search, last accessed 30 October 2007.

[85] Notice that for sixteenth-century Protestants even weeping *not* intended for the dead was 'overtly associated ... with Catholicism'. See Shell, p. 57.

you from God'.[86] The emerging language of emotional ration, which treats grief as measurable ('mean', 'excess', 'measure') and invites distinctions between 'rational' and 'irrational' on the basis of what will or will not 'keep you from God', is striking. That both more and less godly among Reformed took such ration for 'rationality' is clear. We have noted already Thomas Browne's uneasy refrain from the 'over-mourning' of prayer, but he was not alone. As Houlbrooke notes, Puritans such as Simmonds D'Ewes as well as 'a Protestant, but hardly a Puritan' like Sir Ralph Verney guiltily blamed their mournings for having 'made the loved one an idol, a focus of excessive affection'.[87]

Since G.W. Pigman observed the inadequacy of 'the history of the emotions and of the family' in 1985, the topic has received much attention.[88] Pigman's own tentative but grand narrative 'of the emergence of a more compassionate and less anxious attitude towards mourning' in the sixteenth and seventeenth centuries now itself appears untenable.[89] Regarding anxiety, it misses how the emerging, Reformed concern that the dead not be prayed for increased strictures over the breadth of rites of commemoration; and during the two centuries in question, it fails to distinguish sufficiently between periodic differences of emphasis – not all heading toward 'compassion'[90] – on how one might mourn. Nevertheless, Pigman's study of a variety of writings (essays, sermons, formularies, disputations, tracts) anticipates in detail the present, developing interest in the 'measuring' of mourning of the period. I therefore turn to that detail, noting especially the prescriptions for mourning by Elizabethan and Jacobean divines.

Such prescriptions include writings by so-called 'moderates', such as the Archbishops of Canterbury Matthew Parker and John Whitgift, as well as of 'radicals' such as Thomas Cartwright. In the controversy between Whitgift and Cartwright

---

[86] See Calvin's *Institutes* 1.11.8 and Foxe's *Acts and Monuments* 8:702 as cited by Diehl, pp. 121–2.

[87] See Ralph Houlbrooke, *Death, Religion and the Family in England, 1400–1750* (Oxford: Clarendon Press, 1998), p. 243.

[88] G.W. Pigman III, *Grief and English Renaissance Elegy* (Cambridge: Cambridge University Press, 1985), p. 2. I have cited a number of the developers of the topic above.

[89] I say 'tentative', here, because Pigman acknowledged the origins of the purported 'shift in attitudes' to be 'obscure'; indeed: 'it seems to me that it is too early too offer an explanation [of it]' (Pigman, p. 2). To avoid returning to the issue in successive footnotes, I note that this inconsistency between offering and not offering a complete thesis of the 'the emergence of a more compassionate and less anxious attitude towards mourning' dogs Pigman's study more largely. This is because he expands his grand narrative of historical development over a number of chapters, but also rightly acknowledges that the process 'is neither uniform nor unilateral' (Pigman, p. 2).

[90] The rigorous Edwardine attempts of 1547–1553 to restrict mourning present a substantial obstacle to even a broad thesis of *sixteenth*-century progress towards compassionate mourning. In larger historical perspective, moreover, historians remain unclear as to whether the Reformation's abolition of effective prayer for the dead was not itself a development uncompassionate towards the living. Houlbrooke, for example, argues that in teaching that the prayers of the living aided the dead, 'the Roman Catholic Church offered the possibility of therapeutic positive action on behalf of the survivors' (Houlbrooke, *Death, Religion and the Family*, p. 243).

over the *Admonition to Parliament*, however, 'moderation of mourning is one of the very few things that Thomas Cartwright and John Whitgift agree upon'.[91] Indeed, with occasional exceptions of the late 1620s, in which the first sustained defences of emotional mourning emerge and to which I shall return, extant examples of Reformed opinion on the topic divide into two broad types: 'rigorism' and '*de facto* rigorism'.[92] More precisely, in the period:

> Unrestricted mourning never finds a theological champion, but some advocates of moderation insist upon mourning as a necessary expression of humanity. This second position is really a matter of emphasis because the necessity of moderation is never lost sight of. The third position ... [r]igorism ... prohibits and condemns all grief for those who have died virtuously and are in heaven.[93]

That the differences were merely 'of emphasis' is illustrated in the characteristic *de facto* rigour of Thomas Wilson, who in his *Arte of Rhetorique* (1553), fearing that mourning may be a sin, and certain it becomes one unless quickly suppressed, permits the bereaved only a single day to master his grief.[94]

Clearly by 'modern' standards this is not moderation; Freud's claim that human beings know interference in mourning to be 'useless or even harmful' looks sadly optimistic.[95] But Reformed prescriptions – particularly in texts like the *Arte of Rhetorique* – bear on the age's mourning literature, including revenge tragedy; in presenting a *performative* ideal, moreover, the prescriptions present a measure for the *staging* of mourning. Against that ideal standard of Reformers, thus, this study will 'measure' the Reformed-ness of revenge tragedy. How specifically Reformed mournful 'rigour' is, however, requires inspection.

One relevant consideration is the self-perception of Reformers. We have seen how over-elaborate, allegedly 'superstitious' rites of funeral continued to be interpreted as 'popish' long after Elizabeth's accession. But contemporaries linked such rites with a specific culture of emotion. According to Hugh Latimer in a sermon of 1553, for example, it was specifically 'In the time of popery, before the gospel came amongst us, [that] we went to burials, with weeping and wailing, as thoughe there wer no god.'[96] Similarly, in his consolatory treatise on the death of Elizabeth I, Radford Mavericke advised: 'mourne as Christians, and not as the Heathen and the Papists doe'.[97] In such sermons and treatises, expansive commemorative emotion is a very sign of popery, which in turn is conceived of as un-Christian ('before the gospel came amongst us'; 'not as the Heathen') and indeed atheistic ('as thoughe there wer no god').

---

[91] Pigman, p. 33.
[92] Pigman, pp. 27–39; the phrase '*de facto* rigorism' appears on p. 39.
[93] Pigman, p. 27.
[94] Pigman, p. 17.
[95] Freud, p. 244.
[96] Cited in Pigman, p. 32.
[97] Cited by Patricia Phillippy in *Women, Death and Literature in Post-Reformation England* (Cambridge: Cambridge University Press, 2002), p. 11.

Nor were Latimer and Mavericke alone in making strong, cultural distinctions between Catholic and Reformed, 'un-Christian' and 'Christian', indeed, 'beastly' and 'reasonable'. 'Make small weeping for the dead', advised Matthew Parker in a sermon of 1551, at what was Martin Bucer's showcase funeral; for 'it is both unseemly and wicked to use any howling or blubbering for him [the dead], unless we desire to be accounted endued rather with beastly nature then furnished with the use of reason; to be deemed Heathen people rather then true christians'.[98] Like Latimer especially, Parker advises a 'small' grief, and presents 'howling or blubbering' as the mark both of 'heathens' and of Christians who are not 'true', such truth being discerned through a 'reason' we shall notice as 'godly'. However, as Patricia Phillippy observes generally, to Reformed writers 'the excesses of ancient ritual lamentation were easily aligned with those of Catholic superstition'.[99]

But despite such influential historical perspective, the reality was different from the self-perception and ideology of Reformers – and to this second consideration I now turn. Though the Reformed interpreted anything more than *de facto* 'rigour' in remembrance of the dead as popery, their prescriptions inevitably derived much both from the Roman 'heathens' and from their Roman 'Catholic' successors whose cultures preceded. Assessing the full extent of this problematic debt is beyond the scope of the present study,[100] but Thomas Wilson's debt to Erasmus sufficiently suggests 'actual', as opposed to 'ideological' (and widely believed), differences between the Reformed and pre-Reformed or 'Romish'.

Despite Reformed contentions that 'Rome' equalled excess in post-mortem memorial, Erasmus, in his 'extraordinarily popular and influential' *De conscribendis epistolis* of 1522, presents a synthesis of ancient arguments against 'excessive' grief for the dead, as well as a variety of strategies for helping the bereaved to overcome grief.[101] Indeed, Reformers drew deeply on this tract, Wilson's *Arte of Rhetorique* being so indebted to its discussion of mourning as to recall it in 'all but one' of its classical exempla.[102] However, three substantial but related developments between Erasmus and Wilson's presentations are discernable:

---

[98] Cited by Pigman, pp. 29–30. Pigman discusses further passages from Parker's sermon, which reiterate this perspective.

[99] Phillippy, p. 15.

[100] Kristian Jensen provides useful comment on the problem in 'Reform of Latin and Latin Teaching', in *The Cambridge Companion to Renaissance Humanism*, ed. by Jill Kraye (Cambridge: Cambridge University Press, 1996; repr. 1997; 1998; 2001; 2003), pp. 63–81 (77–9). Particularly notice how the likes of Martin Bucer considered Latin 'a political instrument, an expression of the Roman Catholic claim to a unity between the Church and ancient Latin culture' (p. 78). For standard discussion of medieval Catholicism's syncretions with 'paganism' – and of the separation of 'pagan' from 'Christian' at 'the Reformation' – see Keith Thomas, *Religion and the Decline of Magic* (London: Weidenfeld and Nicholson, 1973), though its contrast of 'magic' with 'religion' looks biased today and is being questioned more and more.

[101] Pigman, p. 12.

[102] Pigman, p. 16.

> Wilson has greater faith in straightforward appeals to reason and relies less [than Erasmus] on the bereaved's self-image in the battle against grief. His [Wilson's] greater faith in reason accompanies a greater anxiety about the emotions. He [Wilson] is more worried by the theological implications of mourning, which he apparently believes Christianity condemns as despair and faithlessness.[103]

Thus, in opposing excessive mourning, the substantial difference between Erasmus and Wilson lies in the latter's newly *theological* (and thus allegedly reasonable) anxiety. It was not that Christians before the Reformation were excessive mourners *per se*, but that they placed greater emphasis on emotion in the procedure than did their Reformed successors, the latter preferring to emphasize 'godly logic' or 'theology'.[104] It is against the heightened sense of the irreligion (heathen and popish) of emotion in remembrance of the dead, then, that we can measure and interpret the Reformed-ness or otherwise of revenge tragedy. Considering 'godliness', however, clarifies this further.

The historical connotations of 'godly' are Reformed, 'the godly' denoting a religious style and Reformed social identity, but the *O.E.D.* suggests that 'godliness' is integral to English Protestantism: 'godly' originates with the pre-Reformer Wyclif, and Tyndale's English Bible translated 2 Cor. 7:9 as 'for godly sorrowe causeth repentaunce', disseminating 'godly' among Reformed as 'Biblical':

> For when we were com into Macedonia, oure fleshe had no rest, but we were troubled on every side: outwarde was fightynge, inwarde was feare. Nevertheless he that comfortith the abiecte, comforted us at the commynge of Titus.
>
> And nott with his commynge only: butt also with the consolacion wherewith he was comforted of you. For he tolde us youre desire, youre mornynge, youre fervent mynd to mewarde So that I nowe reioyce the more. Wherefore though I mad you sory with a letter I repent not: though I did repent. For I perceived that that same Epistle made you sory though it were but for a ceason. But I nowe reioyce, not that ye were sory, but that ye so sorrowed, that ye repented. Fo ye sorrowed godly [*sic*]: so that in nothynge were ye hurtte by us. for godly sorrowe causeth repentaunce unto health, not to be repented off: when worldly sorrowe causeth deeth.[105]

Distinguishing between the good and bad sorrower as between those 'of god' and those not, and again highlighting the performativity of memorial, Tyndale's 'ye sorrowed godly' implies that godliness entails a specific style of sorrowing (the Authorized Version brings this out in 'ye were made sorry after a godly *manner*'). Specifically, moreover, the godly 'manner' is restricted to one that 'causeth repentance' rather than 'causeth death'. Thus, the style of mourning was integral to godly Reformation: Tyndale's Bible – controversial both in its unprecedented use of 'godly' in Biblical

---

[103] Pigman, p. 16.

[104] According to the *O.E.D.*, the word 'theology' was defined as 'the science of things Divine' in the period (by Richard Hooker); etymologically, the Greek 'theo-' means 'God', theology thus implying 'godly logic'.

[105] Cited from *The New Testament: Translated by William Tyndale: The Text of the Worms Edition of 1526 in Original Spelling*, ed. by W.R. Cooper (London: The British Library, 2000), pp. 386–7.

translation and in its emphasis on 'repentance'[106] – interpreted godliness as a feature of persons restricting sadness to repentance, thus interpreting any other style of grief as 'un-Christian'.

Exemplifying David Cressy's *dictum* that the 'reformation of religion … went hand in hand with the reformation of manners',[107] this Reformed view of an appropriate Christian style of mourning bears on the mourning literature of the period as a whole. Similarly, the styles of performance it encourages (and forbids) bear on funerary revenge tragedy.[108] Reformed Englishmen such as Puttenham or Sidney insisted that proportion and appropriateness (and so 'ration' and 'rationality') were key to literary aesthetics;[109] however, as we shall see, revenge tragedies present their own versions of what is proportionate and appropriate in the prohibitive matter of remembering the dead, thus actively contending with the performative aesthetics of Reformers.

As I shall show in Chapter 1, by defying the rule of restricted mourning for the dead, the excesses or 'melodrama' of *The Spanish Tragedy*, *Titus Andronicus* and *Hamlet* defy the Reformed prohibitions. Highlighting their traditionalism or 'ungodliness', these three plays defend as 'proportionate' performances of mourning which Reformers continued to think of as 'excessive' well into the 1620s.[110] As we

---

[106] Compare the translation from the Greek of The Jerusalem Bible: 'To suffer in God's way [*sic*] means changing for the better and leaves no regrets [*sic*], but to suffer as the world knows suffering brings death.' Except perhaps indirectly and by interpretation, there is nothing about 'repentance' in this newer translation, while even Tyndale's 'godly sorrowe' is 'in God's way'.

[107] Cressy writes: 'The reformation of religion … went hand in hand with the reformation of manners. Along with their attacks on the errors of papism, English protestant reformers urged propriety and decency in social and religious rituals … It was a common cry among godly activists that "we ought … to bury our dead decently, comely and honestly, without the vanity or error of pomp" … Moderate reformers sought a balance between sumptuousness and simplicity, seeking on the one hand to show due respect for the departed, on the other to avoid superstitious ostentation and excess' (Cressy, *Birth, Marriage and Death*, pp. 412–13).

[108] On this substantial point I disagree completely with Zimmerman, for whom 'plays of blood and/or revenge foregrounded an explicit, even outrageous, sensationalism that would seem to preclude serious symbolic import' (Zimmerman, p. 12); all the historical evidence noted previously – none of which Zimmerman investigates – suggests that the 'excess' of revenge tragedy is of a *most* serious import; for more general differences between us, see note 56 of this Introduction.

[109] Sidney notes that the poet 'cometh to you with words set in delightful proportion', praising his 'exquisite observing of number and measure in the words'. He also argues that 'scornful' laughter 'almost ever cometh of things most disproportioned to ourselves and nature'. See his 'The Defense of Poetry', pp. 511, 503, 524. For Puttenham's detailed treatment of the matter, see 'The Second Book, Of Proportion Poetical' in *The Art of English Poesie*.

[110] Pigman cites two tracts of 1629 [*sic*] as both 'more sympathetic' than, and thus 'radically different' from, the rigorist and *de facto* rigorist views of mourning previously dominant among Reformers: Zacharie Boyd's *The Last Battell of the Soul in Death* and James Cole's *Of Death a True Description*. That the rise of such perspectives coincides with the rise of a sometimes anti-Calvinist and 'Anglican' 'Via Media' cannot be coincidental. That it is

shall begin to see in Chapter 2, in which *Antonio's Revenge* at St Paul's also highlights interaction between 'Church' and 'theatre', and as we shall further see of the later *The Revenger's Tragedy*, *The Atheist's Tragedy*, *The White Devil* and *The Duchess of Malfi* in Chapter 3, mourning becomes – though for the most part not properly Reformed – much more uncertain. Seeming to confirm from a literary standpoint the 'long Reformation' historians now argue for, however, what is perhaps most interesting in these developed revenges is how largely traditional their memorials remain.

Yet although we shall encounter versions of it again, what is already clear, even from this discussion confined largely to rituals of the dead, is the inadequacy of the Broudian view with which this study – and modern criticism of the genre's religion – began. Since Protestants maintained rituals condemned by their Reformed masters, Broude's assumption that 'Protestant interpreters' [*sic*] each viewed Catholicism as the same, absolute Babylon is mistaken. Especially in regard to the dead, it turns out, and thus especially relevantly for revenge tragedy, too many Protestants maintained that 'Babylon' in their own rituals. However, my interpretative claim is that remembrance of the dead is indeed the focal context for revenge tragedy and its religion – a claim requiring large demonstration. We must turn to the plays.

---

not until as late as 1629 that such opinion even *begins* to emerge substantially, however, is evidence of how ingrained Reformed 'rigour' had become. The commemorative triumph of 'active Protestants' in the *Public Directory* of 1644 (as Puritan replaces 'High Anglican' in power) shows how controversial even this alternative perspective would remain.

Chapter 1

'Outrage Fits': Revenge and the 'Melodrama' of Mourning in *The Spanish Tragedy*, *Titus Andronicus* and *Hamlet*[1]

*The Spanish Tragedy, c.*1586–1587[2]

The persistence of 'Broudian' readings of *The Spanish Tragedy* is visible in an essay by J.R. Mulryne published in 1996, in which he discusses Hieronimo's play 'Soliman and Perseda' as follows: 'If we accept the Hispanophobic prejudice drawn out by [Ronald] Broude and [Eugene] Hill as pertinent to the play as a whole, then the relevance of the Turkish tragedy of Soliman and Perseda to the play's portrayal of the fall of the papist realm of Spain becomes obvious.'[3] Reflecting the importance of *The Spanish Tragedy* in Broude's theory of 'classic' revenges, this tragedy was the only one to which Broude accorded a whole essay on matters religious.[4] Since this essay presents Broude's most detailed and developed illustration of his theory, it is without apology that I begin with a consideration of Hill *and* Broude's specific arguments: on them both, as Mulryne recognized, *The Spanish Tragedy*'s alleged anti-Catholicism has substantially rested, while Broude's particular attention to the play deserves a particular response. Despite Mulryne, however, notice from the outset that although given focus by a Spanish Armada both threatened and in 1588 delivered, English antipathy to Imperial Spain is not to be equated simply with anti-Catholicism: irrespective of their religion, Elizabethans (including Catholics)

---

[1] Parts of the first section of this chapter have been previously published in a journal as: Thomas Rist, 'Memorial Revenge at the Reformations(s): Kyd's *The Spanish Tragedy*', in *Cahiers Elisabéthains*: *A Biannual Journal of English Renaissance Studies* 71 (Spring 2007), pp. 15–25.

[2] Although the initial dates for contemporary plays are rarely known exactly, I shall provide approximate dates for each of our plays – based on standard scholarly assessments and normally accurate to within a year or two – to provide a broad sense of chronology. I shall provide further details where necessary. Thus, notice that *The Spanish Tragedy* is unusually difficult to date: though normally placed between 1586 and 1587, it has been dated from as early as 1582 and as late as 1590.

[3] See J.R. Mulryne, 'Nationality and Language in Kyd's *The Spanish Tragedy*', in *Travel and Drama in Shakespeare's Time*, ed. by Jean-Pierre Maquerlot and Michèle Willems (Cambridge: Cambridge University Press, 1996), pp. 87–105 (97).

[4] For this essay especially focused on *The Spanish Tragedy*, see Ronald Broude, 'Truth, Time and Right in *The Spanish Tragedy*', in *Studies in Philology* 68 (1971), pp. 130–45.

could resent Spain on grounds purely patriotic.⁵ Pointed though it *may* be – I shall challenge this too – *The Spanish Tragedy*'s 'Iberian history'⁶ is therefore not in itself anti-Catholic; and since we can no longer infer a Protestant audience holistically anti-Catholic, we should not thus delimit the play.

This chapter argues a further point against Broude and Hill: that their anti-Catholic readings ignore vital pieces of information and therefore *cannot* be said (again despite Mulryne) to describe *The Spanish Tragedy* 'as a whole'. Bearing in mind the historical observations of the Introduction, this argument will demonstrate textually how substantial the *un-Reformed* aspect of the play is, and thus how incomplete (and occasionally unlikely) anti-Catholic readings are – especially as there is only one direct allusion to 'Babylon' in *The Spanish Tragedy*.⁷ Fending off suspicions of misrepresentation by drawing on his established (and sympathetic) accounts, however, I begin with Mulryne's useful summaries of Broude and Hill's positions.

Mulryne summarizes Broude as follows:

> Broude argues that Kyd's play may be seen to turn on the fulcrum of Isabella's line (II.v.59):
> *'Time is the author both of truth and right.'*
> He [Broude] tells us:
> Time as the revealer of truth and bringer of justice was a topos well known in Humanist circles ... It was particularly prominent in Protestant thought ... During the ominous 1580's and 90's ... the *topos* [*sic*.] enjoyed special currency and seemed to promise not only that England would come through individual trials but that Divine Providence would guide English Protestantism through all its perils to ultimate victory.
>
> The narrative of *The Spanish Tragedy*, Broude says, functions to reveal this humanist (but here sectarian) *topos* in action. Four narrative threads bind the play together in a series of revelations. Innocence is vindicated, calumny is unmasked, secret murder is revealed and avenged, and the wickedness of the Spanish royal house is brought to light. The play's ultimate catastrophe shows Time as not merely serial but providential. Broude takes this to mean that *The Spanish Tragedy* must have jingoistic appeal for its English audience.⁸

Superficially this seems plausible enough, but a moment's consideration reveals inherent problems. If the 'innocence' of Hieronimo is vindicated, what are we to make of his death? And if Spain presents 'wickedness', what are we to make of

---

⁵ For detailed discussion of English, Catholic 'loyalism' addressing both Elizabethan and Stuart eras, see Shell, pp. 107–68. Regarding Catholic responses to the Armada specifically, notice Asquith's following observation: 'even exiles in the English College in Rome leapt to their feet and cheered at the news [of the Armada's defeat]'. See Asquith, p. 17.

⁶ The phrase is Mulryne's. See Mulryne, p. 101.

⁷ Thus, anticipating 'Soliman and Perseda' (of which more), Hieronimo says: 'Now shall I see the fall of Babylon / Wrought by the heavens' (IV.i.189–90). Broudian critics have taken this single allusion to 'Babylon' to imply a sectarian perspective, arguing their reading is borne out by the play's wider view of a providential 'time'. I consider and challenge such reading below. All quotations from *The Spanish Tragedy* are from *Four Revenge Tragedies*, ed. by Katharine Eisaman Maus (Oxford and New York: Oxford University Press, 1995).

⁸ Mulryne, pp. 88–9.

its 'innocent' conqueror's Spanish-ness? Perhaps these paradoxes can be resolved – especially if we recognize the paradox of a Reformed England still largely in the thrall of Catholic customs – but in the Broudian reading they reveal a discordance. Further discordance is revealed by Broude himself: his reading, he acknowledges, is 'symbolic', rather than strictly historical, because 'the Spain of Kyd's play cannot be taken literally as the historical Spain'.[9] This acknowledgement implies that less 'symbolic', more strictly historical (and perhaps other), readings of *The Spanish Tragedy* will reveal differing views of its religio-politic; in addition, notice that if the anti-Spanish reading is 'symbolic', then an interpretative leap is needed to achieve it which is not textually self-evident – a point worth emphasizing as anti-Spanish readings tacitly but fallaciously imply the play's contemporary reference to a corrupt Spain implies hostility to *all* things Spanish. However, even leaving each of these difficulties aside, there remains a more substantial problem: one should not but hesitate to endorse the reading of an entire play which centres on a single idea – let alone a single line. Nor, being the basis of the play's holistic interpretation, should the line thus bear so powerfully on the interpretation of the genre! Illustratively, in what follows I shall argue that the implication of different lines belonging to Isabella – especially 'O, gush out, tears, fountains and floods of tears; / Blow, sighs, and raise an everlasting storm; / For outrage fits our cursed wretchedness' (II.iv.105–7) – offer a very different perspective of *The Spanish Tragedy*.

Next, however, I consider Hill's argument, again making use of Mulryne's established and sympathetic summary. Highlighting another drawback of Broude's analysis, this view 'takes in, as Broude does not, the framing action of Andrea and Revenge':[10]

> For Hill, *The Spanish Tragedy* evokes, foregrounds and enacts 'a *translatio studii*, an historical rearticulating of privileged cultural models', these models being the creative insights associated with Virgil (in the framing action largely) and with Seneca. Recent studies, Hill argues, have recovered something of the Elizabethan Seneca as a writer who 'has no peer among classical poets in conveying the texture of evil in a hopelessly corrupt polity'. Virgil, by contrast, evokes in the *Aeneid* the burying of a regretted past, and the foundation of an enduring kingdom. 'In Seneca', Hill writes, 'we observe with horror a hell-bent royal house, foundering in corruption. In Virgil we participate with wonderment

---

[9] See Broude, pp. 144–5. Broude would repeat this point two years later when transforming his reading of *The Spanish Tragedy* into a reading of revenge tragedy as a whole: 'The Spain of Kyd's play is not the historical Spain, but rather a symbol of the vice-ridden kingdom smitten by divine vengeance.' See '*Vindicta Filia Temporis*', p. 497.

[10] Mulryne, pp. 89–90. In view of all the above shortcomings in Broude's analysis, I dispense with anti-Catholic interpretations – for example, Frank Ardolino's – in which the religio-politic does not in *essence* develop Broude. Arguing that *The Spanish Tragedy* 'cannot be reduced to a piece of Protestant propaganda', however, Janette Dillon directly challenges Ardolino *and* Mulryne's views of the play in Dillon, pp. 35, 40. For Ardolino's articles, see '"Now Shall I See the Fall of Babylon": *The Spanish Tragedy*', in *Shakespeare Yearbook* 1 (1990), pp. 106–13. Also, 'Hieronimo Agonistes: Kyd's Use of Hieronimo as Sanctified Revenger in *The Spanish Tragedy*', in *Journal of Evolutionary Psychology* 15 (1994), pp. 161–5. Mapping Milton's known Reformist outlook back onto Kyd, the second article is especially problematic in its inferences.

in a rite of passage which inaugurates a new era of history. The Senecan emphasis of *The Spanish Tragedy* is perhaps clear enough; the Virgilian perhaps needs some clarification. The Senecan prologue of the play, Hill explains, has been rewritten as an inversion of *Aeneid* VI:

'In place of *pious* Aeneas ... Kyd gives us proud Andrea ... Aeneas is led into the underworld by the ever-vigilant Sybil ... Andrea is taken from the underworld by Revenge, who falls asleep. Aeneas learns the glorious destiny of his Trojan line and sees the future Emperor of Rome; Andrea watches the downfall of the Spanish royal house...'

Hill shows how such sentiments would chime with popular myth-making among the Elizabethans. Spain came to be regarded as a kingdom 'too arrogant to note that it is ripe for downfall', while England began to cherish imperialist visions of London as the new Troy (following Rome) and Englishmen as the new Romans. Thus anti-Spanish propaganda achieves in Kyd's play a culturally secure expression, making the energies of Senecan theatre expressively present for the Elizabethan popular stage.[11]

We cannot suggest this view is as reductive as Broude's: on the face of it, its persuasiveness derives from the very holistic-ness of its approach. Yet sophisticated as it is, it is not a 'secure expression' because it was never intended to present 'popular myth-making' in any holistic sense. Hill himself makes this clear, claiming his reading only 'speaks for a significant body of *advanced* Elizabethan opinion'.[12] The implication of this claim would seem to be that the less 'advanced' saw differently.

Hill's reading has three further limitations of a serious kind. First, it says nothing of that *other* source for revenge tragedy noted in the Introduction: Aeschylus, specifically his funerary remembrance;[13] and as we shall observe, it omits the substantial ultimately Homeric – view of funerals to which Aeschylus himself was indebted. Lukas Erne's recent claim that Horatio's funeral in *The Spanish Tragedy* derives from *The First Part of Hieronimo*, and that 'both plays stress Horatio's funeral for his dead friend', further emphasizes the mistake of underplaying funerals.[14] Second, however, though this applies to all the anti-Catholic reading cited in this study, Hill takes no account of Kyd's more general confrontation of Reformed and un-Reformed attitudes to the dead – which make it most unlikely that 'active' (or 'advanced') Reformers would have looked favourably on *The Spanish Tragedy* or, indeed, any other play of this chapter. Third, and finally, Hill's reading of Virgil omits a point vital to considerations of the afterlife at the Reformation: that contemporaries widely considered Virgil's underworld a source of the Roman Catholic Purgatory. To begin: Aeschylus.

John Kerrigan, as we partly saw, noticed the influence of Aeschylus and his funerals on Kyd as follows:

---

[11] Mulryne, pp. 89–90.

[12] See Eugene D. Hill, 'Senecan and Vergilian [sic] Perspectives in *The Spanish Tragedy*', in *English Literary Renaissance* 15 (1985), pp. 143–65 (156; my emphasis); Mulryne has here misunderstood Hill. Catering only to a *limited* audience, thus, Hill's reading is like Ardolino's.

[13] See the Introduction, p. 11.

[14] See Lukas Erne, '"Enter the Ghost of Andrea": Recovering Thomas Kyd's Two-Part Play', in *English Literary Renaissance* 30 (2000), pp. 339–71 (354).

At the start of *The Libation Bearers*, Orestes stands beside his father's tomb, thinking about the past. Apparently sunk in passive grief, he offers Agamemnon a lock of hair and laments that he was not in Argos to mourn at his funeral. Then, however, retrospective modulates into a cry for revenge: 'Zeus, Zeus, grant me vengeance for my father's / murder. Stand and fight beside me, of your grace (17–18). Exactly the same movement of feeling is experienced by Electra when she, in turn, comes to the tomb with the chorus of libation bearers. Recalling the circumstances of Agamemnon's murder, she shifts abruptly to revenge: 'father, I pray that your avenger come that they / who killed you shall be killed in turn' (143–4).[15]

However, Kerrigan's larger observation is that *The Spanish Tragedy* (and *Hamlet*) echoes *The Libation Bearers* in presenting the funerary memory of a dead man as a spur to revenge, which 'Aeschylean' (and ultimately Homeric, as Kyd's 1602 adapter seemingly recognized[16]) spur can be seen in Hieronimo. With this funerary perspective of *The Spanish Tragedy* in mind, then, we may turn to the Purgatory of Kyd's Virgilian afterlife at last, and, thence, to *The Spanish Tragedy* directly.

To anti-Catholic controversialists as to their respondents, the association of Purgatory with Virgil had become commonplace by the late sixteenth century. As Peter Marshall observes, Reformers argued Purgatory emerged from 'syncretist compromises made by the early-Church with pagan converts'; 'Homer, Pindar, Plato, Ovid and *Virgil* were variously described as purgatory's first begetter.'[17] To encounter Virgil's afterlife in Kyd's play, therefore, was to encounter a motif freighted with Catholic significance. Nor is Kyd shy in bringing out the 'Romishness' (in pre- and post-Christian senses) of Virgil. The play revolves around a series of burials, highlighting the pre-eminent controversy of memorial effects from the first. 'When I was slain', tells Andrea's Ghost,

> my soul descended straight
> To pass the flowing stream of Acheron;
> But churlish Charon, only boatman there,
> Said that, my rites of burial not performed,
> I might not sit amongst his passengers.[18]

Features such as 'Acheron' and 'Charon' imply Andrea's afterlife is pagan, but the ghost also calls the place 'hell' (I.i.64), thus also suggesting Christianity, and the

---

[15] See Kerrigan, p. 170. For my previous citation of Kerrigan, see the Introduction, p. 11.

[16] The fourth addition to the 1602 edition shows Hieronimo imagining himself as Achilles, who after due funeral, avenged himself on Hector for killing Patroclus. Most relevantly to my argument, Achilles's revenge famously includes desecrating Hector's corpse. Thus in the addition Hieronimo says: 'At the last, sir, bring me to one of the murderers: were he as strong as Hector, thus would I tear and drag him up and down.' Thus, Hieronimo comes to imagine himself as vengeful Achilles, this addition's author indicating the play's theme of memorial revenge and his recognition of it. I comment further on this recognition at the end of this section.

[17] Marshall, *Beliefs and the Dead*, p. 143; the italics are mine.

[18] *The Spanish Tragedy*, I.i.18–22.

specifics of Kyd's place of the dead are complex. Recalling classical culture generally in which the dead benefit from burial, Kyd's predominant source is indeed Book VI of Virgil's *Aeneid*. However, his 'hell' also entails punishments appropriately tailored to suit 'sins' (I.i.71) in a frame of reference becoming expansively Christian. This is a place,

> Where usurers are choked with melting gold,
> And wantons are embraced with ugly snakes,
> And murderers groan with never-killing wounds,
> And perjured wights scalded in boiling lead,
> And all foul sins with torments overwhelmed.[19]

As a whole, thus, Kyd's hell is a pagan-Christian syncretism such as Marshall links with Purgatory. Moreover, in its Christian aspect, it is not easily 'hell'. Andrea's affirmation that

> my rites of funeral not performed
> I might not sit amongst his passengers[20]

jars with Christianity's affirmation that damned souls are beyond all help. Thus, at the very moment it claims that post-mortem remembrance benefits the dead (a Purgatorial claim in the sixteenth-century), Andrea also implies that his afterlife *must* be purgatorial. Moreover, these claims in which syncretism is evident are insistent. Eventually, says Andrea,

> By Don Horatio, our Knight Marshall's son
> My funerals and obsequies were done.
> *Then* was the ferryman of hell content
> To pass me over to the slimy strond
> That leads to fell Avernus' ugly waves[21]

For the dead Andrea, post-mortem remembrance, specifically funeral, is unambiguously helpful and necessary. Being a precondition of the plot, moreover, this 'performed' (I.i.21) benefit to the ghost is pivotal for the play. Indeed, even suggesting narrative continuity with funerary ritual, the self-consciousness of 'performed' funeral implicates such rite of remembrance in the activity of the playhouse.

Kyd's sixteenth-century Purgatory, however, goes even beyond this. With regard to Virgil, it highlights what Jacques Le Goff has identified as among 'a number of themes that would later figure in Purgatory': imprisonment, combinations of pleasure and pain, a detailing of penalties for the dead.[22] In presenting three rather than two paths through the afterlife, moreover, it defies Virgil by adapting him, revealing what

---

[19] *The Spanish Tragedy*, I.i.67–71.
[20] *The Spanish Tragedy*, I.i.21–2.
[21] *The Spanish Tragedy*, I.i.25–9; my emphasis.
[22] Jacques Le Goff, *The Birth of Purgatory*, trans. by Arthur Goldhammer (Chicago: University of Chicago Press, 1984), p. 25.

Kerrigan observes as 'some special purpose' on Kyd's part,[23] the most obvious being Purgatorial. Regarding the Christian aspect of this afterlife, however, its 'hell' also reflects the popular but traditional view that Purgatory (the location of which was always a matter of dispute, as Reformers liked to observe) was a temporary outpost of hell.[24] Thus, through its various sixteenth-century adaptations of Virgil, its syncretic and popular invocations of 'hell', and its dramatic demands that funerary memorials help the dead, Kyd's narratologically crucial opening evokes Purgatory. Nor is the narrative logic of the opening the only way Kyd makes Purgatory central: it is not allowed to disappear. The sitting presences of Andrea and Revenge as 'Chorus in this tragedy' (I.i.91) keep it before our eyes, while the well-known conflicts of pleasure and pain pervading the drama infuse it with the paradoxes of Andrea's afterlife.[25] Structurally, thematically, unsurprisingly, but nevertheless controversially (since England's view of remembrance was unsettled), Purgatory inhabits 'Spain'.

Funeral remembrance recurs variously in *The Spanish Tragedy*. Notably counter-pointing Andrea's affirmation of the value of funeral, however, is the punishment of Pedringano. Attending to this short-lived subplot highlights the funerary theme, for the Deputy enacting justice specifies more than death as punishment:

So, executioner, convey him hence,
But let his body be unburièd.
Let not the earth be chokèd or infect
With that which heaven contemns and men neglect.[26]

According to the Deputy, the ultimate punishment is not death but being deprived of a burial. In contrast to the increasingly de-ritualized modes of memorial valued by strict, English Reformers, his is an outlook implicitly valuing funerary ceremony. Moreover, that he assumes an association between what 'heaven contemns' and a death without ceremony implies that he presents not only his own, but a widespread view, pointedly thereby suggesting other views of funeral are abnormal.

Memories of the dead are pervasive, however, not least in the play's series of laments, some of which attend self-consciously to their own lamentation. Thus, in act I, scene ii, the Viceroy of Portugal's thirty-eight-line lament for the son he presumes dead highlights its act of remembrance by questioning it. Considering his lack of a fortune he personifies, he asks,

What help can be expected at her hands
Whose foot is standing on a rolling stone,

---

[23] Kerrigan, p. 175.

[24] See Rosemary Horrox, 'Purgatory, Prayer and Plague, 1150–1380', in *Death in England: An Illustrated History*, ed. by Peter C. Jupp and Clare Gittings (Manchester: Manchester University Press, 1999), p. 112; also Greenblatt, *Hamlet in Purgatory*, pp. 53–4.

[25] That such contrasts are well known is shown in David Bevington's discussion of the 'word games of military-amorous encounter', in his Introduction to *The Spanish Tragedy: Thomas Kyd*, ed. by David Bevington, Revels Student Editions (Manchester: Manchester University Press, 1996), p. 9.

[26] *The Spanish Tragedy*, III.vi.105–8.

And mind more mutable than fickle winds?
Why wail I then, where's hope of no redress?[27]

The Viceroy's memorial is extravagant: during the prolonged outburst, he falls from his throne, removing his crown. Interrogating his actions, however, his question 'Why wail I then, where's hope of no redress?' reflects the Reformed contention that (however largely performed) remembrance of the dead does not help them. Yet the case is not clear-cut: 'redress' implying 'an amendment' or 'improvement',[28] the Viceroy both seeks *and* doubts an improvement for his son. Justifying his lamentation a moment later, however, he explains it in Reformist terms: 'O yes, complaining makes my grief seem less' (I.ii.32). Resolving the dilemma, post-mortem memorial is eventually not for the dead, but for the living; moreover, 'less' grief emerges as an ideal.

The Viceroy is not alone in addressing the significance of enacted memorials. Asked by Bel-Imperia 'was Don Andrea's carcass lost?' in battle (I.iv.31), Horatio replies at length:

No, that was it for which I chiefly strove;
Nor stepped I back till I recovered him.
I took him up and wound him in mine arms,
And wielding him unto my private tent,
There laid him down, and dewed him with my tears,
And sighed and sorrowed as became a friend.
But neither friendly sorrow, sighs, nor tears
Could win pale Death from his usurpèd right.
Yet this I did, and less I could not do:
I saw him honoured with due funeral.
This scarf I plucked from off his lifeless arm,
And wear it in remembrance of my friend.[29]

For both dramatic persons recovering the body is important, but so is memorializing it. Bel-Imperia's question enacts a remembrance; Horatio says he risked life 'chiefly' to give Andrea sorrow, sighs, tears and 'due funeral'. Although it is not specified if this obligation is to help the dead, and though, troublingly, death is not denied its 'usurpèd right', extensive mourning 'becomes' friends, the living and the dead being a community to die for. Horatio's highlight of the scarf as a 'remembrance of my friend' materializes this memorial, providing audiences with a visual reminder of funerary devotion: a reminder reappearing in key moments of dramatic transition. And thus, as an indicator of the drama's structure,[30] remembrance of the dead

---

[27] *The Spanish Tragedy*, I.iii.28–31.
[28] See definition 3a of the noun 'redress' in the *O.E.D.*
[29] *The Spanish Tragedy*, I.vi.32–43.
[30] The structural significance of the handkerchief in this respect has been noticed by a variety of commentators. See for example, Ejner J. Jensen, 'Kyd's *Spanish Tragedy*: The Play Explains Itself', in *Journal of English and Germanic Philology* 64 (1965), pp. 7–16; Marion Lomax, *Stage Images and Traditions: Shakespeare to Ford* (Cambridge: Cambridge University Press, 1978), pp. 34–44; Erne, '"Enter the Ghost of Andrea"', p. 351.

shapes the play. I shall comment on the 'Catholicism' of such structure when the handkerchief next appears.

In acknowledging love for dead Andrea in her next soliloquy, Bel-Imperia also memorializes. However, she instructs Horatio to wear the scarf 'both for him [Andrea] and me' (I.iv.48), presenting a dilemma between loyalty to the dead and love for the living. The question is whether Bel-Imperia's 'devotion' belongs primarily to the dead Andrea ('my love'; I.iv.30) or to Horatio; thus, even as it recalls the burden of late medieval religion (so often 'the living in the service of the dead'[31]), it presents the controversy as urgent.

Horatio's exit provides Bel-Imperia with an empty stage and opportunity for private expression:

> Ay, go, Horatio; leave me here alone;
> For solitude best fits my cheerless mood.
> Yet what avails to wail Andrea's death,
> From whence Horatio proves my second love?
> Had he not loved Andrea as he did,
> He could not sit in Bel-Imperia's thoughts.
> But how can love find harbour in my breast,
> Till I revenge the death of my beloved?
> Yes, second love shall further my revenge;
> I'll love Horatio, my Andrea's friend,
> The more to spite the Prince that wrought his end.[32]

Besides developing her personal, cultural and female burden, these lines reiterate the thematic question: 'what avails to wail ... death?' However, Bel-Imperia sidesteps any analytic answer, instead embracing 'love' and 'revenge' as responses to Andrea's 'end', thus moulding her life and actions in remembrance of him. Although the morality of such revenge remains to be considered, remembrance of the dead thus becomes defiantly inscribed – in this era of Reformation – in the drama.

Such inscription is still more visible in what C.L. Barber has called the 'total devotion' of Hieronimo to his dead son.[33] As in Bel-Imperia's memory of Andrea, Hieronimo's revenge also emerges from the memory of a dead man, though this time from a grief and anger emerging at length. As previously, moreover, the ritual treatment of the corpse is also paramount. It is not just a revenger's unfolding memory

---

[31] 'Late medieval religion, as has often been observed, was frequently the living in the service of the dead.' See Philip Morgan, 'Of Worms and War, 1380–1558', in *Death in England: An Illustrated History*, ed. by Peter C. Jupp and Clare Gittings (Manchester: Manchester University Press, 1999), pp. 119–46 (132).

[32] *The Spanish Tragedy*, I.iv.58–68.

[33] See C.L. Barber, *Creating Elizabethan Tragedy: The Theatre of Marlowe and Kyd*, ed. by Richard P. Wheeler (Chicago and London: The University of Chicago Press, 1988), p. 152. Notably suggesting the origin of Hieronimo's devotion lies in 'meditation on Christ's suffering and wounds', although 'it will not do to call athletic young Horatio ... a Christ figure', Barber goes on to consider the devotion 'to have been shaped by religious prototypes'. My reading of Horatio's corpse as a Southwell-like relic, below, resolves the simultaneous likeness and un-likeness to Christ of Horatio over which Barber hesitates.

of his lost son, or horror at his unjust murder, which motivates Hieronimo: it is the abandonment of Horatio's body. Horatio's 'bloody corpse', Hieronimo implies, lacks the 'honour' of funeral:

> What savage monster, not of human kind,
> Hath here been glutted with thy harmless blood,
> And left thy bloody corpse dishonoured here,
> For me, amidst this dark and deathful shades,
> To drown thee with an ocean of my tears?[34]

Two points of religio-political significance emerge from this passage. First, and contrasting with the views of advanced Reformers, ceremony for the dead is emphatically a value. Second, the mourning Hieronimo proposes – the 'ocean' of tears – defies the demand of Reformers for 'rigour' in mourning.

Horatio's 'bloody corpse' lacks 'honour': death lacks the form of memorial Hieronimo considers due. Linking funeral with vengeance, therefore, Hieronimo implies his vengeance and 'tears' (II.iv.99) will stand in. Notably, at this moment, the handkerchief reappears:

> Seest thou this handkerchief besmeared with blood?
> It shall not from me till I take revenge.
> Seest thou those wounds that yet are bleeding fresh?
> I'll not *entomb* them till I have revenged.[35]

At the heart of Hieronimo's vow is the valued, ritual action of burial, and thus again the implicit defiance of England's developing Reform.[36]

However, 'revenge' becomes a substitute for Horatio's tomb, becoming itself commemorative. Vengefully proceeding to the Spanish action's closing funerary remembrances, Hieronimo's life and action are thus a procession winding towards funeral, his monumental revenge presenting the commemoration Horatio lacks. The revenge *tragedy*, thus, is a drama of commemoration. Already suggesting in act II that such tragedy is universal, Hieronimo ritually takes Horatio's scarf – presumably that worn in memory of Andrea – to wear in memory of Horatio. Cyclically, it seems, everyone human and dying remembers the dead.

The close of act II, scene iv is inevitably funereal:

HIERONIMO   Come, Isabella, now let us take him up.
[*Hieronimo and Isabella*] *take him up*

---

[34] *The Spanish Tragedy*, II.iv.81–5.
[35] *The Spanish Tragedy*, II.iv.113–16; my emphasis.
[36] Bringing out the Catholicism of the scene and, indeed, in the age, Andrew Hadfield has noted how the preceding lines recall the execution of Robert Southwell, after which a clamouring crowd 'dipped handkerchiefs in the sprayed blood'. Too far under the influence of Mulryne, however, he implies (albeit tentatively) that he considers this act of veneration for the dead – which no English Reformer would have countenanced – evidence of anti-Catholicism. See Andrew Hadfield, 'A Handkerchief Dipped in Blood in *The Spanish Tragedy*: An Anti-Catholic Reference?', in *Notes & Queries* 46 (1999), p. 197.

And bear him in from out this cursèd place.
I'll say his dirge; singing fits not this case.[37]

However, the funerary rite here merits comment. Despite the objection to singing, the formal taking up of the body, accompanied by the pointedly Latin 'dirge' (itself a synonym for the Latin Office of the Dead and suggesting requiem mass[38]) strongly suggests the superstitions roundly condemned by Reformers. And further 'superstition' emerges in what is said – in translation:

> O let someone mix me herbs which beautiful spring brings forth, and let medicine be given for our pain; or let him offer potions, if there be any which cause forgetfulness of the years; may I myself throughout the great world gather whatever plants the sun brings forth into the beauteous realms of light; may I myself drink whatever poison the sorceress concocts and whatever herbs and incantations unites through occult power. Let me endure all, even death, provided that all feeling may die in a heart already dead. Shall I then never again see your eyes, my life, and has eternal sleep buried your light? Let me die with you; thus, thus would I go to the shades below. But nevertheless I shall refrain from yielding to hasty death, lest then, no vengeance should follow your death.[39]

By no means is this a rendering of the Roman *dirige*, but even for those who could look beyond the Latin (a marker of sacramental and Catholic rite[40]), the subjects treated (death, forgetfulness, memory, dirge, incantation, ghosts) are provocative.

The association of remembrance and revenge is briefly disturbed by the scene's final stage direction: 'He [Hieronimo] throws the sword from him and bears the body away'. But despite such hesitation, in all his following scenes Hieronimo dwells on his son: all his complaining, his scheming and his struggling – what, developing Barber, I have called his 'total devotion' to Horatio – remembers the dead man. Like Fate itself, thus, remembrance for the dead is dramatically inescapable – as Revenge stresses when assuring Andrea he will not be forgotten:

> Content thyself, Andrea; though I sleep,
> Yet is my mood soliciting their souls.
> Sufficeth thee that poor Hieronimo
> Cannot forget his son Horatio.
> Nor dies Revenge, although he sleep awhile;
> For in unquiet, quietness is feigned,
> And slumbering is a common worldly wile.
> Behold, Andrea, for an instance, how
> Revenge hath slept, and then imagine thou
> What 'tis to be subject to destiny.[41]

---

[37] *The Spanish Tragedy*, II.iv.126–8.
[38] See definition 1 in the *O.E.D.*
[39] Translation by John Gassner and William Green (eds), *Elizabethan Drama: Eight Plays* (New York: Applause, 1967; 1990), p. 108.
[40] See my discussion of 'Latin' (evoking Dillon's essay '*The Spanish Tragedy* and Staging Languages in Renaissance Drama) in the Introduction, p. 14, note 59, continuing on p. 15.
[41] *The Spanish Tragedy*, III.xv.17–26.

In sixteenth-century England, Revenge highlights what every scene with mourning Hieronimo shows: a father '*Cannot* forget his son'; despite the calls of contemporary Reformers for moderation in mourning, passionate remembrance is 'What 'tis to be subject to destiny.'

In the last moments before the revenge, remembering the dead is as present as ever. Alone on stage, Hieronimo inspects and highlights his motives:

> Bethink thyself, Hieronimo,
> Recall thy wits, recount thy former wrongs
> Thou hast received by murder of thy son;
> And lastly, not least, how Isabel,
> Once his mother and thy dearest wife
> All woebegone for him, hath slain herself.
> Behoves thee then, Hieronimo, to be revenged.
> The plot is laid of dire revenge;
> On, then, Hieronimo, pursue revenge,
> For nothing wants but acting of revenge.[42]

Underlining the 'behoving-ness' of revenge, and between the introspective pause to 'Bethink' and the eventual decision, the same motive re-surfaces: the dishonourable death of a son, now further fuelled by the dishonourable death of a wife. Pertinently, as Ophelia's better-known death and burial in *Hamlet* reminds us, suspected suicides like Isabella's received only a 'maimed rite' of funeral.[43]

After the unforgettable revenge and revenge *tragedy* of 'Soliman and Perseda', Hieronimo does not cease to avow his motives; instead, he reveals that remembrance is 'destiny' and 'tragedy' again:

> I see your looks urge instance of these words;
> Behold the reason urging me to this!
> *Shows his dead son.*
> See here my show; look on this spectacle![44]

Following S.F. Johnson, 'Broudian' interpretations of 'Soliman and Perseda' argue that Hieronimo's specification of a play performed in a variety of languages implies its association with Babylon and thus anti-Catholicism.[45] However, despite Hieronimo (whom we should not mistake for Kyd[46]) the extant text presents 'Soliman and Perseda' only in English. We therefore only have what even Johnson admits

---

[42] *The Spanish Tragedy*, IV.iii.18–27.
[43] I discuss the burial of Ophelia, and its religio-political implication, later in this chapter. See p. 71–2.
[44] *The Spanish Tragedy*, IV.iv.86–8.
[45] See Johnson, pp. 23–5; Mulryne, however, is notably tentative on the point, claiming his reading is only good '*if* the play was indeed performed in "sundry languages"'. See Mulryne, p. 93. I commented on Broude's debt to Johnson on p. 1. of the Introduction. Finally, recall that 'Babylon' only figures once in *The Spanish Tragedy*.
[46] Dillon, whom I previously noted for rejecting the Broudian interpretation of the play, makes precisely this mistake, thus giving more to her critical antagonists than she need. See Dillon, p. 15.

is 'unusual editorial interpolation' to imply 'Soliman and Perseda' was otherwise performed[47] – interpolation especially suspect in view of the sensitive matter at stake, and hard to credit since clarity of *language* is necessary to appreciate Kyd's carefully wrought meta-drama.[48]

What is clear, however, is that the previous extract seeks to foreground Horatio's corpse exclusively; and the motive for revenge it stages so self-consciously is that disfigured, possibly rotting, but unforgettable corpse. Though Hieronimo will later also recall Isabella, Horatio's corpse is alone here the 'instance' and 'the reason urging'. Indeed, the dead body is thus 'my show' in the various senses of Hieronimo's on-stage play, of his own funerary show as dramatic character, and of the play *The Spanish Tragedy* itself. Essentially entailing an outlook no strict sixteenth-century Reformer could accept, the very 'spectacle' is thus a testament to extravagantly performed remembrance.

As Hieronimo escapes punishment through a suicide less dishonourable for crowning that performance, there is little left but to bury the dead. Suggestively, the 'bloody handkerchief' emerges again, but avenging the newly dead being now impossible, it simply disappears. As the Spanish action concludes in renewed funeral, the language of revenge has gone too:

> KING   Go, bear his [Castile's] body hence, that we may mourn
> The loss of our beloved brother's death,
> That he may be entombed, whate'er befall.
> I am the next, the nearest, last of all.
> VICEROY   And thou, Don Pedro, do the like for us:
> Take up our hapless son, untimely slain;
> Set me with him and he with woeful me
> Upon the mainmast of a ship unmanned,
> And let the wind and tide haul me along
> To Scylla's barking and untamed gulf,
> Or to the loathsome pool of Acheron,
> To weep my want for my sweet Balthazar;
> Spain hath no refuge for a Portingale.
> *The trumpets sound a dead march. [Exeunt] the King of*
> *Spain mourning after his brother's body and the Viceroy of*
> *Portingale bearing the body of his son.*[49]

Despite the 'symbolism' of the reading, the implied fall of an Imperial Spain might well have resonated with an English happiness, but the claim that the '*Spanish* tragedy implies an *English* comedy' is too neat.[50] Besides the fact (reiterated repeatedly now) that in any strict sense England was far from holistically Reformed, this passage links the fall of Spain with emphatic rites of funeral, thus highlighting an English confusion. And though advanced Reformers might have wished to link

---

[47] See Johnson, p. 23.
[48] This last point is actually implicit in the interpolation: it claims to translate the 'sundry languages' for 'the easier understanding [*sic*] of every public reader'.
[49] *The Spanish Tragedy*, IV.iv.205–17.
[50] See Hill, p. 151; Mulryne, p. 91.

that confusion with Spain's 'Babylon' to derive a funerary lesson, the text resists the move in two ways. First, it implies that Spanish-style funeral survives the fall of Imperial Spain, thus also distinguishing religious ritual from religious empire – a distinction to please traditionalists rather than active Reformers. Second, the extract makes its extravagant funerary remembrance the condition of dramatic closure.[51] Indeed, the King and Viceroy round off the action of this world with a fullest funerary: one to outlast the play. *Whatever* befalls – and the wording here is notable – extravagant funerals defying Reformed 'rigour' will continue: Castile will be further mourned once his body is entombed; while suggesting funerary continuity, the Viceroy begins a mythic mourning recalling Virgil's flowing Acheron (IV.iv.15; IV.v.42), the play thus ending in the controversial afterlife where it started. Rulers come and go, the play thus seems to say, but traditions of burial do not. Significantly, as the last scene shows, a vengeance allegedly 'just and sharp' (IV.v.16) awaits these funerals. However, in the last seen of the Latins ('trumpets sound a dead march', 'mourning', 'bearing the body') music and gesture attune to a funerary rite resonant with the death of the drama.

Being even highlighted by the bloody handkerchief, in *The Spanish Tragedy* funereal remembrance marks the dramatic transitions of 'destiny' from Andrea, to Horatio, to Hieronimo, and thence to the Portuguese Viceroy and King of Spain. It is thus a marked feature of the drama's structure and holistic self-consciousness. In an age in which, as we have seen, Reformers actively confronted and reduced traditional acts of remembrance for the dead, *The Spanish Tragedy* overwhelmingly emphasizes that diminished funerary memorial is incomplete, a cause of revenge, conversely equating extensive funerary rites with aid to the dead, honour, friendship and 'destiny'. It also distinguishes extensive funerary memorial *per se* from the politics of Spanish Empire. Thus, as a play of the late sixteenth century, it delivers a drama both 'Latinate' *and* opposing England's advancing Reform.

Or does it? For if perceived failings of memorial practice are an emphatic cause of revenge, might not the play's more general association of post-mortem memorial with revenge suggest hesitation about such memorial, perhaps even Reform of it?[52] The answer is that it might, but only if one assumes that revenge is an evil – as we shall see, a far from self-evident claim for early modern Christians. As we shall also see, *The Spanish Tragedy* comes down heavily in favour of traditional memorials, and not just because, as we have observed, characters so often speak up for them. For as I now argue (developing my observation of *The Spanish Tragedy*'s self-consciousness) the play's specific and detailed presentation of its 'aesthetic' underpins and holistically reinforces what such characters say. The effect is to dress

---

[51] Though Dillon is otherwise correct that 'the play cannot be reduced to a piece of Protestant propaganda', therefore, it is incorrect that the final 'loss of rhythm and control' she discerns becomes 'a problem of closure', making *The Spanish Tragedy* not 'a predominantly Christian play' (Dillon, p. 35). Rather, the disruptions of 'Soliman and Perseda' are resolved into the funerary mourning, a matter of keen, contemporary Christian interest being thus Spain's closing note.

[52] This perspective is proposed by Huston Diehl, who argues therefore that 'the drama of the English Renaissance can also be understood as the drama of the English Reformation'. See Diehl, p. 93.

the action in traditionalism incompatible with Reforming prescriptions of how to remember the dead.

A central problem in criticism of *The Spanish Tragedy,* as of its genre, has been the paradoxical, even contradictory, way in which revenge relates to justice. Katharine Maus summarizes such moral difficulties in a series of questions: 'How ... are we to evaluate the actions of the revenger? Does the protagonist's victimization exonerate him, partially or fully? Do we condone crimes that retaliate for previous crimes?'[53] Addressing these questions, however, presents a further question: 'How *appropriate* is Hieronimo's vengeance to his grievance?' 'How just is Hieronimo's final vengeance in view of the wrongs he suffers?' implies 'How appropriate is Hieronimo's revenge?'

To circumvent the paradoxes of justice, a 'Christian' argument against *all* vengeance has invoked the Biblical injunction to leave revenge to God (Romans 12:19); however, early modern Christians traditionally saw so little contradiction between feuds (themselves ritual acts of vengeance) and their religion that across Europe feuding expressed the 'principal framework for all social relationships'.[54] Citing the violent revenge by Israel on the children of Babylon in Psalm 137, in England Catholics as well as Protestants used the Bible to *justify* violence.[55]

More helpfully, therefore, a second answer notes the more obviously 'inappropriate' aspects of Hieronimo's vengeance: Castile's death, as he has no direct hand in Hieronimo's suffering and would even be a 'benevolent peacemaker',[56] and the suicide of Bel-Imperia, Hieronimo's ally, suggested by his final play.[57] Yet in terms of the vendetta logic of *The Spanish Tragedy,* in which one murder requires another, even these deaths may seem 'collateral damage' of Hieronimo's initially proper search for justice.[58] Thus, Castile and Bel-Imperia are unfortunate victims of a broadly just cause – and thus we are confronted with an uncertainty as

---

[53] See Maus (ed.), 'Introduction', in *Four Revenge Tragedies*, p. x.

[54] See Muir, p. 106. For similar observation of an early modern Christianity at home with revenge (though characteristically focusing on English Protestantism), see Ronald Broude, 'Revenge and Revenge Tragedy in Renaissance England', in *Renaissance Quarterly* 28 (1975), pp. 38–58, Broude remaining helpful when addressing matters other than the overtly 'Babylonian'.

[55] For details, see Hannibal Hamlin, 'Psalm Culture in the English Renaissance: Readings of Psalm 137 by Shakespeare, Spenser, Milton, and Others', in *Renaissance Quarterly* 55/1 (2002), pp. 224–57. Notice too, therefore, that 'Babylon' could refer to both Catholic *or* Protestant.

[56] See Erne, '"Enter the Ghost of Andrea"', pp. 364–5. This discussion is useful both as a generous summary of different critical responses to the killing of Castile and also because from it emerges a point underlying the present study: that the Ghost of Andrea and Revenge are important to the meaning of *The Spanish Tragedy* as a whole.

[57] In *The Spanish Tragedy*, IV.iv.139–42, Hieronimo seems to imply he did not intend Bel-Imperia to die, but there is ambiguity about this in his claim that strictly she 'should have' died and in his further claim – especially in view of the sinister associations of the word with death in the play – that he had another 'end' for her in mind.

[58] James P. Hammersmith, for example, argues that 'the thematic design of the play, not the plot, generates the inevitability of Castile's death'. See Hammersmith, 'The Death of Castile in *The Spanish Tragedy*', in *Renaissance Drama* 16 (1985), pp. 1–16 (3).

pressing as apparently irresolvable. Such uncertainty, indeed, will polarize opinion along contradictory lines, as questions of justice and appropriateness become (especially in the play's rhetorically heightened emotionalism,[59] but also in view of its contemporary religio-politics) questions of sympathies and 'feeling'. Yet crucially, *The Spanish Tragedy* presents perspective on such *felt* response and, thus, on vengeance in memory of the dead.

At the end of his twenty-line lament for the newly dead Horatio in act II, Hieronimo exhorts his wife to ever-greater grief:

> Here, Isabella, help me to lament;
> For sighs are stopped, and all my tears are spent.[60]

Mourning on the largest scale, he claims, is the appropriate response to Horatio's death. In a language itself highly charged, Isabella spells out this view:

> O, gush out, tears, fountains and floods of tears;
> Blow, sighs, and raise an everlasting storm;
> For outrage fits our cursed wretchedness.[61]

Suggestively, this 'outrage' combines Isabella's lamentation and 'rage': her vengefulness is mournful. However, in total contrast to the active restraint advocated by Reformers, Hieronimo and Isabella agree that emotionally *maximized* commemorations are 'fit'.

This goes to the heart of the play's larger paradoxes of justice, appropriateness and feeling: a response allegedly excessive here *befits* ('is appropriate to') the memory of the dead. Moreover, Isabella's view still expresses Hieronimo's developed perspective as revenger: 'rage fits'. Indeed, the play's persistent 'melodrama' – its extravagant language, action, madness – makes sense in light of Isabella's memorial outlook: in response to a death like Horatio's, allegedly disproportionate action is proportionate. Thus, Isabella spells out the revenge tragedy's paradoxical rationale. As a very drama of excess – and bearing in mind that Reformed commentators like Sidney or Puttenham considered 'proportion' key to artistry[62] – Isabella's 'proportionate disproportion' provides a hermeneutical key to the drama.

Her key also bears on the play's religio-politic of remembrance. Audiences need not accept that 'outrage fits' in all cases, but to deny it in act II, scene v is to deny the immediate appeal of a mother grieving for her son. Thus, the treatment of feeling itself emerges by reference to a remembrance of the dead; *and* the audience is invited to share in 'outrage' before its implication is fully evident. With a deceptively pervasive implication, thus, the drama challenges the 'rigour' of Reform. The bloodiness of

---

[59] In subsequent theatrical allusion to *The Spanish Tragedy*'s rhetoric, the play is 'inextricably linked with deep emotional feeling'. See Rebekah Owens, 'Parody and *The Spanish Tragedy*', in *Cahiers Elisabéthains: A Biannual Journal of English Renaissance Studies* 71 (Spring 2007), pp. 27–36 (30).

[60] *The Spanish Tragedy*, II.iv.98–9.

[61] *The Spanish Tragedy*, II.iv.105–7.

[62] See my discussion in the Introduction, p. 25.

Hieronimo's final vengeance may suggest hesitation towards the play's memorials, but that hesitation is itself conditioned in the mournful revenge's launch.

Even more pervasively, in linking remembrance of the dead with proportionate behaviour in the claim that 'outrage fits', Isabella points, as I have noted, not only to a contemporary religio-political but also an artistic or 'aesthetic' concern. As we have observed, Renaissance theorists of literature such as Sidney and Puttenham considered proportionality key in literary aesthetics, so Isabella's claim about proportion implies an aesthetic claim – which in the first instance points to this most self-consciously artful tragedy. Deriving from her extravagant memorial, thus, Isabella's *aesthetic* description of the vengeful logic of the drama presents the very art – as a whole – as at odds with the Reform. To the contemporary audience, the implication is therefore this: the artistry before you is against the Reform; to enjoy it, even to partake in it, endorses a resistance to Reform.

How many of Kyd's audience would have understood this? Perhaps the particularities of 'aesthetics' escaped many, but the play's broad, memorial sweep and thus traditionalism could not have gone unnoticed: 'Hieronimo's discovery of the body of Horatio and the descent in his speech from confusion to grief' is the most referenced scene of the play in the 'recorded responses we possess.'[63] Moreover, two kinds of evidence suggest that remembrance of the dead *and* its aesthetic were noted. The first concerns the additions made to *The Spanish Tragedy* in 1602, for the disputed author seems to have recognized not only the thematic nature of remembrance, but also its aesthetic import; and since this author sought to enhance these features, it seems he considered them important. Thus, the fourth addition of 1602 introduces the painter, Bazardo, showing him in conversation with Hieronimo. Remembering as ever the death of his son, Hieronimo asks whether Bazardo can paint his family in contrasting styles, thus emphasizing aesthetic differences. The first style emerges as follows:

> I'd have you paint me [in] my gallery, in your oil colours matted, and draw me five years younger than I am – do ye see, sir, let five years go; let them go like the Marshal of Spain – my wife Isabella standing by me, with a speaking look to my son Horatio, which should intend to this or some such purpose: 'God bless thee, my sweet son'; and my hand leaning upon his head...[64]

This is a portrait of dignified, domestic harmony. Hieronimo is the successful Marshal of Spain, his wife by his side; Isabella looks affectionately at Horatio, and Hieronimo's hand draped on his son's shoulder is affectionate too. It is the family 'staged' for the public, domestic disharmonies painted out.

The contrasting family-portrait emerges in dialogue:

> HIERONIMO   Well, sir, paint me a youth run through and through with villains' swords, hanging upon this tree. Canst thou draw a murderer?

---

[63] Owens, p. 29. Relevantly, the second most referenced passage is the opening of the play by Andrea's Ghost.

[64] *The Spanish Tragedy*, Fourth Addition.

PAINTER   I'll warrant you, sir; I have the pattern of the most notorious villains that ever lived in all Spain.
HIERONIMO   O let them be worse, worse; stretch thine art, and let their beards be of Judas his own colour; and let their eyebrows jutty over: in any case observe that. Then, sir, after some violent noise, bring me forth in my shirt, and my gown under mine arm, with my torch in my hand, an my sword reared up thus; and with these words:
'What noise is this? Who calls Hieronimo?'[65]

This portrait is a reverse of the first. The family is in disarray: hanging bloodily, in dishabille or absent. Hieronimo's observation that to produce this painting Bazardo will have to 'stretch' his art summarizes the comparative treatment of the two pictures: 'stretching' his first, proportionate art, the painter disproportions it. Drawing attention to the destruction of Hieronimo's family through paintings, however, the disputed author plays aesthetics up. Either he noticed Isabella's aesthetic commentary and sought to enhance it, or he responded to Kyd's more general (though 'generic') memorial aesthetic. To the disputed author, however, that memorial aesthetic – at odds with the advancing Reform – was clear. Developing, indeed, its emphasis on the painfulness of reduced memorials ('stretching' also connotes 'torture'), he thereby also expanded Kyd's Elizabethan protest against the Reform's advance.

The second evidence that both remembrance of the dead and its aesthetic were recognized is the persistent return to these themes of later revenge tragedy. Kyd's influence on such later tragedy is well known, but in developing Kyd's theme, revenge tragedians also developed his treatment of remembrance. However, to see quite how, we must look beyond Kyd.

Titus Andronicus, c.1592

Citing 'most notably' Aaron's allusion to 'popish tricks and ceremonies', the 'purposeful' anachronism of the Second Goth's 'ruinous monastery', Lavinia's presentation as a 'martyr', and the 'cannibalistic feast' served by Titus to Tamora (allegedly presenting a Reformed parody of the Catholic Eucharist), latest Arden editor Jonathan Bate has not been alone in finding 'a Reformation context' in *Titus Andronicus*.[66] Since monasteries were '"purgatorial institutions", established to offer

---

[65]   *The Spanish Tragedy*, Fourth Addition.

[66]   See *Titus Andronicus*, ed. by Jonathan Bate (London: The Arden Shakespeare, 1995; 2002), pp. 19–20. Other commentators finding such context, though interpreting it differently, include, Dorothea Kehler, '*Titus Andronicus*: From Limbo to Bliss', in *Shakespeare Jahrbuch* 128 (1992), pp. 125–31; Lukas Erne, '"Popish Tricks" and "a Ruinous Monastery": *Titus Andronicus* and the Question of Shakespeare's Catholicism', in *The Limits of Textuality*, ed. by Lukas Erne and Guillemette Bolens, Swiss Papers in English Language and Literature 13 (Tübingen: Narr, 2000), pp. 135–55; John Klause, 'Politics, Heresy and Martyrdom in Shakespeare's Sonnet 124 and *Titus Andronicus*', in *Shakespeare's Sonnets: Critical Essays*, ed. by James Schiffer, Shakespeare Criticism 20, Garland Reference Library of the Humanities 1988 (New York: Garland, 2000), pp. 219–40; Anna Swärdh, *Rape and Religion in English Renaissance Literature: A Topical Study of Four Texts by Shakespeare, Drayton and Middleton*

masses and prayers for their founders and benefactors in perpetuity',[67] a second monastic image, of Titus 'perfect / As begging hermits in their holy prayers' (III. ii.40–1), can be added to the list.[68] However, Bate's Reformist interpretation of the play's religious context depends on theories by two commentators: Samuel Kliger and, inevitably, Ronald Broude.[69] Since Broude's only essays directly addressing *Titus Andronicus* add nothing on religion to the flawed, general theory of revenge tragedy we have persistently addressed,[70] and since Bate presents Broude as only a vague index to the religion of revenge tragedy,[71] we need only attend to Kliger.

The history Kliger recounts, to which Bate is 'much indebted',[72] shows that 'German reformers' mythologized their own 'rejuvenation' of Christianity as like the (alleged) 'moral purity' with which Goths cleansed 'decadent Roman civilization':[73] the Goths were, in this Reformed myth, a Reformed prototype. Plausibly, Bate considers this myth a key to the Reformation context of *Titus Andronicus*, the Goths of the play thus presenting Reformers, the Romans (unsurprisingly) presenting their 'Roman' opponents. Various cautions, however, are necessary. First, as John Klause and Anna Swärdh emphasize, *Titus Andronicus* is thick with the motifs of tears poetry associated especially, though not exclusively, with Robert Southwell and so Roman Catholicism, suggesting Reformist interpretations are not inevitable.[74] Second, Bate claims his Reformist use of Kliger is necessary because 'until we know what the Elizabethans thought about the Goths' it will be 'puzzling' that 'the Goths who join with Lucius are a very civilized lot in comparison with the ones who are

---

(Uppsala: University of Uppsala Press, 2003), pp. 76–132; Asquith, pp. 90–100. However, none of these observes the play's pervasive concern with *funerals* as a Reformation context and thus how *Titus Andronicus* reflects what I show is a central concern of revenge tragedy's genre.

[67] See Marshall, p. 81.

[68] Other derivatively Christian imagery includes the Clown playfully invoking the dead in the form of 'Saint Stephen' (IV.iv.42) and swearing 'by [Our] Lady' and (in more sinister mode) the Nurse bidding Aaron to 'christen' his son 'with thy dagger's point' (IV.ii.70). All references to Shakespeare derive from *The Norton Shakespeare*, ed. by Greenblatt *et al.*

[69] Bate (ed.), p. 19.

[70] See Ronald Broude, 'Four Forms of Vengeance in *Titus Andronicus*', in *Journal of English and Germanic Philology* 78 (1979), pp. 494–507. As its title implies, Broude is not primarily concerned with religion in this essay; when he does directly address that topic (p. 501), he simply refers us to the earlier essay of 1973 (familiar to us from the Introduction of this study) '*Vindicta Filia Temporis*'. Similarly, Broude's still earlier essay 'Roman and Goth in *Titus Andronicus*', in *Shakespeare Studies* 6 (1970), pp. 27–34, adds nothing fundamental to the theory of providential time and thus Protestant outlook of '*Vindicta Filia Temporis*'.

[71] Bate simply invites us to 'see also Broude'; see Bate (ed.), p. 19.

[72] Bate (ed.), p. 19.

[73] Samuel Kliger, 'The Gothic Revival and the German "Translatio"', in *Modern Philology* 45 (1947), pp. 73–103 (73). See also Kliger, 'The "Goths" in England: An Introduction to the Gothic Vogue in Eighteenth-Century Aesthetic Discussion', in *Modern Philology* 43 (1945), pp. 107–17 (111), and, with most bearing on sixteenth-century England, Kliger, *The Goths in England: A Study in Seventeenth- and Eighteenth-Century Thought* (Cambridge, MA: Harvard University Press, 1952).

[74] See Klause, p. 224 and 335; Swärdh, p. 78 and 107–17.

paraded through the streets in the first act'.[75] However, this is a problem of Bate's devising. Thus, unobserved by Bate, in the final act, unlike in the first, the Goths explicitly acknowledge the command of Lucius and consider Titus 'once our terror, now our comfort' (V.i.10),[76] making their transformation clearly a matter of Lucius's (Roman) influence. And thus, despite Bate, between 'Roman' and 'Goth' by the end of the play, there is no clear distinction; moreover, presenting peace on Roman terms, unity between the rival groups is eventually achieved under an accepted Roman leadership.[77] Finally, notice a highly implausible feature of Bate's reading necessary to any Reformist interpretation: the placing of criticism of 'popish tricks and ceremonies' in the mouth of Aaron. If one wished persuasively to condemn such ceremonial, could one intelligently place the condemnation in the mouth of this (arguably) most villainous of Shakespearean villains? The effect of giving the Reformed condemnation to Aaron is, implicitly, to rubbish it; indeed, by associating the condemnation with such a villain, Shakespeare – for I treat the play as his[78] – smears Reformers. Goths and Romans in *Titus Andronicus* do – as others have also argued – suggest English Protestants and Catholics, but the play is not therefore Reformed.[79]

---

[75] Bate (ed.), p. 19.

[76] For the explicit acknowledgement of Lucius's command by the Goths, see the First Goth's statement to Lucius: 'We'll follow where thou lead'st' (V.i.13).

[77] In this respect, *Titus Andronicus* anticipates the unity eventually achieved between Britain and Rome in Shakespeare's *Cymbeline*.

[78] Historically, parts of the play have been ascribed elsewhere. Arguing forcefully for Shakespeare's authorship of the complete play, however, Jonathan Bate has placed the burden of proof on those advocating a second author (see Bate [ed.], pp. 79–83). Although Bate has encountered such disagreement, the play can certainly be considered Shakespeare's: 'To make a claim for Peele as part-author of *Titus Andronicus* is not, however, to deny ... that the bulk of the verse is Shakespeare's, or that in its design the tragedy bears the unmistakable imprint of Shakespeare's shaping imagination.' See Thomas Merriam, 'Indefinite Articles in *Titus Andronicus*, Peele and Shakespeare', in *Notes & Queries* 43/3 (1998), pp. 308–10 (310). Brian Vickers argues that George Peele and Shakespeare 'shared the planning of the whole play', pertinently adding that writing *Titus Andronicus* was 'an integral part of Shakespeare's development in tragedy'. See Brian Vickers, *Shakespeare, Co-Author: A Historical Study of Five Collaborative Plays* (Oxford and New York: Oxford University Press, 2002), pp. 148–243, especially p. 243 and p. 161.

[79] See especially Klause, Swärdh and Asquith, who present different reasons for associating Romans and Goths with Roman Catholics and Protestants, but agree the play cannot be read as Reformist. Richard Wilson sees in the play a 'group-portrait of the old Roman nobility at the court of the Caesars, with barbarians at the gates', which 'seems to sum up the historical predicament of Shakespeare's Catholic patrons [sic] in the empire of the Tudors, waiting on the Protestant "Goths"'. See Wilson, p. 22. Bate has elsewhere elaborated on his reading of Aaron on 'popish tricks and ceremonies' to the effect that because the speaker, Aaron, is untrustworthy, 'Lucius should in fact be regarded as the very opposite of a Catholic', but this reading is unpersuasive. Given Bate's broad view (developing Kliger) that the play presents the two contrasting groups, Catholics and Reformers, the implication of the claim that Lucius is 'the very opposite of a Catholic' is that Aaron, his antagonist here, *is* a Catholic – which most improbably implies a Catholic referring to his *own religion* as

The beauty of explaining in terms of *remembrance of the dead* the brief but striking features observed of the play by Bate is that such remembrance exists as a textually and indeed generically pervasive discourse, presenting the otherwise occasional features with an immediate and persistent context.[80] Recalling generally that Shakespeare's 'Roman' plays show a city of memorials,[81] however, we may usefully begin to observe such remembrance by more fully considering Aaron's Reformist condemnation of popery. This, then, is Aaron's address to Lucius:

> thou art religious
> And hast a thing within thee called conscience,
> With twenty popish tricks and ceremonies
> Which I have seen thee careful to observe.[82]

Although it may seem largely unprecedented to the unhistorical reader, this pointed allusion in act V to Lucius's performance of popish 'tricks' does not emerge from nowhere. Rather, as I now illustrate, the Andronicus family of which Lucius is a member is characterized by such performance.

From the opening, the dead have a central role in Rome. Thus, couching his appeal for political support in terms of a dead father whose honour he claims even to reanimate, Saturninus tells Rome: 'let my father's honours live in me' (I.i.7). His rival for power similarly presents his claim in commemorative terms: elect me Emperor, he says,

> If ever Basanius, *Caesar's son*,
> Were gracious in the eyes of royal Rome.[83]

With the introduction of Titus, such political remembrance is quickly associated with remembrances more heart-felt, funerary and ritualized. As if presenting a ritual action, Marcus recalls Titus returning five times

> Bleeding to Rome, bearing his valiant sons
> In coffins from the field.[84]

'popish tricks and ceremonies'. My further reading of the play will show that Bate's view of the passage is not only thus improbable, but also wholly inconsistent with the larger treatment of 'ceremonies' in the play. For this second treatment of the passage by Bate, however, see 'Lucius, The Severely Flawed Redeemer of *Titus Andronicus*: A Reply', in *Connotations* 6/3 (1996–1997), pp. 330–33 (332).

[80] Thus, we cannot agree with Erne that the Reformation context exists only in 'occasional hints'. See Erne, '"Popish Tricks"', p. 151.

[81] Consider, for example, the statue of Pompey beneath which 'Caesar' is murdered; or 'Pompey's Theatre'; conversations like that of Flavius and Murellus (*Julius Caesar*, I.ii.63–8) evoke a Rome thick with statues of ancestors.

[82] *Titus Andronicus*, V.i.74–7. This and all following citations from Shakespeare are from *The Norton Shakespeare: Based on the Oxford Edition*, ed. by Stephen Greenblatt et al. (New York and London: Norton, 1997).

[83] *Titus Andronicus*, I.i.10–11; my emphasis.

[84] *Titus Andronicus*, I.i.33–5.

Setting the scene for a repeat performance, Titus remembers burying 'one-and-twenty valiant sons' (I.i.195). For Titus, notably, Rome is mourning personified: his opening words are 'Hail, Rome, victorious in thy mourning weeds' (I.i.70).

Before the family tomb, the family then enacts a remembrance for the dead and a sacrifice which Titus names a 'rite' (I.i.77). That the rite is *for* the dead, and thus of the kind Aaron would (in Reforming mode) call 'popish ceremony' is clear. Thus, condemning himself for wasting time, Titus asks,

> Why suffer'st thou thy sons unburied yet
> To hover on the dreadful shore of Styx?[85]

Categorically, in this view, the dead are dependent on the remembrances of the living – as Titus repeats at the sacrifice of Alarbus:

> die he must
> T'appease their groaning shadows that are gone.[86]

If anything, however, this association of remembrance with *sacrifice* makes the rite more 'popish' still: as we have observed, Catholic funerals included the 'sacrifice' of the mass.[87] For those missing *this* popery, Lucius repeats a popular (or 'superstitious') version of it: Alarbus dies in the ritual

> That so the shadows be not unappeased,
> Nor we disturbed with prodigies on earth.[88]

Finally, amid this heavily suggestive scene, a clash of religions emerges specifically: for Titus, 'Religiously they [the dead] ask a sacrifice' (I.i.124); Tamora, however, presents the Reformist critique of a 'cruel' religion and paradoxical 'irreligious piety' (I.i.130).

The killing shortly after by Titus of his son, Mutius, provokes further funerary focus, but this time in a controversy between Romans concerning not the value of rite for the dead, but its appropriate expression. Thus, disowning Mutius as a disgrace, Titus denies him burial, insisting 'he rests not in this tomb' (I.i.346) and 'Bury him where you can' (I.i.351). Further highlighting the importance of burial style, however, his denial provokes dissent in the family. Quintus refuses to withdraw from the argument 'till Mutius' bones be buried' (I.i.366); Marcus tells Titus 'this is impiety in you' (I.i.352); and Lucius begs:

> let us give burial as becomes,
> Give Mutius burial with his brethren.[89]

---

[85] *Titus Andronicus*, I.i.86–7.
[86] *Titus Andronicus*, I.i.125–6.
[87] See the Introduction, p. 4.
[88] *Titus Andronicus*, I.i.100.
[89] *Titus Andronicus*, I.i.344–5.

Eventually, sustained pleading all entailing how styles of burial are important prevails:

[MARCUS, LUCIUS, QUINTUS, *and* MARTIUS *kneel*]
MARCUS   Brother, for in that name doth nature plead –
QUINTUS Father, and in that name doth nature speak –
TITUS   Speak thou no more, if all the rest will speak.
MARCUS   Renowned Titus, more than half my soul –
LUCIUS   Dear Father, soul and substance of us all –
MARCUS   Suffer thy brother Marcus to inter
         His noble nephew here in virtue's nest,
         That died in honour and Lavinia's cause.
         Thou art a Roman; be not barbarous.
         The Greeks upon advice did bury Ajax,
         That slew himself, and wise Laertes' son
         Did graciously plead for his funerals.
         Let not young Mutius then, that was thy joy,
         Be barred his entrance here.
TITUS   Rise, Marcus, rise,
         The dismall'st day is this that e'er I saw,
         To be dishonoured by my sons in Rome.
         Well, bury him, and bury me the next.
         They put [Mutius] *in the tomb*
LUCIUS   There lie thy bones, sweet Mutius, with thy friends',
         Till we with trophies do adorn thy tomb.[90]

For all concerned in this passage, getting the style of burial right is paramount. However, the importance of burying a companion correctly does not emerge as only a matter of emphasis. Marcus makes an absolute, cultural distinction between those who do and do not commemorate the dead properly: 'Thou art a Roman; be not barbarous.' Thus, the performance of burial is inextricably linked to what it is to be 'Roman'. Moreover, suggesting a notably un-Reformed outlook in sixteenth-century England, the *ritual* of a burial is central, its reduction 'barbarous'.

Act I, scene i explains this love of ritual in terms of 'honour' – an obvious virtue of ancient Rome, but also one we have observed in sixteenth-century discussion of remembrance.[91] Thus highlighting honour, as we have seen, the play's very opening, in which Saturninus asked 'let my father's honours live in me', presents the honour of the dead as integral to the living – and like views on the virtue of honouring the dead emerge persistently. Self-consciously performing remembrance for his brother, for example, Lucius seeks approval from his father, or perhaps his God:

See, lord and father, how we have performed
Our roman rite.[92]

---

[90]   *Titus Andronicus*, I.i.367–85.
[91]   See the Introduction, p. 20.
[92]   *Titus Andronicus*, I.i.141–2. In view of the play's other Christian features, 'lord and father' *might* suggest the Christian God.

Marcus's previously cited *moral* argument is also illustrative:

> Thou art a Roman; be not barbarous.
> The Greeks upon advice did bury Ajax
> That slew himself, and wise Laertes' son
> Did graciously plead for funerals.

In such an argument, the dead – mythological or otherwise – are a precedent of virtuous action, thus valuable. As a Titus, a Lucius or a Marcus honours his cultural forebears, so he too 'performs' honourable actions.

This understanding of 'honour' is pivotal in the family dispute over burying Mutius. In that quarrel, occasioned by Lavinia's marriage, the centre of Titus's disavowal of Mutius and, briefly, of Lucius, is the disregard of precedent:

> Nor thou nor he are any sons of mine.
> My sons would never so dishonour me.
> Traitor, restore Lavinia to the Emperor.[93]

It is an argument he will reiterate time and again:

> Titus, when wert thou wont to walk alone,
> Dishonoured thus and challenged of wrongs?[94]

> No foolish Tribune, no; no son of mine,
> Nor thou, nor these confederates in the deed
> That hath dishonoured all our family;
> Unworthy brother and unworthy sons![95]

> Marcus, even thou hast struck upon my crest,
> And with these boys mine honour thou hast wounded.[96]

Such insistence explains Titus's ironic 'bury me the next' when eventually he gives way to his family. In giving way, precedent – that guarantee of honour, of which Titus as senior patriarch is the living representative – seems 'buried'. In fact, Titus is only eventually swayed by the *weightier* precedent of 'the Greeks' and 'Laertes' son' appealed to by Marcus (I.i.376–7 above), and thus persistently in the dispute, the hierarchy of precedent – depending on the dead – governs each attempt to perform honourably by the living.

Being precedents of honour, the dead also underpin the family's performances of emotion. 'For two-and-twenty sons I never wept', pleads Titus for the lives of Martius and Quintus, 'Because they died in honour's lofty bed' (III.i.10–11): like Hieronimo in *The Spanish Tragedy*, Titus is not just troubled by the death of sons, or even by the injustice shown them. Rather, he weeps if 'honour's bed' is denied them in death, this scrupulousness about burial taking him to extraordinary lengths. Thus,

---

[93] *Titus Andronicus*, I.i.290–2.
[94] *Titus Andronicus*, I.i.336–7.
[95] *Titus Andronicus*, I.i.340–3.
[96] *Titus Andronicus*, I.i.361–2.

at the end of act III, scene i, he ensures the lopped heads of his sons and his own lopped hand are ritually removed from the stage, and having cut off his hand for the Emperor, his instruction is simple: 'bid him bury it' (III.i.194).

However, the honour of the dead reflecting on that of the living, Titus even comes to imagine himself transformed into the 'dead' matter of a funerary memorial. Thus, his tearful eyes are 'two ancient ruins' (III.i.17) and his body 'this feeble ruin' (III.i.206), such images presenting him as simultaneously man and broken monument of remembrance – a combination also found in the regard for the family of Marcus:

> Now farewell, flatt'ry, die, Andronicus.
> Thou dost not slumber. See thy two sons' heads,
> Thy warlike hand, thy mangled daughter here,
> Thy other banished son with this dear sight
> Struck pale and bloodless, and thy brother, I,
> Even like a stony image, cold and numb.[97]

Even as he commemorates it, Marcus is like a 'stony' memorial to a dead family; moreover, he is a monument iconoclastically 'struck', thus 'numb'.

However, the associated dishonour of the dead and living is most fully explored in another of Titus's motives for revenge: the rape of Lavinia. According to Lavinia, rape entails not only a 'worse-than killing lust' (II.iii.175): it is worse than a death without funerary celebration. Rather than be raped, thus, Lavinia begs Tamora to

> tumble me into some loathsome pit
> Where never man's eye may behold my body[98]

implying thereby, however, an unremembered death to be itself an appalling evil, being even twinned with rape as both involve a 'tumble'. And the association dishonour–rape–improper remembrance recurs in the rape itself: with horrid appropriateness, Chiron and Demetrius have a *specific* rape in mind – over the mutilated corpse of Bassianus and in his unmarked grave:

> Drag hence her husband to some secret hole,
> And make his dead trunk pillow to our lust.[99]

Implying de-ritualized burial is a violation, the connection between rape and interment in a 'pit' is remarkably emphatic. The on-stage 'hole' presents simultaneously a metaphor for Lavinia's injured sexual organs and for the uncommemorative site of Bassianus's burial. Thus, the

> subtle hole
> Whose mouth is covered with rude-growing briars
> Upon whose leaves are drops of new-shed blood[100]

---

[97] *Titus Andronicus*, III.i.252–7.
[98] *Titus Andronicus*, II.iii.176–7.
[99] *Titus Andronicus*, II.iii.129–30.
[100] *Titus Andronicus*, II.iii.198–200.

is also

> the swallowing womb
> Of this deep pit, poor Bassianus' grave.[101]

Moreover, the rape of living and dead within this site carries notably religious overtones:[102]

> Upon his bloody finger he doth wear
> A precious ring that lightens all this hole,
> Which like a taper in some monument
> Doth shine upon the dead man's earthy cheeks.[103]

The 'taper' shining over a darkened monument containing a corpse presents a traditional memorial scene, Shakespeare thus persistently emphasizing the deathliness of rape *and* the 'rape' implicit in a de-ritualized burial. Moreover, not for the first time in this metaphorical association, people – here, Lavinia and Bassianus – are themselves like injured memorials.

Religious significance also emerges elsewhere. Martius refers to 'this *unhallowed* and bloodstained hole' (II.iii.210; my emphasis), and a play on the 'unholy' in this hole that is 'hell' is evident in Tamora's description:

> And when they showed me this abhorréd pit
> They told me here at dead time of the night
> A thousand fiends, a thousand hissing snakes,
> Ten thousand swelling toads, as many urchins,
> Would make such fearful and confused cries
> As any mortal body hearing it
> Should straight fall mad or else die suddenly.[104]

The pit is a place of evil: morally appropriate, thus, for an evil such as rape even as for a rite-less burial telling a 'hellish tale' (II.iii.105). And, as we have seen, the honour of the dead and living being associated, the violation of the daughter is an experience of (popularly conceived) Christian hell:

---

[101] *Titus Andronicus*, II.iii.239–40.

[102] In emphasizing the passage's religion, I develop John Kerrigan's discussion of this scene in 'Shakespeare and the Comic Strain', in *Revenge Tragedy*, pp. 196–7, though Kerrigan's reading of the play as a whole bears little relation to mine. His essay does not consider 'religion', and its description of a humour derived from the violence of generalized and 'rigid' characters such as 'A' and 'B' says little about particular characters such as Lavinia or their tearful and vocal fluidity. But see Kerrigan, pp. 200–1. My reading of the religious significance of the scene differs from Swärdh's, moreover, in that she focuses on the 'pit' as a prison, though since prisons could be entombing (and were seen as such) our readings are compatible.

[103] *Titus Andronicus*, II.iii.226–9.

[104] *Titus Andronicus*, II.iii.98–104.

O, what a sympathy of woe is this –
As far from help as *limbo* is from bliss.[105]

That the living are 'unhallowed' by the violation of 'the dead' is clear when, deciding on revenge, Titus rhetorically asks, 'Then which way shall I find Revenge's cave?' (III.iii.269). 'Cave' having been another label for the 'bloody hole',[106] in seeking revenge Titus returns, metaphorically, to a key source of his grief. Images of hell which each recall the place of violation increasing, Marcus's demand that his heart 'be an ever-burning hell' (III.i.241) also suggests how the rite-less 'hole' affects the family. The importance of revenging the injury done to the *dead*, however, is visible in Titus's exact revenge:

You know your mother means to feast with me,
And calls herself Revenge, and thinks me mad.
Hark, villains, I will grind your bones to dust,
And with your blood and it I'll make a paste,
And of the paste a coffin I will rear,
And make two pasties of your shameful heads,
And bid that strumpet, your unhallowed dam,
Like to the earth swallow her own increase.[107]

Students often respond loosely to the 'yuk-factor' here, but observing the exact symmetry of Titus's revenge is more precisely instructive. Titus's 'Ovidian' revenge is not only to feed Tamora her own sons: he imagines his pie as a 'coffin' that, like the earth, the 'unhallowed dam' Tamora will 'swallow', thus denying the sons *any* rite of remembrance and *thus* turning Tamora into their 'unhallowed/damned' grave.

The religious aspect of Titus's revenge bears emphasis. Recalling how he and Lucius repeatedly considered the damaged Lavinia 'martyred' (III.i.81; 107; III.ii.36), Titus tells Tamora's sons: 'I mean to martyr you' (V.iii.179): *religious* sacrifice is key to the revenge. Associatively therefore, as Bate suggests,[108] there may indeed be a Eucharistic echo in the blood and 'paste' offered to Tamora, but if so the scene is *not* anti-Catholic. As I have shown, to feed Chiron and Demetrius to Tamora specifically punishes the sons by denying them any and all rites of remembrance: implicit in such punishment is the value not just of funerary ritual but of memorial rituals generally – including requiem (or any other) masses. Emphasizing the *value* of remembrance, thus, Titus's revenge is consonant with traditional and Catholic funeral, but *not* with the reduced remembrances persistently proposed by Reformers.

The close of *Titus Andronicus* will also emphasize unambiguously that a reduced funerary remembrance is a punishment. First, however, I consider Aaron.

The play's grouping of Romans as commemorators of the dead and of others, hitherto Goths, as violators of remembrance, includes Aaron who, as partner to

---

[105] *Titus Andronicus*, III.i.148–9; my emphasis.
[106] See, for example, II.iii.24.
[107] *Titus Andronicus*, V.iii.183–90.
[108] See my discussion on p. 44. above.

Tamora and non-Roman, sides naturally against remembrances. Thus, among a catalogue of villainies in act V, Aaron boasts,

> Oft have I digged up dead men from their graves
> And set them upright at their dear friends' door,
> Even when their sorrows almost was forgot,
> And on their skins, as on the bark of trees,
> Have with my knife carved in Roman letters,
> 'Let not your sorrow die though I am dead.'[109]

The play's consciousness of differences of skin colour and faith – in its latter stages this open critic of popish ceremony is increasingly an 'irreligious Moor' (V.iii.120) and a 'misbelieving Moor' (V.iii.142) – suggests that this reported attack on Roman 'skins' is no coincidence. However, in violating the burial places of the dead, the all-but-unregenerate Aaron is like Tamora, Chiron and Demetrius in their attitude to Bassianus's corpse. Nor can we regard his villainous boast as ironic self-parody: having killed the Nurse in act IV *not* out of revenge or any sense of justice but because she is a 'long-tongued babbling gossip' (IV.ii.149), Aaron shows his general disregard for ritual funeral in instructions to Chiron and Demetrius:

> you must needs bestow her funeral.
> The fields are near, and you are gallant grooms.[110]

The burial will consist of no more than a hole in the ground, its accompaniment no more, in Aaron's ironic image, than the 'gallant grooms' of the careless sons: recalling the 'natural' burial of Bassianus, this funeral in the fields too is a violation.

Still presenting de-ritualized (or 'natural') burial as a sign of evil, the close of *Titus Andronicus* continues to emphasize distinctions between Romans and others in funerary terms. Asked by 'A Roman' to pronounce sentence on Aaron, Lucius directs:

> Set him breast-deep in earth and famish him,
> There let him stand, and rave, and cry for food.
> If anyone relieves or pities him,
> For the offence he dies. This is our doom.
> Some stay to see him fastened in the earth.[111]

The burial is a deliberate humiliation: deprived of a tomb, Aaron will be a visible sign of dishonour in death. Indeed, his burial is – in proposed, Roman perspective – a means of re-enforcing Roman attitudes toward remembrance: 'If anyone relieves or pities him, / For the offence he dies.' The re-iteration that Aaron be buried only 'in earth' adds to the prevailing Roman view that 'natural' burial is violation.

Even this, however, is not the end: the distinctions are unrelenting. Lucius orders:

---

[109] *Titus Andronicus*, V.i.135–40.
[110] *Titus Andronicus*, IV.ii.162–3.
[111] *Titus Andronicus*, V.iii.178–82.

> Some loving friends convey the Emperor hence,
> And give him burial in his father's grave.
> My father and Lavinia shall forthwith
> Be closed in our household's monument.
> As for that ravenous tiger, Tamora,
> No funeral rite nor man in mourning weed,
> Nor mournful bell shall ring her burial;
> But throw her fourth to beasts and birds to prey.
> Her life was beastly and devoid of pity,
> And being dead, let birds on her take pity.[112]

Romans – including, pointedly, Saturninus – are buried in their family tombs and with their dead. Since she was 'beastly', however, Tamora will rot without mourning or 'funeral rite', with wild beasts in the open air. As when he begged Titus 'Thou art a Roman; be not barbarous', the distinction by Lucius here between 'Roman' rite for the dead and the burials of barbarians is sharp. In reference to the historical controversies over the dead observed in the Introduction, the affirmation of 'popish ceremonies' (in Aaron's explicit phrase) resounds.

Two more points deserve attention, the first being a surprisingly pointed series of anti-Elizabethan allusions running alongside the sustained treatment of remembrance. For Tamora is presented as Diana and Phoebe, as was so often Elizabeth, the 'Queen of the Goths' thus implying the Queen of the English not obliquely. The context of such labelling is also suggestive. Evoking not unusual comparisons between Elizabeth and her enemies, the besotted Saturninus says Tamora

> like the stately Phoebe 'mongst her nymphs
> Dost overshine the gallant'st dames of Rome.[113]

However, comparing Elizabeth to the far-from-chaste *Tamora* is insulting. Similarly, this question relating to Tamora suggests Elizabeth:

> is it Dian, habited like her
> Who hath abandoned her holy groves
> To see the general hunting in this forest?[114]

Dian, like Phoebe, regularly stood for Elizabeth, but to suggest she might have abandoned 'holy groves' – especially in a play saturated with violated, thus unholy, 'holes' – smears Elizabeth with a religious un-chastity.

Though often *very* pointed, none of this absolutely requires audiences to respond positively to the play's Roman ceremonial. Consciously reflecting on the matter of appropriate response, however, in *Titus Andronicus* even more than in *The Spanish Tragedy*, the question of the appropriateness of punishments to crimes is prominent. The question can be asked in a dizzying variety of ways. Does Alarbus deserve to be sacrificed at the opening? Is Tamora justified in seeking revenge for

---

[112] *Titus Andronicus*, V.iii.190–9.
[113] *Titus Andronicus*, I.i.313–14.
[114] *Titus Andronicus*, II.iii.57–9.

this sacrifice – and even if so, does this justify her role in the rape of Lavinia? Is Titus's revenge on Tamora (and her sons) justified by Lavinia's rape? Ultimately, are Lucius's blank distinctions between 'Roman' and 'un-Roman', good and bad, civilized and uncivilized, just? Indeed, though the theme is relatively undeveloped in this Shakespearean play – though not in others – in addition to such potentially accumulating uncertainty we might even wonder if Aaron's apparently irredeemable evil is not in fact a response, thereby 'justified', to his excluded status as dark-skinned Moor. To adapt Katharine Maus's question cited previously: 'Do we – or to what extent do we – condone crimes that retaliate for other crimes?' As in *The Spanish Tragedy*, such counter-balancing questions will eventually provoke arguments over sympathy and 'feeling', but *Titus Andronicus* too presents perspective on felt responses, allowing assessment of its Roman rituals of funeral.

It has been observed that distinctions between 'life' and 'death' in sixteenth- and seventeenth-century England were unclear,[115] and even that among Shakespeare's 'most common and least noticed', though 'basic dramatic situations', are characters appearing 'simultaneously in death and life'.[116] One such character is Lavinia – as the three previously cited allusions to her 'martyrdom' and four further passages imply. Thus, in the first of these further passages, immediately after Lavinia has walked off stage, the banished Lucius says:

> now nor Lucius nor Lavinia lives
> But in oblivion and hateful griefs.[117]

Thus, Lucius and Lavinia at this point exist in parallel states of death, oblivion and dishonour. Titus reiterates the focal point regarding Lavinia immediately before he 'slays' her, in a second, further passage. Typically, it opens with Titus appealing to precedent:

TITUS	My lord the Emperor, resolve me this:
	Was it well done of rash Virginius
	To slay his daughter with his own right hand
	Because she was enforced, stained, and deflowered?
SATURNINUS	It was Andronicus.
TITUS	Your reason, mighty Lord?

---

[115] As suggested in the Introduction, distinctions between living and dead were growing, but as Cressy notes, 'St Augustine taught that life was death and death was life, and this inverted notion found many English exponents in the sixteenth and seventeenth centuries.' See Cressy, p. 382. However, the perspective Cressy here outlines is only an 'inversion' by modern standards. The view that life is death considerably pre-dates Augustine. Suggesting such long understanding, Robert Pogue Harrison claims the etymological association of the Latin *humanitas* ('humanity') with *humando* ('burying'). To be human, he argues, is to be 'humic'. See *The Dominion of the Dead* (Chicago and London: University of Chicago Press, 2003), p. x–xi.

[116] Duncan Harris, 'Tombs, Guidebooks and Shakespearean Drama: Death in the Renaissance', in *Mosaic: A Journal for the Interdisciplinary Study of Literature* 15/1: 'Death and Dying' (1982), pp. 13–28 (13–14).

[117] *Titus Andronicus*, III.ii.293–4.

SATURNINUS	Because the girl should not survive her shame,
	And by her presence still renew his sorrows.
TITUS	A reason right, strong, effectual;
	A pattern, precedent, and lively warrant
	For me, most wretched, to perform the like.[118]

The distinction between life and death here proposed by Saturninus and accepted by Titus is 'shame'; being dishonoured, therefore, Lavinia is dead already. In the third further passage, immediately after Lavinia's slaying, Saturninus initially expresses shock, but then he asks, 'What, was she ravished?' (V.iii.52), implying he sees the relation between Lavinia's violation and death. Asked by Tamora why he has killed his daughter, fourthly, Titus reiterates the essential point: 'Not I, 'twas Chiron and Demetrius' (V.iii.55). Thus, in a total of seven separate occasions, the text insists the walking Lavinia is to be considered dead – helping us to interpret why Shakespeare should have dramatized so unflinchingly her horrific presence. For being dead, Lavinia embodies a corpse freed of funeral's ceremonial *requiescat in pace*, registering this as a most visible affront.

This all bears directly on the play's treatment of felt responses. Finding Lavinia following the rape – in weaker if more recent parlance her 'symbolic death' – Marcus embarks on a forty-four-line speech expressing shock, sadness and anger – but also the rationale for such large emotion:

Sorrow concealed, like an oven stopped,
Doth burn the heart to cinders where it is.[119]

Large emotion for the dead must be expressed – as Lavinia's very attempts to speak from her disfiguring silence expresses. Indeed, though at this point Marcus only considers an anger to 'rail at' Lavinia's unknown assailants (II.iv.35), we already verge on Isabella's perspective in *The Spanish Tragedy*: that in mourning 'out*rage* fits'.

However, in *Titus Andronicus*, the treatment of how appropriately to remember deathly Lavinia is extensive. Thus, learning of Lavinia's state, and in self-consciously performative language, Titus wonders what style of emotion would be appropriate:

Gentle Lavinia, let me kiss thy lips;
Or make some sign how I may do thee ease.
Shall thy good uncle, and thy brother Lucius,
And thou, and I, sit round about some fountain,
Looking all downwards to behold our cheeks
How they are stained, like meadows yet not dry
With miry slime left on them by a flood?
And in the fountain shall we gaze so long
Till the fresh taste be taken from that clearness,
And make a brine pit with our bitter tears?
Or shall we cut away our hands like thine?

---

[118] *Titus Andronicus*, V.iii.35–44.
[119] *Titus Andronicus*, II.vi.36–7.

> Or shall we bite our tongues, and in dumb shows
> Pass the remainder of our hateful days?
> What shall we do?[120]

It is a complex passage. Repeatedly it asks: what *is* the appropriate way to show feeling towards 'death'? Yet it also emphasizes that emotion requires performance. First, Titus examines his grief in the imagined fountain, concerning himself extensively with the self-reflection it *shows* him. Second, he presents Lavinia as a 'dumb show', delineating the on-looking family who 'behold' as a theatrical audience searching for the right emotional response. Nor does concern with the art of emotion stop here. Transferring from metaphors of theatrical to pictorial art, Titus says,

> Had I but seen thy picture in this plight
> It would have madded me. What shall I do
> Now I behold thy lively body so?[121]

In each case, deathly Lavinia gives rise not only to questions of emotion, but also to matters of its performance. Subtly, however, the overwrought Titus also implies what the correct performance is: in considering a show of feeling which is 'dumb', he links such a response to the violated Lavinia, thus presenting it as a violation. He thus implies only a *voluble* emotion for the dead is appropriate, telling the audience two things: perform emotive memorial, and perform it *largely*.

However, even this suggestion is only the beginning. Confronted by Titus's overwhelming distress at Lavinia's state, Lucius and Marcus initially try to repress his emotion – at least before Lavinia:

> Sweet father, cease your tears, for at your grief
> See how my wretched sister sobs and weeps.[122]
>
> Patience, dear niece. Good Titus, dry thine eyes[123]

When these arguments fail, they attempt more abstract reasoning:

> MARCUS   O brother, speak with possibility
>   And do not break into these deep extremes.
> TITUS   Is not my sorrows deep, having no bottom?
>   Then be my passions bottomless with them.
> MARCUS   But yet let reason govern your lament.
> TITUS   If there were reason for these miseries,
>   Then into limits could I bind my woes.
>   When heaven doth weep, doth not the earth o'erflow?
>   If the winds rage, doth not the sea wax mad,
>   Threat'ning the welkin with his big-swoll'n face?

---

[120] *Titus Andronicus*, III.i.120–35.
[121] *Titus Andronicus*, III.i.103–5.
[122] *Titus Andronicus*, III.i.135–6.
[123] *Titus Andronicus*, III.i.138.

> And wilt thou have a reason for this coil?
> I am the sea. Hark how her sighs doth blow.[124]

There are no theatrical or pictorial metaphors here, but this passage persists in focusing on the appropriate act of feeling. Thus, in response to appeals against 'extremes' of behaviour (and much as we saw in *The Spanish Tragedy*), Titus pronounces 'disproportionate' grief proportionate. 'If there were reason for these miseries', he explains, 'Then into limits could I bind my woes'. However, as he sees no sufficient reason, his grief will have no limit. Grief turning to anger, therefore, like the sighing sea Titus will 'wax mad, / Threat'ning' as the 'winds rage'. Thus, through a sustained consideration of appropriate commemorative action, the play explains the logic of its revenge; and in doing so it implies the most *extravagant* remembrances of the dead – despite sixteenth-century Reformers – are appropriate.

The end shows that Lucius and Marcus have learnt – and are concerned to teach – Titus's extravagant style of remembrance. Addressing 'gentle Romans' (V.iii.146) over Titus's body, they give voice to their grief with justifications of its appropriateness:

> LUCIUS   Stand all aloof, but uncle, draw you near
>   To shed obsequious tears upon this trunk.
>   [*Kissing Titus*] O, take this warm kiss on thy pale cold lips,
>   These sorrowful drops upon thy bloodstained face,
>   The last true duties of thy noble son.
> MARCUS   [*Kissing Titus*] Tear for tear, and loving kiss for kiss,
>   Thy brother Marcus tenders on thy lips.
>   O were the sum of these that I should pay
>   Countless and infinite, yet would I pay them.
> LUCIUS   [*to Young Lucius*] Come hither, boy, come, come and learn of us
>   To melt in showers.[125]

Thus, even while justifying it, Lucius and Marcus publicly illustrate their large and ritual mourning; they also specifically invite Young Lucius to 'learn' their style of grief. Lucius calls such remembrance 'true duties', Marcus emphasizing not only such performance is appropriate 'Tear for tear, and loving kiss for kiss', but also the particular correctness of memorial *largesse*: 'were the sum of these that I should pay / Countless and infinite, yet would I pay them'. The echo here of the 'limitless' emotion in mourning previously endorsed by Titus himself is clear.

Yet even this lesson in remembrance is prefaced by a more pointed one. Appealing to 'sons of Rome' now including Goths, Marcus asks:

> O let me teach you how to knit again
> This scattered corn into one mutual sheaf,
> These broken limbs again into one body.[126]

Thus, the consciously educational close seeks to transform the whole bloodletting and mutilation of the drama into a Christian redemption story, the broken limbs reunited in one body inevitably echoing – for the third time in the play – the redemptive

---

[124] *Titus Andronicus*, III.i.213–24.
[125] *Titus Andronicus*, V.iii.150–60.
[126] *Titus Andronicus*, V.iii.69–71.

but broken body celebrated in the Roman Eucharist.[127] This lesson extrapolated by Lucius, in which the drama becomes an emblem of Christianity, may ring hollowly today; however, it reminds us that sacrifice – even sacrifice as terrible as that of Alarbus or Lavinia – is part of a traditional, Christian 'mystery' in which vendetta, sacrifice and therefore mourning are central.

Hamlet, c.1600, revised 1600–1604[128]

As there has been a 'long series of debates' as to whether its Ghost 'is "Catholic" or "Protestant"',[129] the Broudian thesis that classic revenge tragedy is unambiguously Protestant is already doubtful regarding *Hamlet*. However, because there has seemed to be 'evidence on all sides' of the religious question, the debate appears, in Stephen Greenblatt's phrase, 'doomed to inconclusiveness'.[130] Following the approach advanced generally in this study, therefore, it is appropriate to change the focus of the debate, considering not whether the *Ghost* is Catholic or Protestant, but in what styles the play's *characters* seek remembrance of the dead King. In doing this, we shall observe divergent styles of remembrance denoting religion spread across the play, thus far more pervasively than traditionally observed. For whether the former King 'is' a spirit of health or a goblin damned, Elsinore is united in seeing him as a memory.

Remembrance of the dead King is already focal in the opening scene, but it is in act I, scene ii that the question of what *style* to remember him in emerges. Grounding his argument on the good of the state, this is Claudius's view:

> Though yet of Hamlet our dear brother's death
> The memory be green, and that it us befitted
> To bear our hearts in grief and our whole kingdom
> To be contracted in one brow of woe,
> Yet so far hath discretion fought with nature
> That we with wisest sorrow think on him
> Together with remembrance of ourselves.[131]

Claudius first remembers the dead King as having mournful claims on those surviving him, but he then argues that in 'remembrance of ourselves' attention

---

[127] Erne and Swärdh see in these lines allusion to 'the Pauline body, the Church', but since we have twice previously found allusion to the Eucharist, that would seem the dominant allusion. See Erne, 'Popish Tricks', p. 149, Swärdh, p. 122.

[128] 'It is our belief that Shakespeare wrote *Hamlet* about 1600, and revised it later; that the 1604 version was printed from his original papers; and that the 1603 edition represents a very imperfect report of an abridged version of the revision.' See *The Oxford Shakespeare: The Complete Works*, ed. by Stanley Wells and Gary Taylor (Oxford: Oxford University Press, 1988), p. 653.

[129] Greenblatt, *Hamlet in Purgatory*, p. 239. I cited prominent essays in the debate in the Introduction, p. 14, note 58.

[130] Greenblatt, *Hamlet in Purgatory*, p. 239.

[131] *Hamlet*, I.ii.1–7.

should turn away from the former King. Signifying opposition to this even in his mourning garb, however, to Hamlet the claims of the dead man are unchallengeable, his remembrance impossible to ignore. Highlighting their difference in Reformist mode, Claudius will argue at length that persisting in remembrance is a very 'fault against the dead' (I.ii.102), but the antagonism persisting to the end, act I, scene ii shows differences over memorial performance are a key cause of the tragedy.

Hamlet expresses in detail his view of remembrance in rebuking Gertrude over his 'customary' style of mourning:

> 'Tis not alone my inky cloak, good-mother,
> Nor customary suits of solemn black,
> Nor windy suspiration of forced breath,
> No, nor the fruitful river in the eye,
> Nor the dejected haviour of the visage,
> Together with all forms, moods, shows of grief
> That can denote me truly. These may 'seem',
> For they are actions that a man might play;
> But I have that within which passeth show –
> These but the trappings and the suits of woe.[132]

In this rebuke, Hamlet asserts that Gertrude mistakes the externals of mourning for what is 'within', certainly not dismissing his 'suits of woe' as irrelevant or excessive. These 'trappings' entail a performance – 'actions that a man might play' – but Hamlet's central point is that the clothes cannot be *reduced* to 'mere theatre' in the sense of empty ritual. That Hamlet's 'suits of woe' are to be considered as not 'alone' denoting him is specifically an argument against reductive claims that ceremonial mourning is empty. Indeed, by acknowledging that externals 'may' be merely played at line 83, Hamlet distinguishes as truly representative his own action and 'show' – precisely because 'that within which passeth show' guarantees the memorials he presents 'without'. Thus, presenting a definition of truth that will recur, his mournful act denotes him 'truly' (line 83). Hamlet thus justifies enlarged performances of funerary remembrance despite contemporary Reformers.

Hamlet's soliloquies in particular link what he has 'within' with (external) expression,[133] *showing* his public remembrance to be true. Thus, in his first soliloquy, his imperative question 'Heaven and earth, / Must I remember?' (I.ii.142–3) shows the memory – in this case of the dead King and his relations with his wife – manifesting itself against Hamlet's will. The speech continues to register memory as unwanted but irrepressible, both explicitly ('Let me not think on't') and in the continued way in

---

[132] *Hamlet*, I.ii.77–86.

[133] The following discussion of Hamlet utilizes a number of ideas – for example, contained or repressed emotion, involuntary manifestations – which often suggest psychoanalytic and particularly Freudian interpretation. My own use of these terms, however, is not Freudian and avoids at least the more obvious historical difficulties of retrospective reading. Instead, my thinking on 'repressed' emotion derives from Seneca, a vital source for revenge tragedy, particularly as interpreted by Braden in *Renaissance Tragedy and the Senecan Tradition*. I have commented previously on the usefulness of this study.

which memory erupts disturbingly into his coherent discourse – as in the following on Gertrude at the old King's funeral:

> those shoes were old
> With which she followed my poor father's body,
> Like Niobe all tears, why she, even she –
> O God, a beast that wants discourse of reason
> Would have mourned longer![134]

Emerging from him as if in spite of himself, the interjected appeal to God (as earlier to 'Heavens and earth') presents Hamlet's remembrance of 'my poor father's body' *and* of *Gertrude*'s former remembrance of it as an unwanted intruder in Hamlet's narrative.

Moreover, in each of the soliloquies, Hamlet's mourning emerges in the actions of remembrance which he previously championed: 'windy suspiration of forced breath'; 'dejected haviour of the visage'; and, we may imagine, 'the fruitful river in the eye'. That we are not to discount the insights into 'Hamlet' provided by the soliloquies as 'empty theatre' is obvious. Yet if we acknowledge that they are no mere melodrama (in the negative sense of empty drama), then these persistent performances of remembrance are contrary to Reformed 'measure'. Contrary to the prescribed mourning of Reformers, Hamlet consistently implies that in both action and emotion, performing mourning extensively – but to Reformers 'disproportionately' – is appropriate. Notably, his ideal picture of Gertrude – in contrast to her now more settled state – is of Niobe, who wept for lack of funeral for her slaughtered family,[135] herself 'all tears': an embodiment and epitome of endless mourning for the misremembered. Developing understandings of post-mortem memorial and theatre already visible in *The Spanish Tragedy*, Shakespeare presents maximized mourning as Hamlet's true ideal, his allegedly human 'psychopathology' connoting religious traditionalism in seventeenth-century England.

Hamlet's levity, which T.S. Eliot called 'a form of emotional relief', owes much to his memorial ideal.[136] A case in point is the following soliloquy in act I, scene ii, when Hamlet asks Horatio why he is no longer at Wittenberg, adding ironically that 'We'll teach you to drink deep ere you depart'. The dialogue continues:

---

[134] *Hamlet*, I.ii.147–51.

[135] Resigning Hector's (unburied) body (in the *Iliad*, book 24), Achilles presents Niobe weeping for her twelve slaughtered children as a paradigm of mourning: 'for nine days they [the children] lay in their blood, and there was no-one to bury them, as the son of Kronos had turned the people into stones ... Now she is somewhere among the rocks, in the mountain pastures of Sipylos ... [and] though she is stone, she still broods on the pain the gods gave her.' Citation from *Homer: The Iliad: A New Prose Translation*, trans. by Martin Hammond (Harmondsworth: Penguin, 1987), p. 406.

[136] T.S. Eliot, 'Hamlet', in *Selected Prose* (Harmondsworth: Penguin, 1953; 1958), pp. 104–10 (108).

> HORATIO   My lord, I came to see your father's funeral.
> HAMLET   I prithee do not mock me, fellow student;
>   I think it was to see my mother's wedding.
> HORATIO   Indeed, my lord, it followed hard upon.
> HAMLET   Thrift, thrift, Horatio. The funeral baked meats
>   Did coldly furnish forth the marriage tables.[137]

As in the soliloquy of act I, scene ii, the performance of brief mourning is a cause of resentment. Now, however, that resentment emerges not as forced breath or the rivers of the eye, but as wit: a performance of irony masking Hamlet's conspicuous distress. Hamlet will himself explain such 'cold' humour in act III: 'What should a man *do* but be merry? For look you how cheerfully my mother looks, and my father died within's two hours' (III.ii.13–15; my emphasis). Implying the value he attaches to funerary remembrance, Hamlet says the interruption of mourning for his father explains his inappropriate levity; had the rites of remembrance been properly observed, he implies, he too would now observe 'proper' canons of behaviour.

A final example illustrates the pervasiveness of this understanding. Responding to Hamlet's explanation of the noise festively emanating from the castle in act I, scene iii, Horatio asks, 'Is it a custom?' Hamlet's answer is ironic:

> Ay, marry is't,
> And to my mind, though I am native here
> And to the manner born, it is a custom,
> More honoured in the breach than the observance.[138]

On the face of it, Hamlet is not addressing remembrance of the dead, but the focus on dishonoured customs – especially as he presently seeks his dead father – echoes his wider concern with his father's ill-performed funeral. Moreover, the all but inevitable pun on 'marry' recalls the original cause of the funeral's disruption, the marriage of Gertrude to Claudius, in which festivity displaced mourning and ceremonial time went 'out of joint' (I.v.189).[139]

Illustrating the value he attaches to it, in act II, scene ii, Hamlet says ceremony is 'Th' appurtenance of welcome' (II.ii.354). However, he then requests of the First Player 'a passionate speech' (II.ii.414) evoking a corpse not treated to ceremony, but mythically violated – so much so that even the Player mourns. The speech addresses Priam's death and the response of Hecuba, who,

> Run barefoot up and down, threat'ning the flames
> With bisson rheum; a clout upon that head
> Where late the diadem stood, and for a robe,

---

[137] *Hamlet*, I.ii.175–80.

[138] *Hamlet*, I.iv.15–18.

[139] The traditional calendar year, itself subject to Reform, revolved around repeated holy days; ceremony thus marked time. For discussion of the Reformation of such time, see C. John Summerville, 'The Secularization of Time and Play', in *The Secularization of Early Modern England: From Religious Culture to Religious Faith* (New York and Oxford: Oxford University Press, 1992), pp. 33–43.

> About her lank, and all o'er-teemèd loins,
> A blanket in th' alarm of fear caught up –
> Who this had seen, with tongue in venom steeped,
> 'Gainst Fortune's state would treason have pronounced.
> But if the gods themselves did see her then,
> When she saw Pyrrhus make malicious sport
> In mincing with his sword her husband's limbs,
> The instant burst of clamour that she made –
> Unless things mortal move them not at all –
> Would have made milch the burning eyes of heaven,
> And passion in the gods.[140]

Beside the wildly mourning Hecuba (a clout for a crown, a blanket for a robe…), the tears flowing from the Player and even ('Unless things move them not at all') from the gods, is the picture of Priam's corpse, his limbs minced in malicious sport by Pyrrhus. As we have already observed repeatedly in this chapter, unceremonious treatment of a corpse is a cause for 'burning eyes', the 'passion' of the gods: anger. Moreover, in this self-consciously theatrical context, the matter of *performing* remembrance is to the fore.

Left alone, Hamlet measures his own actions against those of the First Player, focusing especially on the restraint of his own performed remembrance as exposed by the Player's extravagance. In particular, his emotional restraint troubles him. Thus, as Hieronimo used Bazardo's art to interrogate his art of remembrance, Hamlet questions his style of performance by reference to the drama of the First Player, seemingly at first condemning him:

> Is it not monstrous that this player here,
> But in a fiction, in a dream of passion,
> Could force his soul so to his whole conceit
> That from her working all his visage wanned,
> Tears in his eyes, distraction in's aspect,
> A broken voice, and his whole function suiting
> With forms to his conceit?[141]

However, condemnation of the Player is not where this speech is heading. Hamlet is soon demanding

> What would he do
> Had he the motive and the cue for passion
> That I have?[142]

eventually condemning *himself* as 'A dull and muddy-mettled rascal… /…unpregnant of my cause' who 'can say nothing' (II.ii.568–71). The Player's performance of remembrance is an ideal against which Hamlet claims to fall short.

---

[140] *Hamlet*, II.ii.485–98.
[141] *Hamlet*, II.ii.528–534.
[142] *Hamlet*, II.ii.537–9.

Thematically, extravagant performances of remembrance – what Hamlet previously called the 'fruitful river of the eye', 'suspiration of forced breath', the 'dejected haviour of the visage', the 'forms, moods and shows of grief' – are here reaffirmed, the strictly measured mourning of Reformers being implicitly but forcefully rejected. Indeed, the previous speech picks up the controversy over performing remembrance initiated in act I, scene ii, when Claudius first acknowledged it 'befitted / To bear our hearts in grief and our whole kingdom / To be contracted in one brow of woe', but then rejected such 'fit' remembrance. For to Hamlet, the Player's absolute mourning specifically presents a 'whole function *suiting* / With forms to his conceit', the melodramatic 'excess' of Reformers becoming on the contrary here the *correct* style of remembrance.

That extravagance in remembrance is correct is a point this soliloquy insists on. I quote from it at length, not only to show the persistent use of the Player by Hamlet as 'objective correlative',[143] but also because the length of the response is an aspect of Hamlet's extravagance. Thus, the Player's commemoration is 'all for nothing. For Hecuba' (II.ii.534–5), begging the questions,

> What's Hecuba to him, or he to Hecuba
> That he should weep for her? What would he do
> Had he the motive and the cue for passion
> That I have?[144]

Here, the player is a comparative model for the performance of remembrance. However, Hamlet's answer to his second question is extravagant (but correct) remembrance:

> He would drown the stage with tears,
> And cleave the general ear with horrid speech,
> Make mad the guilty and appal the free,
> Confound the ignorant, and amaze indeed
> The very faculty of eyes and ears.[145]

This *most* extravagant, but according to Hamlet appropriate, display he then compares to his own performance again:

>   Yet I
> A dull and muddy-mettled rascal, peak
> Like John-a-dreams, unpregnant of my cause,
> And can say nothing—[146]

---

[143] Eliot's phrase for 'the formula (in this case, theatre) of that *particular* emotion', 'Hamlet', p. 107. I have commented on the meditative implications of this method in *Shakespeare's Romances and the Politics of Counter-Reformation*, Renaissance Studies 3 (Queenston; Lewiston; Lampeter: Edwin Mellen, 1999), pp. 182–5.
[144] *Hamlet*, II.ii.536–9.
[145] *Hamlet*, II.ii.539–43.
[146] *Hamlet*, II.ii.543–6.

It is the restraint in Hamlet's public memorial that is roundly condemned, and so the speech proceeds – from raving self-condemnation for inaction, to extreme self-condemnation for being extravagant only in words – until a plan to act emerges.

That plan – to catch the conscience of the King in The Mousetrap – is often considered avoiding duty,[147] but this misses the importance of *performing* remembrance in Hamlet's thinking. For The Mousetrap, as I now illustrate, presents an ill-remembered King while also highlighting the matter of *performing* remembrance.[148] Moreover, it allows Hamlet to observe if the action presented by the Players provokes any *remembrance* in Claudius or others, thus helping to verify their guilt. However, I begin my discussion of The Mousetrap with Hamlet's particular instructions about the style in which it is to be performed.

Hamlet highlights to the Players the matter of *appropriate* performance: 'Suit the action to the word, the word to the action ... o'erstep not the modesty of nature. For anything so overdone is from the purpose of playing' (III.ii.16–19). However, 'natural' modesty turns out to be defined in religious terms. Unnatural performance, says Hamlet, has neither 'the accent of Christians, nor the gait of Christian, pagan, nor no man' (III.ii.27–9). Thus, challenging the sharp pagan–Christian distinctions of Reformers, and especially their sharp distinctions regarding performing remembrance,[149] Hamlet presents 'Christian' and 'pagan' actions as similarly natural and human.

The Mousetrap itself not only replays circumstances approximating King Hamlet's murder, it also confronts the range of mournful attitudes that have been focal. Briefly, the Player King suggests his wife will re-marry after his death, but the Player Queen twice interrupts, protesting such marriage is 'treason' and 'accurst' (III.ii.160; 161) and thus implying she will live out her remaining life in remembrance of him. The King pertinently counters that 'Purpose is but the slave of memory' (III.ii.170), but the Player Queen is adamant:

> Nor earth to me give food, nor heaven light,
> Sport and repose lack from me day and night,
> Each opposite that blanks the face of joy
> Meet what I would have well and it destroy,
> Both here and hence pursue me lasting strife
> If, once a widow, ever I be wife.[150]

---

[147] Being thus part of the question surrounding Hamlet's 'delay' that Jenkins still noted in 1995 as having been key in criticism of the play for 'more than two centuries'. See *Hamlet*, ed. by Harold Jenkins, The Arden Shakespeare (London and New York: Routledge, 1982; 1995), pp. 136–40 (136).

[148] In what follows, I expand Neill's view of The Mousetrap's 'double function as both memorial and a fatal memento mori' by highlighting its related matters of performance and religion. For Neill's stated view, see *Issues of Death*, p. 259.

[149] For my discussion of these sharp distinctions, see the Introduction, p. 22–3.

[150] *Hamlet*, III.ii.198–203.

The final punch line does not *quite* rule out second marriage, but the passage reiterates that widowhood – a life in mourning – should be more or less forever. Thus, the play Hamlet has organized for the court repeats his view of ideal remembrance as it was embodied, for example, in his image of Niobe, 'all tears'. Mourning, he emphatically implies, should be extensive and sustained.

The responses to this claim among the play's immediate audience are telling. Reiterating his ideal, Hamlet implies how dishonourable it would be abandoning widowhood after an avowal like the Player Queen's: 'If she should break it now!' (III.ii.204). Gertrude is less enthusiastic, claiming 'The lady protests too much, methinks' (III.ii.210); thus, Hamlet and Gertrude differ in their views of how much remembrance for a dead man is 'too much', the play-within-the-play eliciting the religious controversy of the period.

Claudius's response to the enacted poisoning of the Player King has been deemed problematic. Why is Claudius so frightened by the 'murder' when he has already seen the pouring of poison 'in the King's ears' in the Prologue?[151] However, repetition and elaboration being standard ways of rhetorically enforcing a point, a simple answer is that it is the *repeated* action, and its elaboration in the second presentation, which affects Claudius, eventually making his memory of old King Hamlet's death unbearably vivid. For provoking a remembrance is clearly important in Hamlet's attempt to 'catch the conscience of the king' (II.ii.582).

Making the remembrance forcefully indicate Claudius's guilt is another matter, but as Hamlet says, the play is 'the thing' to do it (III.i.581). Ironically presenting a *weak* remembrance of the murder alleged by the Ghost, Hamlet has good grounds to consider the King guilty when his response to it is so strong. For being highly mannered, presenting clunking couplets and persistent archaisms, being even uneven in its tone – it is said to present both a 'revenge' and a 'comedy' (III.ii.232; 269) – The Mousetrap is a weak drama – compare it to the flowing lines in which the First Player previously remembered Hecuba! As Hamlet puts it, Claudius is frightened with a '*false* fire' (III.ii.244; my italics), his horror suggesting a much more direct remembrance than The Mousetrap actually warrants. Literally, it is Hamlet's joke; The Mousetrap is only strong enough to catch 'mice'; so if a King is caught in it, he has entangled himself. Hamlet can therefore infer Claudius's hand in the murder, thus taking the Ghost's word 'for a thousand pound' (III.ii.64).

Using art – though not, now, performance – to provoke remembrance is also Hamlet's technique in his following confrontation with Gertrude. In act III, scene iv, Hamlet is so extravagantly passionate that Gertrude fears she will be murdered, but his 'excess' centres as ever on his memory of his dead father, the debate between mother and son being still over the competing needs of living and dead. Pointing to Claudius and her own status as queen, Gertrude represents the living: 'Hamlet, thou has thy father much offended'; also, 'Have you forgot me?' (III.iv.9; 14). Seeing the world only in relation to old King Hamlet, Hamlet represents the dead: 'Mother, you have my father much offended', and 'by the rood... / You are the Queen, your husband's brother's wife' (III.iv.10; 14–15). In forcing Gertrude to compare the

---

[151] In 1995, Jenkins considered this question of long-standing to still evoke 'active controversy'. See Jenkins (ed.), p. 123.

pictures of Claudius and King Hamlet – 'a mildewed ear / Blasting his wholesome brother' (III.iv.63–4) – Hamlet emphasizes again how enactments (this time in paint) induce remembrance. Confirming his view, in outcome Gertrude abandons her relationship with Claudius, and so the claims of the living for those of the dead.

Examining it more closely, this conversion of Gertrude has the usual hallmarks of a debate about extravagant and reduced styles of remembrance. Gertrude says Hamlet's forceful words 'like daggers enter in mine ears' (III.iv.85), her responses to his long harangue each begging, by contrast, a reduction of his excess: 'O Hamlet, speak no more!' (III.iv.78), 'O speak to me no more!' (III.iv.84), 'No more' (III.iv.92). Pertinently Gertrude's conversion – juxtaposed with Claudius's prayerful struggle in act III, scene iii – is accompanied by a string of religious referents: 'By the rood' we have observed, but there is also the 'sweet religion' made 'A rhapsody of words', even the 'compound mass / With tristful visage' (III.iv.46–7; 48–9).[152] These point to a world of religious remembrance and 'mass' which, instructing 'the body [of Polonius] / Into the chapel' (IV.iii.35–6), Claudius will claim is just off stage.

But while the play, *Hamlet*, has consistently implied remembrances of the dead are a matter of performance, and that the styles of remembrance condemned by contemporary Reformers are correct, where does Hamlet the man finally stand in the matter? Initially, as we saw, he argued such performance denoted him 'truly'. Confronted by the First Player in act II, scene ii, he embraced his theatricality as 'fitting'. In using The Mousetrap to catch Claudius, he continued to reveal the extensiveness of his remembrance; and in enlarging Gertrude's remembrance of his father his advocacy of sustained remembrance persists. However, a different view of remembrance is briefly visible in his encounter with the Gravediggers or 'Clowns'.

Hamlet makes no immediate objection to the First Clown, who previously queried 'Christian burial' (V.i.1), when he sings,

> A pickaxe and a spade, a spade,
> For and a shrouding-sheet;
> O, a pit of clay for to be made
> For such a guest is meet.[153]

Though presented light-heartedly, the clown's view of the dead contrasts starkly with the view Hamlet has hitherto expressed, suggesting his origin in the 'knavish Sexton' of 'desacralizing' Elizabethan jigs.[154] Thus, in the clown's view, a 'meet' funeral is minimal: the tools of burial, a shroud and a hole in the ground. Hamlet will call the clown 'knave', but he is not so offended as to stop the banter, seemingly entering into a new humour of mock-remembrance. Previously, his humour was directed at the living; now it aims at the dead:

---

[152] It is tempting here to compare Gertrude's ear-induced conversion to the death of King Hamlet, itself induced 'in the porches of mine ears' (I.v.63) and poisoning 'the blood of man' of the whole body-politic. It involves, however, too large a digression for this place.
[153] *Hamlet*, V.i.86–9.
[154] See Neill, 'Feasts Put Down as Funeral', pp. 51–2.

There's another [skull]. Why might not that be the skull of a
lawyer? Where be his quiddits now, his quillets, his cases, his
tenures, and his tricks? Why does he suffer this rude knave
now to knock him about the sconce with a dirty shovel,
and will not tell him of his action of battery?[155]

Though the third of these questions shows he is half-concerned for its good, this skull is a figure of fun. Visibly lacking the power to respond, it appears impotent, deprived of status. Hamlet ends this remembrance unceremoniously:

HAMLET   Dost thou think Alexander looked o' this fashion
i' th' earth?
HORATIO   E'en so.
HAMLET   And smelt so? Pah!
[*He throws the skull down*]
HORATIO   E'en so, my lord.[156]

If, as Horatio affirms, the dead are nothing but stinking matter, why honour them?

Considering that 'We fat all creatures else to fat us, and we fat ourselves for maggots', and therefore 'how a king may go a progress through the guts of a beggar' (IV.iii.23; 30), by act V Hamlet has already intimated a humanity sealed off from, indeed potentially without, afterlife. Offering little reason for ritual in remembrance, that circular and self-consuming universe is now recalled, though more extensively and with less regret:

HAMLET   To what base uses we may return, Horatio! Why
may not imagination trace the noble dust of Alexander
till a find it stopping a bung-hole?
HORATIO   'Twere to consider too curiously to consider so.
HAMLET   No, faith, not a jot; but to follow him thither
with modesty enough, and likelihood to lead it, as thus:
Alexander died, Alexander was buried, Alexander
returneth into dust, the dust is earth, of earth we make
loam, and why of that loam whereto he was converted
might they not stop a beer-barrel?[157]

In this second view, the closed circle of life is not even complete, nor is humanity part even of a grandiose food-chain. Hamlet's 'progress' ends in a beer-barrel and 'post-mortem remembrance' is little more than a joke. Among the Gravediggers, the *Directory for the Public Worship of God* of 1644 seems not far off. Indeed, 'Here's fine revolution, an we had the trick to see't' (V.i.82).[158]

---

[155] *Hamlet*, IV.i.90–5.
[156] *Hamlet*, V.i.182–6.
[157] *Hamlet*, V.i.187–95.
[158] 'Revolution' can be glossed as a 'reversal of fortune', but according to the *O.E.D.* the term gained its contemporary sense of 'overthrow of the established government' in 1600;

Laertes's dramatic function as 'foil' to Hamlet is well known,[159] yet in light of my present focus, their juxtaposition over Ophelia's grave and before the priest demands comment. Like so many revengers remembering family of this chapter – indeed, like Hamlet himself – in act IV Laertes is troubled not only by his father's death, but also by his funeral. However, Laertes explicitly brings forward *rebellious* as well as vengeful remembrance. Thus, fearing Laertes's rebellion, and considering too the distraction of Ophelia, Claudius admits:

> we have done but greenly
> In hugger-mugger to inter him [Polonius].[160]

In his fury at Claudius, Laertes is still more explicit on the relation of rites of burial to rebellion:

> His means of death, his obscure burial –
> No trophy, sword, nor hatchment o'er his bones,
> No noble rite nor formal ostentation –
> Cry to be heard, as 'twere from heaven to earth,
> That I must call't in question.[161]

Unambiguously, the absence of a fully performed, un-obscured and ritual funeral is the cause of rebellion. The Messenger will imply a more general link between 'custom' and maintaining monarchy in his description of the 'rabble' behaving

> as the world were now but to begin,
> Antiquity forgot, custom not known.[162]

However, the relation of customs of *funeral* to rebellion re-emerges with Gertrude telling Laertes to go 'Calmly' (IV.v.113). Laertes's response recalls the Hamlet of earlier soliloquies:

> That drop of blood that's calm proclaims me bastard,
> Cries cuckold to my father, brands the harlot
> Even here between the chaste unsmirchèd brow
> Of my true mother.[163]

Calmness is the antithesis of what Laertes considers due to the dead, being even an insult to his mother and predecessor. For such a rebel, maximizing remembrance is the only response to death appropriate.

---

thus, the scene's anticipation of 1645 looks forward to the 'Puritan' revolution 'an we had the trick to see't.'

[159] For a standard discussion, see Jenkins (ed.), p. 132–4.
[160] *Hamlet*, IV.v.79–80.
[161] *Hamlet*, IV.vi.208–12.
[162] *Hamlet*, IV.v.99–100.
[163] *Hamlet*, IV.v.114–17.

Un-calmness also characterizes Ophelia's remembrance of Polonius. Horatio observes that in her madness she 'speaks much of her father' (IV.v.4) and repeatedly her inconsistent talk focuses on his funeral. One song particularly emphasizes its enacted 'hugger-mugger': 'At his head a grass-green turf, / At his heels a stone' (IV.v.31–2) reverses the 'correct' order of burial (in which the 'headstone' is at the corpse's 'head'), suggesting – in the manner of preceding revenge tragedies[164] – that the 'reversal' of her mind derives from the 'reversal' of his burial rite. The song's further allusion to pilgrims to the relics of Santiago de Compostella in Spain – 'By his cockle hat and staff / And his sandal shoon' (IV.v.26) – makes Ophelia's concern with 'correct' burial a concern over sainthood. Her closing song performs an overt prayer for the dead man defying every Reformed prescription:

> His beard was white as snow,
> All flaxen was his poll.
>   He is gone, he is gone,
>   And we cast away all moan.
> God 'a' mercy on his soul.[165]

Ophelia's additional *envoi* – 'And of all Christian souls, I pray God. God b'wi' ye' (IV.v.195) – re-iterates prayer for the dead, but makes it universal. Moreover, by seemingly addressing the universal prayer to the audience ('ye'), her challenge to Reformers becomes particularly poignant.

As we also saw in the previous revenge tragedies of this chapter, 'un-calmness' (whether in mind or rebellion) is in *Hamlet* a self-consciously 'fit' response to a perceived inadequacy in remembrance of the dead. Unsurprisingly, therefore, in his dispute with the Priest over the burial of Ophelia, Laertes emphatically values the ceremonial enactments that, he believes, should accompany it:

> LAERTES   What ceremony else?
> HAMLET   [*aside to Horatio*] That is Laertes, a very noble youth. Mark.
> LAERTES   What ceremony else?
> PRIEST   Her obsequies have been as far enlarged
>   As we have warrantise. Her death was doubtful,
>   And but that great command o'ersways the order
>   She should in ground unsanctified have lodged
>   Till the last trumpet. For charitable prayers,
>   Shards, flints, and pebbles should be thrown on her,
>   Yet here she is allowed her virgin rites,
>   Her maiden strewments, and the bringing home
>   Of bell and burial.
> LAERTES   Must there no more be done?
> PRIEST   No more be done.
>   We should profane the service of the dead

---

[164] My discussion of *The Spanish Tragedy* touched on similarities between the maddened and suicidal Isabella and Ophelia; here, then, we may particularly note how the madness of both these women derives from the misremembrance of a loved one.

[165] *Hamlet*, IV.v.190–4.

> To sing sage requiem and such rest to her
> As to peace-parted souls.[166]

Laertes's persistent demand for performances of 'ceremony' for the dead – which the Priest takes to imply 'bell and burial', 'the service of the dead', 'charitable prayers', and indeed a sung 'requiem' – defy Reformed 'moderation', showing more than 'universal' concern for a beloved sister. Indeed, these ceremonies being refused not because they are wrong in essence but because they are inappropriate to a suicide, Laertes's open demand is for Roman Catholic rites for the dead.

Hamlet *may* present a different view as he confronts Laertes at Ophelia's grave. His comment to Laertes, 'Thou pray'st not well' (V.i.244), perhaps ironizes Laertes's requests for Catholic rites and 'excessive' emotion in Reformist style. The case, however, is not clear. Certainly, Hamlet presents Laertes's emotion as theatrical:

> Woot weep, woot fight, woot fast, woot tear thyself,
> Woot drink up eisel, eat a crocodile?
> I'll do't. Dost thou come here to whine
> To outface me with leaping in her grave?
> Be buried quick with her, and so will I.
> And if thou prate of mountains, let them throw
> Millions of acres on us, till our ground,
> Singeing his pate against the burning zone,
> Make Ossa like a wart. Nay, an thou'lt mouth,
> I'll rant as well as thou.[167]

However, these lines can be read in two, contrary ways. In them Hamlet either mocks Laertes's emotional remembrance (showing it to be an imitable and so 'empty' act), or he also 'rants', being as carried away at the grave as Laertes. These perspectives reflecting the remembrances of both more and less Reformed in the era, the matter is noteworthy; but as Hamlet has previously advocated sustained performances of remembrance for the dead, while also showing a certain disrespect for them among the Gravediggers, we may consider the ambiguity sophistical.

The matter is ultimately sophistical for another reason too. In soon admitting himself 'very sorry... / That to Laertes I forgot myself' (V.ii.76–7), Hamlet not only regrets offending Laertes in his remembrance, but he also reclaims the 'self' he initially presented in the play, in which pronounced remembrance denoted him 'truly'. Drawing parallels between himself and Laertes, and thus alluding to their shared grief for dead fathers, Hamlet explains this change:

> For by the image of my cause I see
> The portraiture of his.[168]

---

[166] *Hamlet*, V.i.205–21.
[167] *Hamlet*, V.i.260–69.
[168] *Hamlet*, V.ii.78–9.

However, Shakespeare never discloses how precisely Hamlet reflects Laertes's vengeful rebellion in memory of the dead: Hamlet kills the King, but there is inadvertency in the killing.[169]

Performing remembrance dominates the play's close. Hamlet's dying desire is to be remembered truthfully ('aright') and as a 'story' for the future:

> HAMLET   I am dead.
>   Thou liv'st. Report me and my cause aright
>   To the unsatisfied.
> HORATIO   Never believe it.
>   I am more antique Roman than a Dane.
>   Here's yet some liquor left.
> HAMLET   As thou'rt a man,
>   Give me the cup. Let go. By heaven, I'll ha't.
>   O God, Horatio, what a wounded name,
>   Things standing thus unknown, shall live behind me!
>   If thou didst ever hold me in thy heart,
>   Absent thee from felicity a while,
>   And in this harsh world draw thy breath in pain
>   To tell my story.[170]

That stories may be told 'aright' reiterates Hamlet's opening argument that performed remembrance need not be empty melodrama. Indeed, as in act I, scene ii Hamlet guaranteed the true denotation of his mourning-garb by reference to the commemoration 'within', so he here seeks the performance of his story as 'thou didst ever hold me in thy heart'. In both instances, what is within validates what is performed, *and* emotion is key, Hamlet thus defying contemporary Reformers to the end.

Horatio's demand that he perform that memory 'High on a stage [to] be placèd to the view' (V.ii.322) celebrates both Hamlet himself and his performing view of remembrance. Moreover, he also celebrates Hamlet's view of *truly* performed remembrance: 'All this', he tells pointedly, 'can I / Truly deliver' (V.ii.328–9). And in presenting a taste of that performance to come, he anticipates action attuned to the funeral he celebrates: recalling the ritual hugger-mugger of the play, his story is

---

[169] Considering it the very mark of Shakespeare, Wilson argues evasion is evidence of an author who was 'one of those moderate Catholics who reacted against the suicidal violence of [the age's religious] fanatics with a project of freedom of conscience' and of 'respect for the secrecy of the human heart'. See Wilson, p. ix. Suggesting Shakespeare was less *'politique'* than Wilson claims, however, this evasion by Hamlet is largely notable by contrast with the play's previously sustained addresses to the controversy of remembrance. Thus, in *Hamlet*'s (and *Titus Andronicus*'s) case at least, Shakespeare is controversial, our unfamiliarity with such controversy seeming to stem *less* from the deliberate ploy of the author than from a critical unfamiliarity with the controversies of the age – though Wilson's further observation of a critical establishment still 'deeply invested in building a Protestant canon' also bears consideration. See Wilson, p. ix and 4.

[170] *Hamlet*, V.ii.280–91.

'Of carnal, bloody, and unnatural acts, / ... accidental judgements, casual slaughters' (V.ii.325–6).

Appropriately, then, as the play thus looks forward, it is the most bloody of *Hamlet*'s three younger men, Fortinbras, who has the last word; appropriately too, it addresses a funeral:

> Let four captains,
> Bear Hamlet like a soldier to the stage,
> For he was likely, had he been put on,
> To have proved most royally; and for his passage,
> The soldiers' music and the rites of war
> Speak loudly for him. Take up the body. Such a sight as this
> Becomes the field, but here shows much amiss.
> Go, bid the soldiers shoot.[171]

Being underscored by the death of the play,[172] this call for funeral must be solemn. Invoking a soldier's musical 'rites', however, Fortinbras places this ritual of funeral in a martial context, his final call for ordnance extending a sequence of gun-shots which at his entrance gave 'To th' ambassadors of England ... warlike volley' (V.ii.393–4). Literally aiming at England, thus, Fortinbras's remembrance for Hamlet is a very 'show' of ritualized funeral – such as traditionalists, but *not* active Reformers, held dear.

Yet most remarkable of all in Fortinbras's speech (and substantiating his funerary 'show') is his particular metaphor for the place of burial: 'the stage'. It recalls Andrea's allusion to 'performed' rites of funeral with which this chapter opened, as it recalls each of the self-conscious, funerary performances we have observed since. What each of these instances implies is the extensive debt of the contemporary playhouses to the age's funerals as, inevitably, to the religious controversy surrounding them. To explore that debt further, I now turn to *Antonio's Revenge* at the theatre at St Paul's, thereby examining a playhouse contiguously bearing on Kyd and Shakespeare's in which funerary remembrance was part of the monument.

---

[171] *Hamlet*, V.ii.339–47.
[172] Thus, similar to the closing style of action 'on earth' in *The Spanish Tragedy*.

Chapter 2

Funerary Theatre: Mourning, *Antonio's Revenge* and Paul's Theatre

In *The Spanish Tragedy*, *Titus Andronicus* and *Hamlet*, being 'theatrical' or 'melodramatic' in remembrance of the dead carried a positively construed sense of being 'extensive' in such performance, the plays thus denoting and championing popish 'excesses' in Protestant England. However, a question that arises is how a Protestant more ideologically committed than Kyd and Shakespeare thus might have written a revenge tragedy, a genre extravagant even in its classical origins, and therefore likely to present 'excessive' remembrances?[1] Written by John Marston, who suffered public censorship by Archbishop Whitgift and Bishop Bancroft in 1599 before taking 'Anglican' orders in 1609,[2] *Antonio's Revenge* (c.1599–1601) provides an answer. Crucially, it reduces the dramatic centrality and impact of mourning in two ways. First, in place of the view that extensive funerary ritual 'fits' in remembrance of the dead, its absence justifying revenge, Marston presents in Pandulpho an active dissenter from such ritual, which he persistently and openly criticizes as inappropriate. Second, in presenting 'Piero Sforza' ('rapacious' or 'forceful Peter') as the corrupt power of the play, Marston implies a corrupt 'Peter' – coming to suggest, as we shall observe, the See of Peter – lies *directly* behind the remembrance challenged by Pandulpho. This proto-Reformer does not by any means have it all his way, but *Antonio's Revenge* thus distinguishes itself from the plays of the previous chapter through a sustained contrast of views on remembrance,[3]

---

[1] I considered such classical origins in relation to remembrance in my Introduction to the study on p. 10–11.

[2] 'On 1 June 1599 Archbishop Whitgift of Canterbury and Bishop Bancroft of London commanded the destruction of sundry satirical and offensive publications: [Marston's] *Pigmalion* and *The Scourge* were burnt by the common hangman.' See John Marston, *Antonio's Revenge*, ed. by W. Reavley Gair (Manchester: Manchester University Press; Baltimore, MD: Johns Hopkins University Press, 1978; 1999), p. 7. All my textual quotations are from this edition. I consider censorship in regard to Paul's Theatre below. For a fuller but succinct account of Marston's life (including the further 'censorship' of imprisonment in 1608) see 'John Marston', by David Stymeist (Queen's University, Ontario) in *Literary Encyclopedia*, http://www.litencyc.com/php/speople. php?rec=true&UID=4987, last accessed 31 October 2007. I use the term 'Anglican' carefully because it is historically problematic. According to the *O.E.D.*, and suggesting the emergence of Laudianism in the English Church, 'Anglican' (in a sense approximating to the modern) was first used in 1635 – some years after Marston took orders. For further discussion of such historical problems, see my comments on the emergence of a religious 'Via Media' on p. 25–6, note 110.

[3] My reading of *Hamlet* did present contending views of remembrance, but the traditional view was clearly the dominant. This is much less the case in *Antonio's Revenge*.

the Reformist presence being heightened. Marston thus emerges as a playwright deeply interested in Reform, though not as yet convinced of it fully. Presenting little settled ideology and much controversy, however, *Antonio's Revenge* thus also seems an important forebear of the better-known tragedies of Chapter 3. For following Marston's play in different ways, these each make largely problematic the self-conscious and dramatic claim observed in Chapter 1: that extensive and ritualized remembrances for the dead were 'fit', as traditionally dictated. However, to illustrate the close involvement of the contemporary theatricality in religion, and thus for the study as a whole, I begin with the theatre for which *Antonio's Revenge* was written – Old St Paul's:[4] a contested monument containing subsidiary, contested monuments, as we shall see, and thus a theatre *bearing on* the theatricality of the age yet *inextricably* bound up in the remembrance of the dead.[5]

The playhouse at Paul's was located 'in the immediate area of the cathedral church', where it was identified by contemporaries (not distinguishing between 'cathedral' and 'theatre') as 'part of the cathedral'.[6] The playhouse 'extended into and across the cloisters' of St Paul's, and its principal historian considers not only that 'the stage itself may have been built between the first two main pillars of the cloister',[7] but even that 'the cloister itself served as the tiring house'.[8] Whether or not, however, the inter-relation of this theatre and its church is undoubted. Thus, contemporaries observing the relation between the two, religious activities clearly spilled over into the theatrical at Paul's and vice versa. For example, referring to a series of 'Pastoralls and 'Comoedyes' played at Paul's in a memorandum of *c*.1600–1601, William Percy, younger brother to the Earl of Northumberland, instructed that 'The children [are] not to begin before Four *after Prayers*.'[9] In similar illustration, the theatre sought only to use quieter musical instruments because – in the words of the verger John Howe – by 'meanes of the dailie knockinge and noyse, the Churche is greatlie disturbed': in both these contemporary views, the activities of the church bear directly on the theatre.[10]

---

[4] 'Old' because the St Paul's to which I refer was destroyed in the Great Fire of London in 1666.

[5] As the *O.E.D.* makes plain, 'monument', from the Latin, implies a commemorative statue, building or tomb. Gair indirectly alludes to the play's religious exploitation of its 'monument': its final moments are, he says, a 'liturgical, almost monastic statement ... solemnized by the closing requiem for the departed sung by the choristers in a specifically ecclesiastic setting' (Gair [ed.], p. 39). Gair regarded this end as symptomatic of a larger, 'complex, and it must be admitted not always explicit, statement' which he does not pursue, but which I here clarify.

[6] See W. Reavley Gair, 'Paul's Playhouse', in *The Children of Paul's: The Story of a Theatre Company, 1553–1608* (Cambridge: Cambridge University Press, 1982), pp. 52–4.

[7] Gair (ed.), *Antonio's Revenge*, p. 27.

[8] Gair, *The Children of Paul's*, p. 66.

[9] Cited in *The Children of Paul's*, p. 53; my emphasis.

[10] For citation and discussion, see Gair, *The Children of Paul's*, p. 47 and p. 65. Church concerns with noise pollution similarly determined 'theatre' at the Blackfriars in 1596. When

Such examples show that contemporaries saw theatrical activity in direct relation to contemporary religious rituals; but lest Paul's example be dismissed as an anomaly, consider the following. Until forbidden in 1598, Paul's playhouse staged sermons; and thereafter, it remained in competition for its *theatrical* audiences with the *sermons* at Paul's Cross.[11] In such contemporary understandings of performance and staging, the categories 'drama' and 'religion' are indistinct.[12] What, then, of performed remembrance of the dead?

As a church – London's foremost – St Paul's was a prime site of remembrance. Audiences to the playhouse entered through (and left by) the churchyard gate,[13] travelling not only through ramshackle shops and houses, but also through the graveyard and tombs in the monument's shadow.[14] Such procession constituted a *de facto* extension of the drama I shall observe: a merging of the audience in and out of the drama which Paul's playwrights, 'custom-designing' plays to suit the conditions of performance,[15] must have recognized. For though it cannot fail to be striking today, the standard, contemporary name for the location of the playhouse was 'the shrowdes', the very theatre thus denoting the dead.[16] Thus, in London's heart, and within the religious monument of St Paul's, the playhouse presented *shrouded* remembrance. Addressing its sensitivity to religious disputes is apt.

Like the liberties of the Blackfriars, the liberties of St Paul's were outside the jurisdiction of the City Magistrates.[17] However, in the country at large, the early seventeenth century saw a proliferation of enquiries by religious authorities into the use of churches and their surrounds for theatrical and other performance.[18] Thus, in a Visitation to Paul's of 1598, Bishop Bancroft asked searching questions of the Master and choristers about their behaviour. Did they, he asked, leave services 'wth owt [without] licence first asked of Mr Deane…and whoe doe offend herein, or have offended herein, and when and howe often'; and, 'is that decree and ordinance of

---

Burbage attempted to transform the Blackfriars into a 'public' (i.e. open-air) playhouse, local residents complained that the playhouse was 'so neere the Church that the noyse of the drummes and trumpets will greatlie disturbe and hinder both the ministers and parishioners in tyme of devine service and sermons'. Burbage's plan was consequently thwarted and – 'to evade the objections' – the Blackfriars was established as a 'private' theatre. See *The Children of Paul's*, p. 11.

[11] See *The Children of Paul's*, p. 47, 69 and 181.

[12] Gair even wonders if seating arrangements from Paul's Cross were not adapted for the playhouse: further 'indistinct' theatre and religion. See *The Children of Paul's*, p. 69.

[13] *The Children of Paul's*, p. 56.

[14] For a description of the churchyard, with its houses, shops and sheds encroaching on the burial ground, see 'The Decay of Paul's', in *The Children of Paul's*, p. 23.

[15] For discussion of such 'custom-designed-ness', see *The Children of Paul's*, pp. 61–6.

[16] Gair's passages alluding to the playhouse in 'the shrowdes' are too numerous to cite, but see under 'Paul's Playhouse' and 'shrowdes' in his index, *The Children of Paul's*, p. 211. I cite one instance of a contemporary referring to the playhouse in the 'shrouds' below.

[17] *The Children of Paul's*, p. 72.

[18] See, for example, the Visitation Articles for the Diocese of Gloucester, in *Records of Early English Drama: Cumberland, Westmorland, Gloucestershire*, ed. by Audrey Douglas and Peter Greenfield (Toronto; Buffalo; London: University of Toronto Press, 1986), pp. 345–6.

yours observed, that all the peticanons and vicars of the Churche should diligently attend in the quier the whole tyme of all sermons on Sundaies and holidaies in the afternoons from whence none of them should depart wth out leave askinge'; and again, 'what be their names that bee, or have bynn most offensive therein and when and howe often they have offended'.[19]

Bancroft addressed specifically searching questions to the use of the playhouse. Thus, 'In whose custody are the lower Cloisters, and the place Caled the shrowdes how are they implyd, and by whome and whose license and whether is there any doore of any private mans use made into them, and for what use.' The Bishop's interest in hidden doors in the playhouse, and a seeming suspicion concerning their use, emerges in another enquiry: 'how is the Cloyster by the Chapter howse imployed, and wheather is theire any extraordinary doore for any private mans use made into it, by whom and by whose consent'.[20] In asking these searching questions, we cannot know certainly what Bancroft was seeking; illustrating the aptness of the playhouse for religious investigation, however, the Bishop's suspicion of the theatre's activity is clear.

Another example of religious investigation into Paul's playhouse this time highlighting contemporary suspicion of its *plays* emerges in 1575. The *Repertories of the Court of Council* for 8 December note a complaint against Sebastian Westcott, the establisher of Paul's first playhouse and Master of the Choristers until 1582.[21] The *Repertories* state: 'this Courte ys enformed that one Sebastian that wyll not communicate with the Church of England kepeth playes and resorte of the people to great gain and peryll of the Corruptinge of the Chyldren with papistrie'. Responding to these suspicions, the court sent one 'Master Morton' to the Deane of Paul's 'to give him notice of that disorder, and to praye him to gyve suche remeadye therin, within his iurysdyccion, as he shall see meete, for Christan Relygion and good order'.[22] In view of this complaint against 'papistry' to uphold 'good order', one wonders if Bancroft's interest in hidden passages and doors was not an interest in priest-holes,[23] but the matter is beside the point. For present purposes, what is important is that the reputation of the theatre made it a target for open investigation by religious authorities, that its founding-member and plays were openly suspected of Catholicism, and that the plays themselves were openly considered propagators of Catholicism in such persons involved in them as 'the Chyldren'. Though Westcott's influence was clearly important in this precarious reputation, the wider history of Paul's monument also reveals why the playhouse was an object of suspicion.

For the history of St Paul's is a microcosm of England's Reformations.[24] Indeed, in his *Microcosmographie* of 1628, the Bishop of Salisbury, John Earles, described

---

[19] For a full transcript of Bancroft's 1598 Visitation relevant to the theatre, see Appendix 1 in *The Children of Paul's*, pp. 176–81; citations from p. 176.

[20] Citations from *The Children of Paul's*, p. 180.

[21] See *The Children of St Paul's*, p. 44.

[22] Court proceedings cited from *The Children of Paul's*, p. 44.

[23] Connections between priest-holes and Renaissance drama have recently been made by Wilson in *Secret Shakespeare*, pp. 23–8; 130–1; 257; 273.

[24] As noted in *A History of St Paul's Cathedral and the Men Associated with It*, ed. by W.R. Matthews and W.M. Atkins (London: Phoenix House, 1957), pp. 122; 132–3.

Paul's Walk as 'the land's epitome, the lesser isle of Great Britain, the whole world's map which you may here discern in its perfected motion, justling and turning'.[25] Thus, Paul's embodied the diversity both of England and the world, presenting, as the Bishop was particular to observe, Roman Catholicism:

> It is a heap of stones and men, with a vast confusion of languages; and were the steeple not sanctified, nothing like Babel ... It is a great exchange of all discourse, the synod of all parties politic; it is the market of young lecturers, the general mint of all famous lies, which are here like the legends of Popery, first coined and stamped in the Church.[26]

The vibrant confusion of Paul's indirectly points to Babel, from which it is only a short step in the stricter Protestant mind to 'Popery'. However, though his description is clouded by anti-Catholic rhetoric, the Bishop reveals the Catholic presence within Paul's, particularly in the way that, as aide-mémoire,[27] it was 'stamped in the Church'. Moreover, his awareness of the 'meaning' of the monument was a common one. Describing the removal of imagery from Paul's and other English churches in *The Annalles of England* (1605), John Stow observed 'textes of scriptures ... written upon the wals of those churches against Images': creating a sub-literary controversy of the Cathedral itself, sprays of contemporary graffiti illustrated the continuing sensitivity of its monument.[28]

Controversy was meaningfully 'stamped in the Church' in other ways too. Through the reign of Edward VI, Paul's suffered what has been called an 'orgy of destruction'.[29] In 1547, the Great Rood and its accompanying figures were removed by royal instruction and – following the Order of Council of 1548 requiring removal of all roods and images as 'things corrupt, vain and superstitious' – the following 'images' were also taken away: pictures, banners, hangings, altar furnishings and frontals, candlesticks and lights – all things, that is, directly presenting religious 'shows'. On the order of Bishop Ridley in 1552, the altars, chapels and parclose screens of the Cathedral were destroyed, the High Altar was replaced with a Holy Table (in an anti-massing move) and – especially significantly from the perspective of this study – the time-honoured tombs adorning the Cathedral were disfigured. Altar and rood – the most necessary props for performing the Mass –were reinstalled under Queen Mary, the rood being thereafter removed with the Latin Mass in 1559.[30]

---

[25] Quoted from G.H. Cook, *Old Saint Paul's Cathedral* (London: Phoenix House, 1955), p. 80.
[26] Quoted from Cook, p. 80.
[27] For contemporary churches as aides-mémoires, see the Introduction, p. 5.
[28] See Andrew Gordon, 'The Act of Libel: Conscripting Civic Space in Early Modern England', in *Journal of Medieval and Early Modern Studies* 32/2 (Spring 2002), pp. 375–97; for citation of Stow, see pp. 394–5.
[29] See Cook, p. 76; except where otherwise noted, the following account of Edwardine, Marian and Elizabethan reforms of the Cathedral combines information from Cook and from Matthews and Atkins.
[30] The change of religion was also theatrically signalled – by the visit of Robert Horne, Dean of Durham on 11 August 1559, when the Litany was deliberately read in English and Horne himself preached. As Matthews and Atkins emphasize (p. 132), Horne's Reforming credentials were impeccable: as Dean of Durham he had removed the founding tomb and

Into the seventeenth century, however, ruined monuments recalling the Catholic past (and its defeat) remained for all to see.

Another example of Paul's involvement in continuing religious differences can be found in the activities of Elizabeth I herself, as her amusing encounters with the Dean Alexander Nowell show. In 1562, she berated the Dean, who was to preach before her, for being 'ignorant'. The Dean had had her Prayer Book decorated with pictures 'resembling angels and saints, nay grosser absurdities', in Elizabeth's words, causing her to ask: 'Have you forgot our proclamation against images, pictures and Romish reliques in the Churches?' However, in 1565, in the middle of a sermon by Nowell *against* such 'relics' but before the Spanish Ambassador, Elizabeth interrupted the Dean, exclaiming: 'To your text! Leave that; we have heard enough of that!' Nowell barely managed a few more words.[31]

That religious silencing may amuse; the next is more sombre. Excited by Pius V's Bull excommunicating Elizabeth in 1571, John Felton, a Roman Catholic, fixed a copy of the Bull on the gates of the Bishop's palace adjoining the Cathedral – for which he was hanged. However, an anti-Catholic ballad composed for the occasion brings us neatly not only to Paul's but also to its microcosmic struggles over remembrance:

> A Pope was wont to be an odius name
> Within our land and scrapped out of our scrowles;
> And now the Pope is come so far past shame
> That he can walk with open face at Poules
> Go home, mad Bull! to Rome and pardon soules,
> That pine away in Purgatorie payne.[32]

Neither John Felton nor the satirical balladeer had forgotten either Rome or its purgatorial cult of the dead. As Earles observed, Paul's was England's religious history in microcosm and (itself constructed as a theatrical aide-mémoire) the controversial dead were remembered in its material.

Thus, presented at Paul's, and even displaying materials of remembrance of their own, to contemporaries plays like *Antonio's Revenge* must have seemed resonant with remembrances of the dead. And since, sharing plays, playwrights, actors and London's audiences with playhouses less obviously religious, Paul's had a stake in the circulating meanings of 'theatre' in the period, we must assume *at least* some of its monumental associations rubbed off on those, on the face of it, 'secular' theatres. Indeed, whether Paul's shared plays, playwrights or audience with such theatres; whether a play presented tombs, skulls or other such materials of remembrance or just the 'material' of a lament and its actor; even if a play bore only a generic or thematic similarity with a tragedy performed at Paul's like *Antonio's Revenge*: *qua*

---

prominent shrine of St Cuthbert (adjoining that of Bede) from Durham Cathedral 'with his own hands'.

[31] A full account of the affair is found in *A History of St Paul's*, pp. 134–6 since, the authors admit, they 'cannot forbear quoting [it] at length'.

[32] See *A History of St Paul's Cathedral*, p. 133.

theatre, the early modern was therefore religious.³³ Mindful of this, we can turn to *Antonio's Revenge*.

The lines with which Piero opens the play's 'Italian' action also open its treatment of remembrance:

> Ho, Gasparo Strotzo, bind Feliche's trunk
> Unto the panting side of Mellida.³⁴

Moments later Piero announces with ironic piety that 'Andrugio sleeps in peace' (I.i.14), soon adding:

> By heaven, I think
> I ha' said my prayers, within this month at least,
> I am so boundless happy.³⁵

Thus, the opening presents two theatrically dishonoured corpses amid the ironic piety and 'prayers' of Piero, whose further claim to be

> great in blood,
> Unequalled in revenge³⁶

makes the essential point: in this public and funerary deprivation and its mistreatment of the dead, Piero has inflicted the worst insult on his enemies he can.

Discovering Feliche's hanging body, Antonio's reaction is a familiar one. His thoughts very quickly turn to the dishonoured status of the corpse:

> See, look, the curtain stirs; shine nature's pride,
> Love's vital spirit, dear Antonio's bride!
> *The curtain's drawn and the body of* FELICHE, *stabbed thick with wounds, appears hung up.*
> What villain bloods the window of my love?
> What slave hath hung yon gory ensign up
> In flat defiance of humanity?³⁷

The second question illustrates Antonio's sense of the abused and 'inhuman' treatment of the corpse, such treatment being also a matter of performed spectacle, thus theatrical – as Antonio's instructions to 'look' and 'see' make clear. Amid all this, however, there prevails the view that active Reformers rejected: reducing rituals for the dead is offensive.

---

³³ For broader discussion of the theatrical relation and interaction (competitive and parasitic) of St Paul's with The Theatre, The Globe, The Rose, The Blackfriars, The Whitefriars, see 'The Children of Paul's and the English Drama', in *The Children of Paul's*, pp. 1–12. But such was the level of interaction between the public and private (i.e. indoor) theatres that between them the age of the actors and general style of the plays 'became indistinguishable' (p. 10).
³⁴ *Antonio's Revenge*, I.i.1–2.
³⁵ *Antonio's Revenge*, I.i.99–101.
³⁶ *Antonio's Revenge*, I.i.17–18.
³⁷ *Antonio's Revenge*, I.iii.128–33.

Remembrance of Feliche is brief in *Antonio's Revenge*, being displaced by Antonio's remembrance of his father – though two bodies are linked in Antonio's dreams even before he learns of the two deaths:

> Last sleep my sense was steeped in horrid dreams:
> Three parts of night were swallowed in the gulf
> Of ravenous time when to my slumbering powers
> Two meagre ghosts made apparition.
> The one's breast seemed fresh-paunched with bleeding wounds
> Whose bubbling gore sprang in frighted eyes:
> The other ghost assumed my father's shape…[38]

In Antonio's anticipation, these most corporeal ghosts display the wounds borne at the moment of death, thus appearing as violated and unburied bodies.[39] That Antonio's horror at such bodies is simultaneously religious and 'Latinate' emerges when he wakes to see the heavens on fire. This is his account:

> Viewing these prodigies,
> I bowed my naked knee and pierced the star
> With an outfacing eye, pronouncing thus:
> *Deus imperat astris.*[40]

In kneeling prayerfully, praying in Latin and 'superstitious' imagination of ghosts, Antonio's performance for the dead is un-Reformed.

The lengthy and detailed stage direction at the opening of act II suggests the importance of funerary performances:

> *Enter two mourners with torches, two with streamers,* CASTILLO *and* FOROBOSCO *with torches, a Herald bearing Andrugio's helm and sword, the coffin,* MARIA, *supported by* LUCIO *and* ALBERTO, ANTONIO *by himself,* PIERO *and* STROTZO *talking,* GALEATZO *and* MATZAGENTE, BALURDO, *and* PANDULPHO; *the coffin set down, helm, sword, and streamers hung up, placed by the Herald, whilst* ANTONIO *and* MARIA *wet their handkerchiefs with their tears, kiss them and lay them on the hearse, kneeling. All go out but* PIERO. *Cornets cease and he speaks.*

Yet it is not only Marston's elaboration of a self-consciously mournful funeral rite that is significant. Piero and Antonio's contrasting actions show they are enemies bound by the same values. Thus, both valuing rituals for the dead, the dead man's enemy seeks to dishonour his funeral while Antonio seeks to honour it: while Piero

---

[38] *Antonio's Revenge*, I.ii.39–45.

[39] Such 'materiality of ghosts' has been observed by Ann Rosalind and Peter Stallybrass in 'Of Ghosts and Garments: the Materiality of Memory on the Renaissance Stage', in *Renaissance Clothing and the Materiality of Memory* (Cambridge: Cambridge University Press, 2000), pp. 245–56. Of particular relevance to my argument is their claim that 'Material ghosts' are 'the logical extension of the material remains (rings, scarves, handkerchiefs, jewels, shoes) that are so frequently staged in the Renaissance theater' (p. 249): Antonio's and like 'ghosts' are thus memorials.

[40] *Antonio's Revenge*, I.iii.56–9.

talks, Antonio is quiet and solitary, kneeling prayerfully at the hearse. Indeed, talkers and mourners are neatly contrasted in groups of two: the murderers Piero and Strotzo talk while Antonio and Maria – initially in her grief unable to stand – kneel and weep.

With the departure of the others, the insult Piero seeks to inflict on the corpse becomes starker. His gaze firmly fixed on the paraphernalia of burial, he begins with an injunction to 'Rot there, thou cerecloth that enfolds the flesh / Of my loathed foe; moulder to crumbling dust' (II.i.1–2), going on to ask that 'Oblivion choke the passage of thy fame' (II.i.3). The entrance of Pandulpho provides a contrasting perspective. To him, the corpse's very lips 'breathe defiance to black obloquy' (II.ii.16).

However, the differences between Piero and Pandulpho extend beyond their views of the dead man to their views on performing remembrances. The disagreement opens with Piero asking whether Pandulpho weeps 'for thy son' (II.ii.66), to which Pandulpho replies

> No, no, Piero, weeping for my sins.
> Had I been a good father he had been
> A gracious son.[41]

That Pandulpho is specifically concerned *not* to weep for his son emerges when he remembers songs he used to sing to him. Noting that 'Such songs as these / I often dittied till my boy did sleep', Pandulpho continues, 'But now I turn plain fool; alas; I weep' (II.ii.23–5). These tears *are* in remembrance of the dead, and Pandulpho considers them 'plain fool'. As we shall see, the Reformist claim that mourners for the dead were 'fools' is one that will recur.

However, Pandulpho's antipathy toward mourning is provoking to Piero, leading to a dispute over styles of mourning. In an aside, Piero remarks that Pandulpho's dislike of his emotion 'makes me shrug' (II.ii.26), thereafter wondering at Pandulpho's calm as a matter of tendency:

> Is he all man?
> Hath he no part of mother in him, ha?
> No lickerish, womanish inquisitiveness?[42]

Thus, Piero seeking to test Pandulpho's emotional resolve, the two men juxtapose in their more and less 'manly' responses to death.

Taking in questions of political obedience, out of this difference there emerges a larger dispute about just and unjust action. Performing emotion, however, remains to the fore, as does funeral since Andrugio's coffin remains in the background. Presenting a fierce competition over emotional performance, therefore, lines like the following resonate with funerary controversy:

---

[41] *Antonio's Revenge*, II.ii.67–9.
[42] *Antonio's Revenge*, II.iii.34–7.

PIERO   Hence, doting stoic. By my hope of bliss,
             I'll make thee wretched.
PANDULPHO   Defiance to thy power, thou rifted yawn!
             Now, by the loved heaven, sooner thou shalt
             Rinse thy foul ribs from the black filth of sin
             That soots thy heart, than make me wretched.[43]

The scene eventually ends with the triumph of Pandulpho's resolve, as Piero concedes: 'His quiet's firmer than I can disease' (II.ii.103). Thus, Pandulpho's restrained emotionalism before the coffin defeats Piero's larger, 'feminine' emotionalism, exposing it as 'excessive'. The implied triumph of a man of strictly Reformed mentality over one minded more traditionally becomes explicit when Pandulpho describes his struggle against Piero as against Catholicism's 'Babylon':

> Hadst thou a jail
> With treble walls like antique Babylon,
> Pandulpho can get out.[44]

As we shall see, the play will confirm *Piero's* Catholicism just as clearly in the final, seemingly damning discovery that he carries about him '*Bede-roles* of mischief' (V.iii.133) – that is, the record of the names of the dead recited aloud in Roman Catholic churches for the purpose of prayer.

The opening of act III offers another deliberate stage direction focusing on attitudes of remembrance:

> *Enter* CASTILLO *and* FORBOSCO, ALBERTO *and* BALURDO *with poleaxes;* STROTZO *talking with* PIERO; [PIERO] *seemeth to send out* STROTZO; *exit* STROTZO. *Enter* STROTZO, MARIA, NUTRICHE *and* LUCIO. PIERO *passeth through his guard and talks with* MARIA *with seeming amorousness; she seemeth to reject his suit and flies to the tomb, kneels and kisseth it.* PIERO *bribes* NUTRICHE *and* LUCIO; *they go to her, seeming to solicit his suit. She riseth, offers to go out;* PIERO *stayeth her, tears open his breast, embraceth and kisseth her; and so they go all out in state.*
>   *Enter two pages, the one with two tapers, the other with a chafing-dish; a perfume in it.* ANTONIO, *in his nightgown and a nightcap, unbraced followeth after.*

As in the previous such tableau, Antonio and Piero's actions before the dead, now materially presented by a tomb, contrast. Piero insultingly makes love to the still mourning Maria, while Antonio remembers the dead 'unbraced' or distractedly. Maria matches his extravagant display: the stage direction presents her flying to and kissing the tomb (showing her emotionalism) as well as kneeling before it (suggesting prayer for the dead). The extravagance of such performance is ironically illustrated in the contrast with Piero's equally expansive but inappropriate show of love: tearing open his doublet or 'breast', embracing and then kissing Maria. However, the two

---

[43] *Antonio's Revenge*, II.iii.70–5.
[44] *Antonio's Revenge*, II.ii.76–8.

'tapers', or candles,⁴⁵ which will burn during Antonio's spoken remembrance over the tomb, are materials of remembrance requiring explanation.

As objects traditionally placed at the shrines of saints and on altars, sixteenth-century candles aroused controversy. In Injunctions issued in 1538, parish clergy were required to preach regular sermons enjoining the English 'not to repose their trust and affiance in any other works devised by men's phantasies, besides Scripture; as in wandering to pilgrimages, offering of money, candles, or tapers to images or relics ... or such like superstition'. And clergy were told:

> ye shall, for avoiding that most detestable sin of idolatry, forthwith take down and delay, and shall suffer from henceforth no candles, tapers or picture but only the light that commonly goeth across the church by the rood loft, the light before the sacrament of the altar, and the light about the sepulcher, which for the adorning of the church and divine service ye shall suffer to remain.⁴⁶

However, this attack on the materials of remembrance was only a beginning. In 1547 there was further Injunction and Reform. Duffy describes its historical motive and effect in one traditional parish:

> The 1538 Injunctions had permitted lights before the Rood and the Sepulchre, and the [Stores of the] Young Men and Maidens at Morebath had accordingly transferred their lights from the tabernacles of the saints to the basins and candlesticks before the High Cross and Sepulchre. But for convinced Protestants, lights above the Sepulchre or the Crucifix were if anything grosser manifestations of idolatry than lights before the lesser images of the saints. The 1547 Injunctions now banned all lights or candles anywhere in the church except the two on the high altar.⁴⁷

In July 1599, Queen Elizabeth 'to all intents and purposes' reinstated these Edwardine reforms in Injunctions expressly 'for the suppression of superstition' and 'to plant true religion'.⁴⁸

So candles *before sepulchres* – as before the tomb of act III, scene i in *Antonio's Revenge* – entailed a controversy. Recalling that *Antonio's Revenge* was first performed at Paul's, and that Elizabeth's homily against idolatry in the *Second Tome of Homilies* states categorically that 'images placed publicly in Temples, cannot *possibly* bee without danger of worshipping and idolatrie',⁴⁹ the controversy implicit in the tableau is direct. Though offset by the ironic emotionalism of Piero, Antonio and Maria's extensive emotions at the candle-lit tomb present Catholic performances in Paul's.

The juxtaposition of Catholic and Reformed becomes still clearer when Antonio asks, 'Is this Saint Mark's Church?' (III.i.3), overlaying not just England with Italy

---

⁴⁵ Though according to the *O.E.D.*, the word 'taper' is particularly associated with wax candles 'in early times used chiefly for devotional or penitential purposes'.
⁴⁶ Cited by Duffy, *The Voices of Morebath*, p. 95.
⁴⁷ *Morebath*, p. 118.
⁴⁸ *Morebath*, p. 170.
⁴⁹ This quotation from the homily is cited by Scodel in *The English Poetic Epitaph*, p. 24; emphasis mine.

amid these rituals, but Paul's with St Mark's and thus a Reformed monument with a Catholic. The First Page's reply is 'It is' (III.i.4), inviting us to affirm what Reformed St Paul's pointedly denies. The narrative, however, requires us to follow the Page. Presenting further Italianisms, Antonio instructs the Second Page to 'Set tapers to the tomb' and 'lamp the church', and as he 'Swings the chafing dish'[50] he tells listeners, 'I purify the air with odorous fume' (III.i.6–8). In St Paul's, such self-consciousness resonates with controversy: amid the contrast of Italian and English churches, 'purification' suggests Paul's theatre is presently *impure*, Antonio's act of cleansing thus seeming to restore the theatre to its religious self.

In this churchly theatre, then, Antonio's extended remembrance begins. It addresses 'Graves, vaults and tombs ... Cold flesh, bleak trunks, wrapped in ... half-rot shrouds', asking them not to 'groan' as Antonio presses them 'softly with a tender foot' (III.i.9–11). At Paul's such language is – again – self-conscious: illustrating the nearness of the theatre and funerary site, in Paul's 'shrouds' the actor's foot does stand on the dead. Thus, drawing on a theatrical reality, Antonio's remembrance addresses Andrugio's tomb. I quote it fully, with its succeeding stage direction and the Ghost's immediate response:

> ANTONIO Thou royal spirit of Andrugio,
>   Where'er thou hover'st, airy intellect,
>   I heave up tapers to thee – view thy son –
>   In celebration of due obsequies.
>   Once every night I'll due thy funeral hearse
>   With my religious tears.
>   O blessed father of a cursed son,
>   Thou died most happy since thou lived'st not
>   To see thy son most wretched and thy wife
>   Pursued by him that seeks my guiltless blood.
>   O, in what orb thy mighty spirit soars,
>   Stoop and beat down this rising fog of shame
>   That strives to blur thy blood and girt defame
>   About my innocent and spotless brows.
>   *Non est mori miserum, sed misere mori.*
>   [*Enter* ANDRUGIO's *ghost from the tomb*]
> GHOST OF ANDRUGIO Thy pangs of anguish rip my cerecloth up
>   And lo, the Ghost of old Andrugio
>   Forsakes his coffin.[51]

It is an extensive remembrance thick with the language of extravagantly performed, religious funeral; moreover, it is an extravagant funerary remembrance claimed to be 'due'. And pointedly, the cause of distress is not death, but dishonour in death: 'Non est mori miserum, sed misere mori' translates as 'it is not a wretched thing to die, but it is to die wretchedly'.[52] Implying the value of ceremonial remembrance denied by Reformers, it is the death that is dishonoured which causes the greatest grief.

---

[50] According to the stage direction.
[51] *Antonio's Revenge*, III.i.17–34.
[52] Translation from *Antonio's Revenge*, p. 104, note 31.

Other features of the remembrance reinforce its controversy. For example, Antonio's phrases about the place of the dead – 'Where'er thou hoverest'; 'in what orb thy mighty spirit soars' – are coy, suggesting to an England still strenuously denying the existence of Purgatory that there is room for doubt.[53] Purgatory is never quite mentioned, but Andrugio's ghost appears in response to Antonio's remembrance, suggesting a connection between living and dead Reformers of all kinds were 'determined to break'.[54] Reciprocity between dead and living, moreover, persists throughout this scene before the tomb as, occasionally, it does for the remainder of the play. Thus, the dead here disappear and re-appear in the candlelight, also echoing Antonio's speech, according to stage directions, 'from beneath the stage' and 'from above and beneath'. Such unreformed 'haunt' is summarized by Antonio towards the end of the scene:

Now croaks the toad, and night-crows screech aloud,
Fluttering 'bout casements of departing souls;
Now gape the graves, and through their yawns let loose
Imprisoned spirits to revisit earth.[55]

In Paul's now allegedly Italianate monument, there is a disturbingly regular traffic between the living and their candle-lit dead.
Revenge too arises from the tomb. For Antonio, it is

By the infectious damps of clammy graves
And by the mould that presseth down
My dead father's skull, I'll be revenged![56]

However, asked specifically why he would be avenged, Antonio answers,

So I may sleep tombed in an honoured hearse;
So may my bones rest in that sepulchre.[57]

---

[53] Such coy reference to the source of punishment for the dead will be repeated in a (Latin) invocation from Seneca's *Thyestes* – in translation: 'O whoer'er thou art, harsh judge of shades, who dost allot fresh punishments to the dead...' Translation from *Antonio's Revenge*, p. 106.

[54] Marshall, p. 210. Marshall continues, 'A recurrent and insistent refrain in the writings of late sixteenth- and early seventeenth-century divines was that the souls of the dead in heaven did not listen to the prayers of the living; indeed, could not hear them; that the dead on their own account could have no knowledge of what transpired in the created world.' He adds that the Elizabethan redefinition of prayer in the homilies describes prayer as 'an inward crying of the heart to God' which 'no virgin, patriarch, or prophet among the dead could apprehend'. (Marshall, pp. 210–11).

[55] *Antonio's Revenge*, III.iii.45–8.
[56] *Antonio's Revenge*, III.ii.26–8.
[57] *Antonio's Revenge*, III.ii.31–2.

As ever, revenge is no simple matter of reflex or of justice: it concerns honoured burial, a monumental revenge being again a funerary monument.[58]

Recalling the sacrifice of Alarbus in *Titus Andronicus*, the ritual killing of Julio over the tomb is the climax of Antonio's extravagantly performed remembrance. Inviting us to 'Behold' Antonio 'spurt warm blood' (III.iii.50), the text instructs we attend the performance.

First, then, Antonio 'spurts' the warm blood and then goes on to 'make incense' of it (III.iii.62). Scattering the blood is key to the killing, as editors have tried to illustrate by inserting stage directions 'on the assumption that the chances of the reader being able to attend the play, except imaginatively, are remote'.[59] One attempt to render the bloodletting is: 'Antonio allows Julio's blood to fall upon the hearse'; another that he 'Sprinkles the tomb with blood'. Either way, though, this scene replays the sacrifice in *Titus Andronicus* of Alarbus, and thus elements suggesting the 'Sacrifice of the Mass', in the full and gruesome view of the audience.[60]

Highlighting Catholic sacrifice, then, is important in the scene; yet despite this, anti-Catholicism is not clear: Antonio blunts any anti-Catholic sting at the moment of the killing:

> Come, pretty, tender child,
> It is not thee I hate, not thee I kill.
> Thy father's blood that flows within thy veins
> Is it I loathe, is that revenge must suck.
> I love thy soul; and were thy heart lapped up
> In any flesh but in Piero's blood,
> I would thus kiss it; but being his, thus, thus,
> And thus I'll punch it.
> [*He stabs Julio*][61]

This crucial passage is a nexus of religious suggestiveness pointing in at least two opposing directions. Antonio emphasizes that his quarrel is not with Julio, even claiming it is not Julio whom he wishes to kill. Rather, it is 'Thy father's blood that flows within thy veins ... I loathe'; thus, divorced by Antonio from its spirit, Julio's body

> is all Piero, father, all; this blood,
> This breast, this heart, Piero all.[62]

The emphasis on Piero's blood is especially suggestive. In the sacrificial context, the imagery of flowing blood, of drinking ('revenge must suck', 'heart lapped up') and of working mouths ('thus kiss it') all plays on the drinking of 'Christ's Blood'

---

[58] For monumental revenge as a funerary monument, see my discussion of *The Spanish Tragedy*, p. 36.
[59] Gair, p. 6.
[60] For my discussion of Alarbus' death in reference to the Sacrifice of the Mass, see Chapter 1, p. 44 and 53.
[61] *Antonio's Revenge*, III.ii.177–84.
[62] *Antonio's Revenge*, III.iii.35–6; 56–7.

which, we have observed, Reformers parodied as a rite of cannibalism.[63] However, this blood is not Christ's but, emphatically, Piero's: the lines 'I love thy soul, and were thy heart lapped up / In any flesh but in Piero's blood, / I would thus kiss it' distinguish the 'soul' of the child from the blood he inherits from his father.

This distinction (between Julio's 'soul' and his 'pierine' blood) implies 'Piero' is an idea as much as a character, and in the moment's detailed and suggestively Catholic memorial, his name inevitably suggests the See of Peter. At this deliberate juncture, therefore, it is not the blood of Christ, but of *Peter* that Antonio seeks to separate from Julio's loved 'soul', the scene thus murdering the *popery* of sacrifice while maintaining its traditional rite. So the message to observe seems this: maintain catholic, but not Roman Catholic, remembrance.

For this ideology, it is tempting to reach for the phrase 'Via Media', especially since Marston went on to take holy orders. Yet the 'Via Media' was groping uncertainly for its settled identity at this stage,[64] and the scene too lacks clarity, as I have noted. For the imagery of blood-*drinking* in the sacrificial passage presents a second train of associations. In this second perspective, 'Peter's' blood is both loathed *and swallowed* – suggesting that, however hateful, Rome too must be swallowed. This may seem contradictory, but that is in keeping with the scene: Antonio surrounds his *chosen* actions with sinister images of night-crows screeching and yawning graves; and finally leaving the scene, he bequeaths it 'peace and rest', while paradoxically heaving

> blood-stained hands to heaven;
> Even like insatiate hell.[65]

Recalling the Sacrifice of the Mass, the sacrifice of Julio is simultaneously a glory, a horror and a laying to rest.

With Antonio's departure from the 'night-ghosts and graves' (III.ii.214) of 'St Mark's', the play presents a more clearly Reformist drama climaxing in the eventual overthrow of Piero. Anticipating that overthrow, Pandulpho, whose Reformist style we have previously observed, picks up a line of religious imagery now familiar, reporting,

> And I do find the citizens grown sick
> With swallowing the bloody crudities
> Of black Piero's acts; they fain would cast
> And vomit him off their government.[66]

According to Pandulpho, the 'bloody crudities' performed by Piero – previously associated, as we have seen such blood, with the Communion of the See of Peter – have literally sickened the citizens: his violent ejection from a body-politic *seeming*

---

[63] For discussion, see Chapter 1, p. 44.
[64] For details, see Tyacke, *Anti-Calvinists*; relevant too is my discussion of English divines on 'mourning' before 1629 in the Introduction, pp. 25–6, note 110.
[65] *Antonio's Revenge*, III.ii.214; 211–12.
[66] *Antonio's Revenge*, V.iii.17–20.

providentially to heal itself is at hand. Interestingly in the meantime, however, Marston presents the alleged sickness of the citizens as a matter of saving Roman Catholicism from itself: in act IV, Piero plans to

> conquer Rome,
> Pop out the light of bright religion
> And then helter skelter[67]

suggesting the foremost danger to Rome's 'light of bright religion' comes from a character who purported defending its remembrance.

Act IV, scene iv opens with Antonio 'alone, in fool's habit' – a costume gracing him since the beginning of the act. Addressing the 'Omnipotence' (IV.iv.1), he acknowledges that Mellida belonged not to him but to God:

> she was all thine,
> All heavenly, I did but humbly beg
> To borrow her of thee a little time.[68]

After some enlargement on this theme, the stage direction says he 'puts off his cap, and lieth just upon his back' in order, in Antonio's words, 'to turn my prostrate breast upon thy [God's] face' (IV.iv.12). Thus, Antonio seeks to argue away his grief in assertions that he had no claim on Mellida; however, his eventually prostrate demeanour, his acknowledged 'beg' of God, and especially his persistent persona as a *fool* (in all but his cap) each suggests irony.

But if Antonio seems mocked for *not* mourning, he is mocked for mourning too. Having mourned Mellida 'so loud' he had seemingly 'brought back' Mellida's soul (IV.iii.182), Antonio was also called a 'fool' and a very 'audacious fool' (IV.iii.181; 184). In response to his wail, the seemingly dead Mellida had briefly revived, as if mourning might be beneficial. Eventually, however, the scene implies a parody of the 'superstition' of extensive mourning: it transpires Mellida was *not* quite dead; thus, Antonio's noise revived her, but not from death and only for a moment, making his lamentation only a foolish noise.

In the same vein, in act IV, scene v, Reformist Pandulpho presents successive arguments against extended mourning. For example, when desolate Antonio explains 'I ha' lost a wife' (IV.v.11), Pandulpho replies: 'Hast lost a wife? / Thrice blessed man that lost her whilst she was good, / Fair, young unblemished, constant, loving, chaste…' (IV.v.15–17); similarly, when Alberto sides with Antonio because he lost 'a true friend' (IV.v.23), Pandulpho argues against both men:

Thou lost a good wife; thou lost a true friend, ha?
Two of the rarest lendings of the heavens;
But lendings: which, at the fixed day of pay
Set down by fate, thou must restore again.[69]

---

[67] *Antonio's Revenge*, IV.i.245–7.
[68] *Antonio's Revenge*, IV.iv.4–6.
[69] *Antonio's Revenge*, IV.v.25–8.

In each case, Pandulpho argues for a cheerful demeanour in mourning. It is because of these arguments that Pandulpho is visibly exasperated that Antonio 'still' dwells on his feelings a little later:

> ANTONIO   I scorn't that any wretch should survive,
> Outmounting me in that superlative,
> Most miserable, most unmatched in woe.
> PANDULPHO   Will't still be so? And will't yon bloodhound live?[70]

Here Pandulpho reiterates a motif familiar to this study: that a dishonoured corpse requires revenge. However, in Pandulpho's Reformist version of this motif, revenge should occur *without* mourning or 'dirge' except the most restricted, as he makes clear in the succeeding burial of Feliche. Thus, the scene ends with Pandulpho's deciding to 'inter the dead' before proceeding to revenge (IV.v.62), Antonio asking the Page to 'sing a dirge' (IV.v.65) and this intervention from Pandulpho: 'No; no song; 'twill be vile out of tune' (IV.v.66). For Pandulpho, indeed, songs for the dead are always inappropriate because 'the strings of nature's symphony / Are cracked' (IV.v.68–9): natural music is flawed. However, performances of remembrance being as crucial as ever, instead of music Pandulpho proposes reciting 'an honest antique rhyme I have' (IV.v.72), thus distinguishing between an 'honest' rhyme and (dishonest) *Dirige* with characteristically Reformed implication.

The Reformed views of Pandulpho's rhyme also deserve notice:

> Death, exile, plaints and woe
> Are but man's lackeys, not his foe.
> No mortal scapes from fortune's war
> Without a wound, at least a scar.
> Many have led these to the grave,
> But all shall follow, none shall save.
> Blood of my youth, rot and consume;
> Virtue in dirt doth life assume
> With this old saw close up this dust;
> Thrice-blessed man that dieth just.[71]

The lines define death not as a cause of great sadness, as it has hitherto been for all but Pandulpho, but as a 'lackey' to the just and virtuous, death serving to get the just to heaven. In particular contrast to traditional Dirges, moreover, the claim that 'none shall save' rules out intercession on behalf of the dead. As a whole, the scene is a lesson in Reformed funeral.

However, there is irony in all this. This burial is for 'Feliche' – it is 'felicity' which is thus here buried. In particular, it is the 'felicity' of the mournful remembrances reformed by Pandulpho that are interred and (however restrainedly) mourned. And there are other ambiguities – especially regarding the persistent theme of 'blood'.

Moments before the rhyme's appeal for the 'Blood of my youth' to 'rot and consume', Antonio had bewailed the loss of Mellida (his 'mel' or sweetness),

---

[70] *Antonio's Revenge*, IV.v.55–9.
[71] *Antonio's Revenge*, IV.v.74–83.

specifically mourning her passing as that of his 'vital blood' (IV.vi.10). Considering himself the 'quicksand that devours all misery', therefore, he continued:

> For all this, I dare live, and I will live,
> Only to numb some others' cursed blood
> With the dead palsy of like misery.[72]

The lines partly imply Antonio infecting others with the 'palsy' of his remembrances, and thus a negative view of mournful funerals. More positively, however, the remembrance of Mellida in these lines is also that for which Antonio 'dare live'. Pointedly, moreover, the 'vital blood' in remembrance of which Antonio 'dare live' – Mellida – is *Piero's* daughter. Thus, the deliberate education of Antonio in a 'correct' style of remembrance we have observed also implies a loss of vitality itself entailing a loss of Piero's (Catholic) lifeblood.

The most substantial irony of the scene, however, is that despite preaching in favour of cheerful remembrances, Pandulpho himself breaks down at the memory of his son:

> ALBERTO   Why weeps mine uncle?
> PANDULPHO Ha, dost ask me why? ha? Ha?
>   Good coz, look here.
>   *He shows him his son's breast*
>   Man will break out, despite philosophy.
>   Why, all this while I ha' but played a part,
>   Like to some boy that acts a tragedy,
>   Speaks burly words and raves out passion;
>   But when he thinks upon his infant weakness
>   He droops his eye.[73]

Especially in view of his hostility to emotional acts of remembrance hitherto, it is Pandulpho's defensiveness about weeping for the dead, and his admission that his 'manly' demeanour is an act beneath which lies a weeping 'infant' (like the boy-player himself), that is striking. For Pandulpho conceding here that his advocated style of mourning is a sham, Marston's depiction of the Reformer – and thus of the Reformation – is fraught with contradiction.

The last act is equally ambivalent. After the departure of the choric Ghost of Andrugio, there follows the rhetoric of anti-Catholic eschatology. Antonio, Pandulpho and Alberto all vie for the credit of having slain Piero, now variously 'the monster's heart', 'huge pollution' and even 'Beelzebub' (V.iii.121; 129; 136). Notably, Pandulpho's insistence that ''twas I / 'Twas I sluiced out his life-blood' (V.iii.124–5) revives the focus on Piero's contentiously vital 'blood', presenting both Paul's and the 'gory spectacle' (V.iii.115) as ritually cleansed. The heroism of the slaughter is made unambiguous in Galleazzo's words to Antonio:

---

[72] *Antonio's Revenge*, IV.iv.16; 18–20.
[73] *Antonio's Revenge*, IV.v.43–51.

Thou art another Hercules to us
In ridding huge pollution from our state.[74]

To the Second Senator, Piero's death is cause for sanctification:

Blessed be you all, and may your honours live
Religiously held sacred, even for ever and ever.[75]

Confirmation of such *religious* heroism emerges in the First Senator's report that 'bede-roles of mischief' were discovered on Piero's person. As I previously observed, the bede-role was a list of a church's dead, read aloud in the Catholic Church for the salvation of those in Purgatory, so the association of these with Piero underlines his Catholic style. The discovery repays close attention:

Antonio, belief is fortified
With most invincible approvements of much wrong
By this Piero to thee. We have found
Bede-roles of mischief, plots of villainy
Laid 'twixt the Duke and Strozzo; which we found
Too firmly acted.[76]

As usual, remembrance of the dead is a matter of theatre: Piero's use of bede-roles was 'too firmly acted'. However, Piero's decisive villainy, and Antonio's equally decided justice, turns on the discovery of the bede-roles as 'invincible approvements of much wrong'. Moreover, implying villains are papists who remember the dead in the un-Reformed style, line 133 suggests 'bede roles of mischief' is a synonym for 'plots of villainy'. Disturbingly but – as Ronald Broude might have told us – unsurprisingly, Antonio and his companions are sanctified for murdering a papist.[77]

Yet a Broudian reading of the scene is insufficient: as I have argued, there remain striking ambiguities. Most immediately, in condemning plots 'Too firmly acted' in a *theatre*, the Senator subverts his own condemning act. The movement of the poetry supports this reading: by presenting 'Too firmly acted' in a new line, the matter of theatricality gains emphasis. Similarly, in condemning Catholic remembrance in Paul's monument – in which, as we have seen, Catholicism was inscribed – the condemnation becomes uncertain.

However, the failure to endorse 'killing' Piero's style of remembrance is clearest in the play's last moments. Picking up on the preceding metaphors of 'cleansing', there emerges a 'cleansing' of hands, 'purging' of hearts and 'entombing' of love (V.iii.153–4), but this is preceded by a surprising, monastic development. Most surprisingly, Pandulpho initiates it:

---

[74] *Antonio's Revenge*, V.iii.128–9.
[75] *Antonio's Revenge*, V.iii.126–7.
[76] *Antonio's Revenge*, V.iii.130–5.
[77] As I observed at the opening of the study, Broude considered *Antonio's Revenge* among the 'classic', Protestant revenge tragedies. See my Introduction, p. 1.

> We know the world, and did we know no more
> We would not live to know. But since constraint
> Of holy bands forceth us keep this lodge
> Of dirt's corruption till dread power calls
> Our soul's appearance, we will live enclosed
> In holy verge of some religious order,
> Most constant votaries.[78]

Pandulpho's invocation of the traditional Christian prohibition against suicide with an equally traditional *contemptus mundi* leads him to consider the rest of his life best served as a monk:[79] seemingly Pandulpho regrets murdering Piero, despite the latter embodying the styles of remembrance Pandulpho has overtly and persistently condemned.

The choice of a *monastery* as an appropriate place of penitence is also significant. Further emphasizing monasticism, the end looks forward to a 'calm, sequestered life' (V.iii.159) of 'contemplation' in which to 'meditate' (V.iii.162; 161), yet monastic life was unavailable in post-Reformation England, the end thus affirming a religion decidedly Italianate. Moreover, given that monasteries were, as I have observed, '"purgatorial institutions", established to offer masses and prayers for their founders and benefactors in perpetuity',[80] the choice of a monastic penitence has special thematic relevance: in committing themselves to a monastery for life, Pandulpho and his fellows embrace the most extensive of remembrances of the dead. Finally, the un-Protestant nature of this penance bears emphasis. As David Beauregard observes, Protestant penance had become 'a completely privatized and interiorized exercise, which merely permitted and allowed for exteriorization in the form of auricular confession'.[81] Thus, Pandulpho and the fellow penitents are clearly proposing a course most controversial and, in Pandulpho's case, unexpected.

Finally, in referring to the penitents as 'The downcast ruins of calamity' (V.vi.53), Maria adds bite to the controversy by linking the monastic discourse to England's monastic heritage: 'downcast ruins'. Simultaneously, however, 'downcast ruins' suggests the surrounds of Paul's, which, suffering from such successive bouts of iconoclasm as we have observed (and to which the text also refers[82]), by 1600 had left the monument in a severe state of disrepair.[83] Thus, the 'ruin' of the dramatic

---

[78] *Antonio's Revenge*, V.iii.145–51.

[79] Gair's view of this development as 'almost monastic' (which I considered in note 4 of this chapter) is not strong enough: Pandulpho explicitly says he will live in a 'religious order'. In what follows, I shall observe – like Gair – the closing requiem of the play accompanying this monasticism, though in view of the persistent funerary theme I have illustrated, we can dispense with Gair's view that Marston's 'statement' is not 'explicit'.

[80] See my discussion (following Peter Marshall) of monasticism in Chapter 1, p. 44–5.

[81] See David Beauregard, 'Shakespeare against the Homilies: The Theology of Penance in the Comedies', in *The Ben Jonson Journal* 7 (2000), pp. 27–54 (35); similarly, see Marshall, pp. 210–11.

[82] See the attack on the 'unconscionable souls' of the play who are like the 'spoke-shaves of *the church*' (*Antonio's Revenge*, IV.v.25–31; my emphasis).

[83] See my discussion of Paul's monument above, on p. 79–80. Cook notes that 'a long period of neglect in Elizabeth's reign had reduced the fabric' of the Cathedral 'to a state of

persons reflects the ruin of the foundation: in the First Senator's words, these theatrical persons are Paul's 'well-seasoned props' (V.v.25). And thus, the tragedy of the dramatic persons eventually reflects the tragedy of England's monasteries, presenting an elision of theatre and monastery especially pertinent to Paul's.

For in the eighth and ninth centuries – a period without clear distinctions between canons regular and canons secular[84] – Paul's was referred to as a 'monasterialis vita' and 'congregatio fratrum'; moreover, having been re-founded in 654 (after a pagan interlude), its first bishop was a monk.[85] Thus, combining with a prospect of both England and Paul's monastic and ruined histories, the play's closing view of monasticism evokes Paul's historical past.

Accompanying the final monasticism is a clear embrace of extensively performed funeral. Thus, burying Mellida – Piero's child – with 'doleful tunes' and 'solemn hymn' (V.vi.54), Antonio concludes with a *hymned* remembrance emphatic about its funerary extravagance: 'Never more woe', we are told, 'in lesser plot was found' (V.vi.59) – a phrase in which Mellida's burial 'plot' also evokes the dramatic plot, the play itself being thus finally conceived as a funeral. And though, in imagining such extravagance as part of 'some [other] black tragedy' Antonio slightly softens this blow, as the play's last lines give way to music, that imagined and ideal tragedy becomes *Antonio's Revenge* itself:

And when the [ideal] closing Epilogue appears,
Instead of claps, may it obtain but tears.
    They sing.[86]

Even as it transforms into a hymn, Antonio's ideal 'black tragedy' will evoke *nothing* but tears. Indeed, in concluding the play with hymned funerary performance – a *Dirige* – *Antonio's Revenge* becomes a tragedy loudly rejecting ideas that emotional performances for the dead are 'unmanly' or 'clownish'. In what must be construed as a loss of nerve by the Protestant-minded dramatist, the logic of creating a figure such as Pandulpho seemingly to undermine the 'excessive' tendencies of the genre ultimately leads nowhere. The picture of Marston emerging is thus of a playwright torn between, indeed confused by, opposing styles of Christianity. Nevertheless, though *Antonio's Revenge* lacks coherence, its divided view of remembrance reveals a development in the emphasis of revenge tragedy and an insight into a divided, Protestant mentality, even as the presentation of mourning in a *monument* reveals a theatre and church entwined.

---

dilapidation' and provides a history of attempted restorations under James. (See especially Cook, p. 81.) However, the dilapidation was already visible in the 1540s, as noted in 'The Decay of St Paul's', in *The Children of Paul's*, pp. 13–43.

[84] I emphasize this as it negates arguments of the type 'Was St Paul's a monastery or not?', though for present purposes what is important is the *perceived* history of the building.

[85] The monk-bishop was Erkenwald; his sister, St Ethelburga, also founded a monastic community for women at Barking. For discussion of this early and monkish history of St Paul's, see Cook, pp. 5–6 and p. 11.

[86] *Antonio's Revenge*, V.vi.68–9.

Chapter 3

Melodrama and Parody: Remembering the Dead in *The Revenger's Tragedy*, *The Atheist's Tragedy*, *The White Devil* and *The Duchess of Malfi*

Three fundamental points are now clear. First, in their repeated presentations of such remembrance, and in their proximity to contemporary monuments like Paul's Cathedral, early revenge tragedies, including the most prominent and influential, are suffused with remembrances of the dead, thus participating in a heated contemporary controversy. Second, by repeatedly stressing *performance* of funerary remembrance, these tragedies take on the most central matter of that controversy – *performing* remembrance. Third, early revenge tragedies are nothing like as Reformed as 'Broudian' critics have persistently implied. On the crucial matter of remembrance – of the dead firstly, but of the meaning of the materials of the Eucharist by extension[1] – *Antonio's Revenge* is divided, though lurching traditionally at the end; but *The Spanish Tragedy*, *Titus Andronicus* and *Hamlet* favour traditionalism almost throughout.

The question therefore arising is: how do later revenge tragedies respond to this debate? To provide an answer, this chapter will consider three examples of the genre of persistent interest: *The Revenger's Tragedy*, *The White Devil* and *The Duchess of Malfi*. I also consider a less admired play, *The Atheist's Tragedy*, because its treatment of the theme is, as we shall see, so singular.

In fascinatingly different ways, all but one of these plays address the performance of remembrance self-consciously, playing with contrasts between extensive and restricted remembrances so that each religiously significant style reflects uncertainly on the other. In particular, ironic parodies of extensive remembrances juxtapose with the real things, presenting dramatic performances of remembrance that are as a whole ambiguous. The exception is Middleton's *The Revenger's Tragedy*: short of removing dramatic focus entirely from the remembrance (and thus becoming irrelevant) but nevertheless suggesting the Reform traditionally associated with Middleton, this play does everything it can to illustrate that remembrance of the dead

---

[1] For my discussion of the association of these among contemporaries, see the Introduction, p. 3–4.

is without value.² Indeed, for this play *distinctively*, the notion of drama 'emptying' the sacred from traditional religious rituals has meaning.³

The Revenger's Tragedy, c.1606

The Revenger's Tragedy is fraught with implied religious views. Thus, aside from the passages I shall specifically discuss in regard to the remembrance of the dead, one persistently finds terms and phrases such as the following: 'It is the Judas of the hours, wherein / Honest salvation is betray'd to sin' (I.iii.71–2); 'O one incestuous kiss picks open hell' (I.ii.173); 'I'll call foul incest but a venial sin' (I.ii.169); 'puritan' (II.ii.30); 'Mahomet' (III.ii.27); 'A very fine religion!' (I.iii.108).⁴ There are far too many other invocations of religious concepts, often to moral effect, to enumerate here, but the persistent presence of such phrases means this play treating a corrupt Italian court is permeated with a religious perspective.⁵ However, the play's especial interest in sexual corruption combines with its interest in the dead. Vindice brings this out notably when asked his identity by Lussurioso:

---

    ²   Like most recent commentators, I am persuaded of Middleton's authorship of *The Revenger's Tragedy*. For discussion of the issue, see the introduction to *The Revenger's Tragedy: A Facsimile of the 1607/8 Quarto*, ed. by MacDonald P. Jackson (Rutherford, NJ: Fairleigh Dickinson University Press, 1983). For further discussion of Middleton's association with Reform – so often, problematically, his 'Puritanism' – see p. 145–6, note 2.
    ³   For my previous discussion of this view associated with Stephen Greenblatt, see the Introduction, pp. 13. I emphasize, however, that regarding 'emptying' of rituals, *The Revenger's Tragedy* is exceptional; though it may point towards secularity, moreover, in Middleton's case it is more likely an expression of Reform.
    ⁴   All quotations from *The Revenger's Tragedy* are taken from Thomas Middleton, *Five Plays*, ed. by Bryan Loughrey and Neil Taylor (London: Penguin, 1988).
    ⁵   The point is especially worth emphasizing in view of Steven Mullaney's previous work on *The Revenger's Tragedy* in 'Mourning and Misogyny: *Hamlet, The Revenger's Tragedy*, and the Final Progress of Elizabeth I', in *Shakespeare Quarterly* 45/2 (Summer 1994), pp. 139–62. Broadly suggesting the approach of this book, Mullaney argues that 'Human emotions are no more free from historical and cultural construction than are genders or ideologies or gestures', adding that 'the popular stage represents a unique historical resource' as 'an affective ... forum' (Mullaney, p. 142; p. 144). However, despite following G.W. Pigman – to whom I give much attention in my Introduction – in the view that 'grief was one of the "natural" human emotions that radical Protestants sought to reform and even eradicate from properly Christian psyches' (Mullaney, p. 141, note 11), the reading of *The Revenger's Tragedy* that Mullaney presents thereafter ignores this potent religious context. My reading of the play therefore rectifies this exclusion; moreover, it can claim to present a more topical context than Mullaney's essay: Elizabeth was a figure of the (recent) past in 1606, while (as detailed in my Introduction) Reformers were still *actively* preaching on the unnaturalness of mourning for the dead up to and well beyond 1606. The fact that Vindice only associates his skull with 'Gloriana' in act III, that he only does so once, and that (according to Mullaney) the play thereafter generalizes 'the memory of Elizabeth' into 'the traditional status of the Petrarchan lady' (Mullaney, p. 161) also cautions us against over-stressing Elizabeth's role in the play.

LUSSURIOSO	What hast been, of what profession?
VINDICE	A bone-setter.
LUSSURIOSO	A bone-setter?
VINDICE	A bawd, my lord, one that sets bones together.[6]

Lussurioso's repetition 'bone-setter' allows time for the play on words to sink in. As a 'bawd', Vindice claims to press the sexual bones of the body together and even to set up the phallic 'bone', but when Lussurioso queries 'bone-setter', he brings out another implication: that is, of one who lays out the dead. However, erotic and remembrance are entwined from the start.

The dramatic premise of *The Revenger's Tragedy* is one we can now recognize as largely conventional. Following the opening torch-lit procession, Vindice appears on stage 'holding a skull', itself once

> the bright face of my betrothed lady
> ...
> ... far beyond the artifical shine
> Of any woman's bought complexion.[7]

Thus, the play opens with a performance of remembrance for a beloved, dead woman.

That such remembrance is extensive, dominating Vindice's thought, soon becomes apparent: the speech lasts for forty-nine lines. Moreover, Vindice calls the skull 'my study's ornament' (I.i.15), so the 'study' has been careful. Implying a most lengthy mourning, Hippolyto more openly observes Vindice '*Still* sighing over Death's vizard' (I.i.49; my emphasis), and as 'nine years' eventually crowd 'into a minute' of revenge for this woman (III.v.121), the full extensiveness of Vindice's remembrance becomes clear.

Conventionally, too, vengeful remembrance is bound up in the dishonour of the deceased. Vindice explains that his former love was murdered for refusing the Duke's 'palsy lust' (I.i.34). Thus, killing the Duke is a response to the dishonour of the dead – a theme also explicit in the parallel plot in which Junior rapes and kills Antonio's wife. Presenting 'the body of her dead' in what Antonio calls 'A sight that strikes man out of me' (I.iv.5), the scene brings out the relation between a desecrated corpse and revenge in a world valuing extravagant funerary honour:

> Her funeral shall be wealthy, for her name
> Merits a tomb of pearl. My lord Antonio,
> For this time wipe your lady from your eyes;
> No doubt our grief and yours will one day court it
> When we are more familiar with revenge.[8]

However, as it is the corrupt Duke who speaks these lines, and as act I, scene ii has already shown him failing to bring about the promised revenge on Junior in court, the integrity of this traditional valuing is ironically compromised. Similarly,

---

[6] *The Revenger's Tragedy*, I.iii.41–4.
[7] *The Revenger's Tragedy*, I.i.16; 21–2.
[8] *The Revenger's Tragedy*, I.iv.69–74.

though perhaps less plainly, the integrity of Vindice's remembrance in act I, scene i is compromised too – for two reasons.

First, Vindice's skull is not his only vengefully motivating remembrance, presenting some confusion as to what really motivates him. Thus, at the close of act I, scene i, Vindice explains his anger in reference not to his betrothed but to his dead father:

> For since my worthy father's funeral,
> My life's unnatural to me, e'en compelled.[9]

Once again, funerary remembrance underlies revenge, and when Hippolyto explains 'our lord and father / Fell sick upon the infection of thy [the Duke's] frowns / And died in sadness' (III.v.167–9), *dishonoured* remembrance becomes again the revenger's theme. However, although presenting *two* funerary motives for vengeance doubles a standard reason for grievance, the different explanations of Vindice's anger – especially when expressed, as here, without relation – present a disconcerting inconsistency in Vindice.

Second, though Vindice's opening remembrance expresses much anger, as we shall see, it also presents his remembrance of the dead as a *generic* motive, exposing his emotion for the dead as a matter of conventional rather than appropriate action. Thus, Vindice ironically calls vengeance 'murder's quit-rent' (I.i.39), too self-consciously explaining the mechanics of dramatic action to suggest sincerity; and, with even greater self-consciousness, he explains that it is for honour that vengeance shows itself 'tenant to Tragedy' (I.i.40). The implication of such lines – as of the very name 'Vindice' – is that despite the fictions of remembrance, the true cause of vengeance is not the skull or the father but the tragic genre.

Though significantly implying the remembrances *of the dead* of revengers are thus inauthentic, such impressions might be overlooked as details were it not that so many other features of *The Revenger's Tragedy* point in the same, Reformist direction. Thus, although the play does evoke funerary motifs, there are notably few monologues presenting direct expressions of mourning, reducing the affective dimension of the drama in remembrance of the dead. Instead, there is a series of alternative spectacles; some of them *are* in remembrance of the dead, but rather than valuing remembrance, they tend to detract from it.

Thus, from the opening presentation of Vindice's meditation and skull, there is, besides inauthenticity, excess. This is partly a matter of tone and partly of place: a Hamlet or Hieronimo works up to a mournful fury, but Vindice is furious from the start. Thus, we never see Vindice in anything other than vengeful mode, suggesting he *has* no other mode – which 'Vindice' again supports. 'Vindice' suggesting vengeance rather than a rounded character, indeed, the personality is excessive.[10]

---

[9] *The Revenger's Tragedy*, I.i.119–20.

[10] As Loughrey and Taylor state more generally (and more negatively): 'The play's characters and action lack the inwardness and specificity of Shakespeare. Vindice is not an individual in the sense that Hamlet is.' See Loughrey and Taylor (ed.), p. xv.

As the years of waiting 'crowd' into the minute of vengeance of act III, the excessiveness of Vindice's action is exemplified. Observing the setting for the revenge brings this out.

The revenge takes place in what Vindice describes as a

> darken'd blushless angle, that is guilty
> Of his [the Duke's] forefathers' lusts and great folks' riots[11]

the dead being thus explicit in a sinister monument. Emphasizing darkness, Hippolito carries a 'torch', and Vindice's instruction to 'raise the perfumes' (III.v.139) implies the use of incense.[12] Seemingly, then, the monument is a church, or perhaps a vault, the riots of the 'great folks' being their elaborate funerary tombs. The scene is thick with puns to this effect. Vindice notes the skull has 'somewhat a grave look' (III.v.134), and in imagery that ironically combines both a 'grave' and a robed cleric, the Duke says:

> In gravest faults the greatest sins seem less;
> Give me that sin that's rob'd in holiness.[13]

Eventually regretting the whorishness of his own beloved relic – and so condemning his very style of remembrance – Vindice wittily notes: 'This would become graves better than the streets' (III.v.115); finally, reminded that he promised to share each 'tragic thought', Vindice replies (with further irony): 'By the mass, I think I did too' (III.v.7). Thus, in this 'faulty, vaulty', Italian setting,[14] graves, whore, robed cleric, and 'mass' assemble sinisterly, the scene being set for an anti-Catholic view of Vindice's revenge.

Highlighting the role of the dead in the revenge as well as the ceremonial, after poisoning the Duke, Vindice remarks:

> The very ragged bone
> Has been sufficiently revenged.[15]

Paradigmatically, thus, the scene presents revenge as an act of remembrance, but equally paradigmatically this remembrance is poisonous – even to its perpetrator, Vindice, who discovers he

> could e'en chide myself
> For doting on her [the skull's] beauty.[16]

---

[11] *The Revenger's Tragedy*, III.v.14–15.

[12] As noted in editorially added stage directions in Maus (ed.), *Four Revenge Tragedies*, p. 340; these directions also present a 'torch'.

[13] *The Revenger's Tragedy*, III.v.137–8.

[14] Since we are dealing with spoken drama, and since 'fault' and 'vault' both begin with labio-dental fricatives (voiceless and voiced) it is hard not to infer a play on the two words, especially as this vault – if such it is – is clearly 'faulty'.

[15] *The Revenger's Tragedy*, III.v.151–2.

[16] *The Revenger's Tragedy*, III.v.68–9.

The act of remembrance – mass, vault, skull, image and murder – is thus ironically offset by the sinister surrounding and a direct moral condemnation. That it is therefore excessive – even to its performer – is implied.

Excessive remembrance is also present in Vindice's language – from the start, as I have suggested, right up until Vindice's revenge. Thus, the terminology of the opening remembrance is made up of evils: 'true-begot in evil', 'will do with devil', 'damned desires', 'infernal fires' (I.i.3; 4; 6; 7) are just a few instances of the evil bubbling from Vindice's mouth, the successive terms implicating him in the corruption he condemns. Spreading from Vindice to the rest as the play proceeds, the climax of this hellish rhetoric is the climax of his vengeance and remembrance: the killing of the Duke. Here, it is as though hell itself emerged on stage. 'Is there a hell besides this, villains?' are among the Duke's last words (III.v.181).

On one hand, then, there is Vindice's over-remembrance; however, on the other, the play presents the *emptiness* of such act. Vindice's stage-setting first soliloquy consistently presents his skull as the reference-point and thus meaning of his life of remembrance. However, he further claims his life and death are hollow. Thus, humans are only 'apparelled in ... flesh', but in this 'marrowless age' the 'hollow bones' are ruled by the 'veins of a dry Duke' – indeed

> One
> That has scarce blood enough to live upon.[17]

Like the actor's clothing, human flesh disguises a skeleton and society that is persistently pronounced insufficient, 'hollow', 'marrowless', such terms also describing Vindice's state of mind. Thus, in Vindice's early words,

> since my worthy father's funeral
> My life's unnatural to me, e'en compelled,
> *As if I lived now when I should be dead.*[18]

It is a mental emptiness persisting to the end: ''Tis time to die when we are ourselves our foes' (V.iii.10) still treats living as worthless. The unusual absence of a ghost in this revenge tragedy's course is worth observing: without a ghost, the play withholds from the audience a dramatic suggestion of life in death.

The play insists on the emptiness of death in various ways, another being to imply the emptiness of memorial tombs. Here, for example, is the Duke on the guilt of Junior and the 'honour' of the dead:

> Duchess, it is your youngest son; we're sorry
> His violent act has e'en drawn blood of honour
> And stained our honours,
> Thrown ink upon the forehead of our state
> Which envious spirits will dip their pens into
> After our death, and blot us in our tombs.
> For that which would seem treason in our lives

---

[17] *The Revenger's Tragedy*, I.i.31; 6–10.
[18] *The Revenger's Tragedy*, I.i.119–21.

> Is laughter when we're dead. Who dares now whisper
> That dares not then speak out, and e'en proclaim
> With loud words and broad pens our closest shame?[19]

Seemingly valuing remembrance, the passage presents life as a time looking forward to 'our tombs'. However, tombs are worthless vehicles of remembrance: in terms historically suggesting the over-writing of Catholic lines of remembrance by Reformers, 'envious pens' will 'blot' us in the tomb, thus 'blotting us out'.

The First Judge's response to the Duke provides a second example of empty monuments for the dead:

> Your Grace hath spoke like to your silver years
> Full of confirmed gravity; for what is it to have
> A flattering false insculption on a tomb,
> And in men's hearts reproach? The bowell'd corpse
> May be cered in, but, with free tongue I speak,
> *The faults of great men through their cerecloths break.*[20]

Presenting 'flattering false insculption', tombs here also are false vehicles of remembrance. And thus, ironically, in his 'confirmed gravity' (presenting yet another play on 'grave'), the Duke himself is like a false tomb: a sign of death externally glamorous yet inviting 'in men's hearts reproach'.

Thus, illustrating the bare and empty bones of remembrance is one of *The Revenger's Tragedy*'s preoccupations. Nine years crowding into the minute of Vindice's revenge, act III, scene v is paradigmatic of this phenomenon. He appears with his skull 'dressed up in tires'. He then repeatedly reveals and hides the skull beneath its clothing in a procedure which culminates in Vindice presenting the skull to the Duke: first he presents the skull as a new mistress, allowing him to kiss its poisoned lips, then he reveals the hidden skull to him. However, in hiding and revealing the skull beneath the clothing repeatedly, the scene plays with three kinds of suggestion. First, it presents the skull as a plaything rather than a thing of honour. Second, it presents the dead as the playthings of the living, implying their powerlessness against 'blottings out' by the living raised earlier by the Duke. Third, it presents, in T.S. Eliot's phrase, 'the skull beneath the skin',[21] illustrating human existence as an empty material. When the Duke then fails to distinguish the living from the dead skull, he too implies the emptiness of human life and matter.

That emptiness is also brought out in Vindice's conversations with the skull. For example:

> Madam, his grace will not be absent long.
> Secret? Ne'er doubt us, madam; 'twill be worth
> Three velvet gowns to your ladyship. Known?
> Few ladies respect that! Disgrace? A poor thin shell,

---

[19] *The Revenger's Tragedy*, I.ii.1–10.
[20] *The Revenger's Tragedy*, I.ii.11–16; emphasis mine.
[21] The famous phrase appears in Eliot's poem 'Whispers of Immortality', where it applies to John Webster, but for the reasons I have outlined it is descriptive of this scene too.

> 'Tis the best grace you have to do it well.
> I'll save your hand that labour, I'll unmask you.
> [*Reveals the skull*]²²

Addressing the skull as 'madam' amounts to treating it as a person. Moreover, Vindice's various questions to the skull each treat it as such, seemingly imagining it might reply and therefore making its repeated silences – each implying the skull is empty – deafening.

The play makes striking dramatic capital of this emptiness. Notably, Vindice observes that the 'show / And useless property' of the skull 'shall bear a *part* / *E'en* in its own revenge' (III.v.99–101; my emphasis), bringing out the generic role of corpses in tragedies of revenge, but also the impossibility of the action since skulls cannot perform. Thus, Vindice again ironizes the mechanics of a genre in which the dead have – through remembrance – had a role. Similarly, in lines referred to previously, Vindice claimed the '*very* ragged bone' would become 'sufficiently revenged'. Such paradoxical 'evens' and 'verys' highlight a dramatic impossibility, satirizing the genre persistently.

Demystifying it in a variety of passages, *The Revenger's Tragedy* mocks remembrances of the dead, presenting a parody of a genre in which, as we have seen, remembrance gives rise to revenge. Here is a final example of such demystification. Having plotted Lussurioso's death, Supervacuo and Ambitioso are surprised to run into him:

> *Enter* LUSSURIOSO.
> LUSSURIOSO   Now, my lords!
> BOTH   O!
> LUSSORIOSO   Why do you shun me, brothers?
>   You may come nearer now,
>   The savour of the prison has forsook me.
>   I thank such kind lords as yourselves, I'm free.
> AMBITIOSO   Alive!
> SUPERVACUO   In health!
> AMBITIOSO   Releas'd!²³

Ambitioso and Supervacuo are surprised by Lussurioso, and shun him, not just because they fear him, but also because they are surprised to find him, in their phrase, 'Alive!' The implication, thus, is that they briefly take him for a ghost. Quickly, however, they realise that is a mistake, the scene thereby suggesting the over-credulity of believers in ghosts. Repeated allusions to prayer for the dead two scenes earlier give the satirical scene an edge: Ambitioso worries about the execution of Junior because

>   the gaping people
> Will trouble him at his prayers
> And make him curse and swear, an so die black.²⁴

---

²² *The Revenger's Tragedy*, III.v.44–9.
²³ *The Revenger's Tragedy*, III.vi.55–61.
²⁴ *The Revenger's Tragedy*, III.iv.20–2.

When Junior does curse, an officer advices that 'those words were better chang'd to prayers, / The time's but brief with you, prepare to die' (III.iv.27–8); and we also hear (at some length) that before his supposed death Lussurioso could not be induced 'once to pray' (III.vi.46). Thus, the drama leading up to the supposed sighting of Lussurioso as a ghost presents notably Catholic views of remembrance, making the demystification of the 'ghost' especially pointed.

The Revenger's Tragedy is, then, the very opposite of a play defending the extensive mourning of traditional revengers as 'fit'. In place of prolonged mournings, a series of passages expresses the futility of remembrance, ironizing the mournful vengefulness of Vindice and distancing us from his act. Yet if Middleton thus 'ignores' the dramatic option of 'exploring sympathetically the sensibility of his hero',[25] *The Revenger's Tragedy* is well aware of the affective and extensively mournful style. To present a striking example, when Ambitioso and Supervacuo hear their plot to murder Lussurioso has – as they think – succeeded, Ambitioso comments directly on funerary emotion:

> Our sorrows are so fluent
> Our eyes o'erflow our tongues. Words spoke in tears
> Are like the murmurs of the waters, the sound
> Is loudly heard but cannot be distinguished.[26]

Again, however, the view of extended remembrance is ironic. Even as Ambitioso performs his sorrow, he pronounces the remembrance a convoluted and confused language in which eyes overflow tongues and sounds are indistinguishable, implying the mourning is without sense. Indeed, though 'Babylon' is not invoked here, it is strongly suggested.

Thus, in stark and telling contrast to all the tragedies considered hitherto, the end of *The Revenger's Tragedy* is an illustration of restraint in mourning. When Vindice and Hippolito announce they were the Duke's murderers, Vindice is initially surprised to find Antonio – the murder's beneficiary – will punish them. Eventually, however, he *reasons* himself into acknowledging the justice of punishment:

> May not we set as well as the Duke's son?
> Thou hast no conscience; are we not revenged?
> Is there no enemy left alive amongst those?
> 'Tis time to die when we are ourselves our foes.[27]

Rather than mourning death, Vindice's rhetorical questions all aim to establish acceptance of it: thus, ''Tis time to die when we are ourselves our foes.' That line implies, I have suggested, an embrace of death in which there is neither sorrow nor complaint.

As a whole, the end is devoid of extravagant emotion. Vindice continues by coolly analyzing his demise:

---

[25] Loughrey and Taylor (ed.), p. xv.
[26] *The Revenger's Tragedy*, III.vi.39–42.
[27] *The Revenger's Tragedy*, V.iii.107–10.

> When murd'rers shut deeds close this curse does seal 'em;
> If none disclose 'em they themselves reveal 'em
> This murder might have slept in tongueless brass,
> But for ourselves, and the world died an ass.[28]

However, notice that Vindice supports his reasoning with an implicit message about remembrance. Thus, the murder sleeps not in evocative tombs, but 'in *tongueless brass*': monuments deprived of the power of speech. And the bodies are 'shut ... close', 'sealed' and dependent on the living ('ourselves') to leave any impression. Thus, it is not the dead that cry out for vengeance, but the living who decide to be revenged, the power of the dead being so little that 'but for ourselves and the world died an ass'.

Still devoid of mournful emotion, the final lines are a formal tidying up of loose ends, being explanatory, to the point, and wholly without melodrama:

> And now, my lord, since we are in for ever
> This work was ours, which else might have been slipp'd,
> And if we list we could have nobles clipp'd
> And go for less than beggars; but we hate
> To bleed so cowardly. We have enough, i'faith:
> We're well, our mother turn'd, our sister true;
> We die after a nest of dukes. Adieu.
> *Exeunt* [Vindice and Hippolito *under guard*].[29]

'We have enough': by contrast to preceding tragedies, this phrase summarizes the determination not to complain pervading both the speech and the little that follows. Moreover, the stage direction removing Vindice and Hippolito denies audiences either the pathos of two dramatized deaths or the funeral and mourning that might have followed. Finally, amid such death, the death of the play is like a quickly 'closed' coffin:

> How subtly was that murder clos'd! Bear up
> Those tragic bodies; 'tis a heavy season.
> Pray heaven their blood may wash away all treason!
>   *Exeunt.*[30]

The resolving of the Duke's murder is briefly wondered at, the bodies briefly removed, the 'season' briefly mourned. There is the briefest prayer – for virtue in the living, not for the dead – and this least melodramatic ending is over, its Reformist remembrances performed.

---

[28] *The Revenger's Tragedy*, V.iii.110–14.
[29] *The Revenger's Tragedy*, V.iii.120–6.
[30] *The Revenger's Tragedy*, V.iii.127–9.

The Atheist's Tragedy, c.1611

Presenting figures overtly puritan as well as atheistic, *The Atheist's Tragedy* is another revenge tragedy foregrounding religious perspective. In the atheist D'Amville, Tourneur presents an obviously 'damned' picture of atheism, but as we shall see, the atheist and puritan are one in their contempt for extensive funerary ritual and the 'superstition' associated with it. Thus, as a drama of the seventeenth century, Tourneur's play is partisan, but it was also prophetic: as we have observed, the 'tantamount to secular' burial service of *The Directory for the Public Worship of God* (1644) was created by 'advanced' Reformers;[31] seemingly, thus, Tourneur foresaw the secularity to which continuing Reform led. Three other unusual features of *The Atheist's Tragedy* demand our preliminary attention too.

The first is the treatment of revenge, for it has been recognized that 'The significance of the *The Atheist's Tragedy* in the tradition of Elizabethan revenge plays lies in the fact that it is the first play in which a revenger is specifically forbidden to take revenge.'[32] Dramatized revenge combining hitherto with funerary remembrance, this seemingly bears on our study. Yet although *The Atheist's Tragedy* cleanly reverses established patterns of revenge, we shall see that with traditional remembrances it makes no clean break. Indeed, although there is a persistently unstable irony in the presentation, as we shall see,[33] the play brings forward more skulls, deaths, laments and performances of ghosts – thus, more deliberate remembrance of the dead – than any tragedy considered until this point.

Belying a scholarly interest in rites of remembrance, the second unusual feature of *The Atheist's Tragedy* is the presence in its midst of Lucretius's *De Rerum Natura*. In act IV, Languebeau Snuff, the Puritan, finds D'Amville sliding toward 'superstition', and therefore rebukes the atheist: 'walking spirits are but imaginary fables. There's no such thing in *rerum natura*' (IV.iii.275).

De Rerum Natura presenting an extended attack on ritual religion, this allusion is conspicuously relevant, especially as the play's Puritan Reformer evokes it. For Lucretius presents *Epicurus* as a champion who, 'When man's life lay for all to see foully grovelling upon the ground, crushed beneath the weight of Superstition ... was the first to raise his mortal eyes against her, the first to make stand against her.' He goes on: 'Therefore Superstition is now in her turn cast down and trampled underfoot, whilst we [humanity] by the victory are exalted high as heaven.'[34] Even anticipating Reformed objections to the Sacrifice of the Mass, Lucretius's paradigm

---

[31] For discussion of the rite, see the Introduction, p. 15–16.

[32] *Cyril Tourneur: The Atheist's Tragedy*, ed. by Brian Morris and Roma Gill (London: A. & C. Black; New York: W.W. Norton, 1976; 1989), p. xxii. All citations from the play will be from this edition.

[33] 'Unstable irony ... offers no fixed standpoint which is not undercut by further ironies'. See *A Glossary of Literary Terms*, ed. by M.H. Abrams, 5th edn (Fort Worth, TX: Holt, Rinehart and Winston, 1988).

[34] Lucretius, *De Rerum Natura*, trans. by W.H.D. Rouse, rev. by Martin Ferguson Smith (Cambridge, MA: Harvard University Press; London: William Heinemann, 1975), pp. 7–9. Such representations of 'superstition', though not always so direct, permeate the poem.

of man superstitiously 'grovelling upon the ground' is ritual human sacrifice. Lucretius makes this clear in his opening address to the reader:

> One thing I fear in this matter, that in this your apprenticeship to philosophy you may perhaps see impiety, and the entering on a path of crime; wheras on the contrary more often it is that very Superstition which has brought forth criminal and impious deeds: as when at Aulis the altar of our Lady of the Crossways [Diana] was foully defiled by the blood of Iphianassa, shed by chosen leaders of the Danai, chieftains of the host. So soon as the ribbon had bound her maiden tresses falling in equal lengths down either cheek, so soon as she saw her father standing sorrowful before the altar, and by his side attendants hiding the knife, and the people shedding tears at the sight of her, dumb with dread, she sank to the ground upon her knees. Alas, poor girl! no help could it be to her at such a time that the name of father had been bestowed on the king first by her; for uplifted by the hands of men, all trembling she was brought to the altar, not that amidst solemn and sacred ritual she might be escorted by loud hymeneal song, but a clean maiden to fall by unclean hands at the very age of wedlock, a victim sorrowful slain by a father's hand: all in order that a fair and fortunate release might be given to the fleet. So potent was Superstition in persuading to evil deeds.[35]

Thus, in making Snuff invoke *rerum natura*, Tourneur presents his anti-massing Puritan as a seventeenth-century Epicurean; moreover, Snuff's view that evoking *rerum natura* will help remind D'Amville to stand against 'superstition' suggests Tourneur considered Puritan intellectualism encouraged atheism.

Also belying deliberate views of religion and ritual, the third unusual feature of *The Atheist's Tragedy* is its direct evocation of the Siege of Ostend (1601–1604). Besides foregrounding a war between Catholic Spain and the Free Protestant Dutch,[36] the play thus evokes a scene of exceptional burial. Dutch casualties alone at the siege exceeded 130,000, and many bodies went unburied: in the twentieth century, 'human skeletons found on the beaches and in the town itself' were still 'as familiar as the driftwood and shells which lie partially buried in sand'.[37] Thus, in conjuring an extensive picture of corpses of solders 'cast upon / The sands' (II.i.74–5) to be noticed further, the play's constant and complex concern with funeral illuminates a historical reality.

---

[35] *De Rerum Natura*, pp. 9–11.

[36] Profiting from a truce between the United Provinces (Holland) and the Spanish Regime in the Southern Netherlands (Belgium), the Free Protestant Dutch took Ostend under the generalship of Prince Maurits in 1601. The Spanish besieged the town, but it was supported by sea, possibly even by the English. In 1604, however, the Spanish general Spinola of Genoa recaptured the town. The siege was part of an ongoing and larger struggle between Spain and Holland for the region. For details, see Pieter Geyl, *The Revolt of the Netherlands, 1555–1609* (London: Cassell, 1988).

[37] See Diane Lesko, 'Ensor in his Milieu', *Artforum* 15/9 (May 1977), pp. 56–62 (56), and Gert Schiff, 'James Ensor: Skeletons in the Studio', in *Annual Bulletin* 4 (1980–1981), pp. 1–4 (1). My previous descriptions of the battle derive from these sources.

Death is already at the centre of the 'baldly conceptual' expression of atheism by D'Amville at the play's opening.[38] Thus, presenting an Epicurean *carpe diem*,[39] it is because 'death casts up / Our total sum of joy and happiness' that D'Amville decides to be 'feasted in / Th' abundant fulness of delight at once' (I.i.16–20). *The Atheist's Tragedy* argues *this* Epicurean is mistaken by showing D'Amville's decline into the very superstitions of the afterlife he here denounces implicitly; however, along the way it presents a series of remembrances of the dead notable, as I have said, for their unstable irony. Regarding the foregrounded religion, extensive performances of mourning become indistinguishable from their ironic parodies, the play performing an uneasy game of *trompe l'œil*, or rather *trompe l'émotion*, in which the religion – Reformist or traditional – becomes challengingly unclear.

The first substantial enactment of post-mortem remembrance in the play is illustrative. In dramatic terms, it is a parody of a remembrance, yet it reflects a historical reality, thus presenting an authentic mourning. In a lengthy speech rich in evocative imagery, Borachio falsely persuades Montferrers that his son has died at the Siege of Ostend.[40] I quote from the passage at length: it is only thus that the extensiveness of this historical remembrance of victims of a religious war is clear:

MONTFERRERS O what became of my dear Charlemont?
BORACHIO   Walking next day upon that fatal shore,
                          Among the slaughtered bodies of their men
                          Which the full-stomached sea had cast upon
                          The sands, it was m'unhappy chance to light
                          Upon a face, whose favour when it lived
                          My astonished mind informed me I had seen.
                          He lay in's armour as if that had been
                          His coffin, and the weeping sea, like one
                          Whose milder temper doth lament the death
                          Of him whom in his rage he slew, runs up
                          The shore, embraces him, kisses his cheek,
                          Goes back again, and forces up the sands
                          To bury him, and every time it parts
                          Sheds tears upon him, till at last, as if
                          It could not longer endure to see the man
                          Whom it had slain, yet loath to leave him, with
                          A kind of unresoloved unwilling pace,
                          Winding her waves one in another, like
                          A man that folds his arms or wrings his hands
                          For grief, ebbed from the body and descends,
                          As if it would sink down into the earth
                          And hide itself for shame of such a deed.[41]

---

[38] For details, see Morris and Gill (ed.), pp. x–xi.
[39] Horace, who humorously styled himself 'a pig from Epicurus's sty', gives us *carpe diem* in reference to Epicurus.
[40] That it is the Battle of Ostend is clear at II.i.27–33.
[41] *The Atheist's Tragedy*, II.i.71–93.

D'Amville has previously told Borachio to feign Charlemont's death, so for the purposes of the plot this performance of grief is feigned and permeated with irony. Yet as I previously observed, Borachio's substantial evocation of Ostend's dead 'cast upon / The sands' reflects a historical reality, the remembrance being in *this* way truthful.[42]

Borachio's picture of 'Charlemont' found by the sea implies a most emotional mourning for the dead: the 'weeping' sea is 'like one / Whose milder temper doth lament the death'; it 'embraces him, kisses his cheek', even 'wrings his [its] hands for grief'. Moreover, the sea performs a burial. Charlemont allegedly 'lay in's armour as if that had been / His coffin' as the sea 'forces up the sands / To bury him, and ... / Sheds tears upon him'. Making the sea a most direct mourner, the passage moves from a simile of a funerary sea ('as if that had been / His coffin') to a metaphorical action of 'burial' in which sea and funeral seem one, subverting irony. For Borachio is, in D'Amville's phrase, a 'sweet *eloquent* villain' (II.i.115; my emphasis): his speech is mournfully moving. And yet, in the play's characteristic style, in thus bringing out Borachio's *rhetorical* eloquence, D'Amville restores somewhat the ironic perspective of the plot, dividing responses to the speech and its remembrance.

The uncertainty of 'unstable irony' occurs again when the 'news' of Montferrers's murder reaches his murderer, D'Amville. For the benefit of those watching, D'Amville pretends great sorrow, his performance for the dead man being 'a sweet comedy. 'T begins with *O Dolentis* and concludes with ha, ha, he.' (II.iv.85). Yet before considering the remembrance and scene further, notice the self-conscious Catholicism of this statement: 'O Dolentis' recalls the *Kyrie Eleison* of the Latin mass; praying for the 'purging' of souls, its final line is: 'Kyrie, expurgator scelerum et largitor gratiæ; quæsumus propter nostras offensas noli nos relinquere, *O consolator dolentis* animæ, eleison.'[43] Thus, in turning the *Kyrie Eleison* to extensive 'comedy', D'Amville makes a joke of Catholicism's remembrance; yet since D'Amville's joke is deeply sinister, it is also and simultaneously the *misuse* of Catholic remembrance the scene condemns.

Being conspicuously related to the *Kyrie Eleison*, D'Amville's self-consciously Catholic remembrance exemplifies the genre's religio-funerary debt: entailing repeated rhetorical questions and exclamations, invocation of the heavens and persistent hyperbole – dead tongues, tennis-ball eyes – the remembrance suggests the characteristically extravagant style of revengers since Hieronimo. A taste of the eighteen-line lament that follows is illustrative:

---

[42] Notably, this speech has been singled out from the play for its evocativeness. See for example the discussion of *The Atheist's Tragedy* in *The Oxford Companion to English Literature*, ed. by Margaret Drabble (Oxford: Oxford University Press, 1985).

[43] The lines translate: 'Lord, *Purger* of sin and Almoner of grace, we beseech Thee abandon us not because of our Sins, O Consoler of the sorrowing soul, have mercy on us' (my emphasis), thus especially focusing on the 'purging' of sin from souls. My quotation from the *Kyrie Eleison* and its translation are taken from the *Catholic Encyclopedia*, www.newadvent.org/cathen/08714a.htm, last accessed 3 November 2007.

> Dead be your tongues! Drop out
> Mine eye-balls, and let envious Fortune play
> At tennis balls with 'em. Have I lived to this?
> Malicious Nature! Hadst thou born me blind,
> Th'hadst yet been something favourable to me.
> No breath? No motion? Prithee tell me, Heaven,
> Hast shut thine eye to wink at murder, or
> Hast put this sable garment on to mourn
> At's death?[44]

Of particular note is the image of Heaven in the 'sable garment' of mourning: it presents a cosmic funeral especially recalling the 'burning eyes of heaven / And passion in the gods' of *Hamlet*.[45]

Making extensive distinctions between correct and incorrect styles of mourning, *The Atheist's Tragedy* deliberately explores contrasting religious views of D'Amville's 'Catholic' remembrance. Knowing nothing of D'Amville's mockery, Belforest (who has Puritan sympathies since Languebeau Snuff is his chaplain) begins a controversy by expressing Reformist views:

> Passion transports you. Recollect yourself.
> Lament him not. Whether our deaths be good
> Or bad, it is not death but life that tries.
> He lived well, therefore questionless well dies.[46]

Belforest identifies D'Amville's supposed 'passion' for the dead as excessive, recommending it therefore cease. He then offers an alternative definition of how death should be approached: by thinking of the living. Ruling out purgatorial trial, his claim 'it is not death but life that tries' is especially pointed, though Belforest dismisses the implied controversy by making it 'questionless'. However, especially as in the era a 'trial' implied 'to purify by fire',[47] Belforest's version of death contains none of the purifying fire of purgatory.

Still emphasizing D'Amville's 'excessive' performance of emotion for the dead, the religious contention continues:

> D'AMVILLE Ay, 'tis an easy thing for him that has
> No pain to talk of patience. Do you think
> That Nature has no feeling?
> BELFOREST Feeling? Yes,
> But has she purposed anything for nothing?
> What good receives this body by your grief?
> Whether is't more unnatural not to grieve
> For him you cannot help with it, or hurt
> Yourself with grieving and yet grieve in vain?[48]

---

[44] *The Atheist's Tragedy*, II.iv.25–33.
[45] For my discussion of these funerary lines in *Hamlet*, see Chapter 1, p. 63–4.
[46] *The Atheist's Tragedy*, II.iv.43–6.
[47] See O.E.D., 2nd edn (1989), definition 3 of 'to try'.
[48] *The Atheist's Tragedy*, II.iv.47–55.

Maintaining his traditionalist act, D'Amville defends his style of remembrance on the grounds that Belforest speaks without experience, the controversy thus coming to centre on 'feeling' for the dead. However, in two further rhetorical questions and one statement, Belforest insists that affectively mourning the dead is useless. Because such mourning 'purposes' nothing, provides no 'good' for the corpse and 'cannot help with it' (and also because the mourner's grief may damage him), Belforest labels D'Amville's style 'unnatural'. Highlighting the implicit Reform, the Puritan chaplain Languebeau Snuff observes '*our* opposition' to D'Amville's style (II.iv.83; my emphasis).

D'Amville's eighteen-line response to Belforest is a combination of seemingly passionate argument and remembrance, itself ending overtly

> wi' tears –
> With tears – yes, faith, with tears.[49]

Still not giving way, however, Belforest demands that any further remembrance is restrained and thus 'reasonable':

> Take up the corpse.
> For wisdom's sake, let reason fortify
> This weakness.[50]

Ironically, of course, in imposing Reformed views of remembrance on D'Amville, Belforest plays into the atheist's hands. With mock-reluctance, D'Amville stops lamenting, claiming his 'shower of tears has laid it [his grief]' – a claim Snuff and Belforest allow on the comically hypocritical grounds that 'Passion resisted grows more violent' (II.iv.78; 83). However, D'Amville wants the body forgotten not only because he is the murderer, but also because, as we have seen, his atheism convinces him of the emptiness of death: implicitly, he too considers remembrances of the dead useless. Prophetically, thus, as the gradual Reform of burial customs ushered in the tantamount to secular burial rite of 1644,[51] so Belforest's Reformist outlook facilitates that of the atheist D'Amville. In D'Amville's ironic words, the 'precisian'

> came religiously and saved
> Our project from suspicion.[52]

And thus, ironically, atheist and Reformer murder Catholic remembrance together: 'O Dolentis concludes with ha, ha, he'.

Throughout the play, ambiguous contrasts of extravagant *and* ironic remembrance endure. The play's response to this ambiguity, however, is an unusually close scrutiny of the psychology of performed remembrance. Thus, although he has yet to learn that Montferrers is dead, in act II, scene vi, Charlemont analyzes the seeming appearance of his father's ghost, his first instinct being to discount supernatural explanations

---

[49] *The Atheist's Tragedy*, II.iv.71–2.
[50] *The Atheist's Tragedy*, II.iv.72–4.
[51] For my discussion of this development, see the Introduction, p. 15–16.
[52] *The Atheist's Tragedy*, II.iv.116; 120–21.

in favour of a trick of memory or of disturbed humours. Rejecting the humoural theory because 'my nature [is not] wont / To trouble me with fantasies of terror' (II.vi.33–4), he considers tricks of memory, initially considering this a more plausible cause of ghostly visions. Highlighting each step of an argument, Charlemont first considers the ghost a dream, defining this as,

> the raised
> Impression of premeditated things
> By serious apprehension left upon
> Our minds…[53]

Thus, dreams are a form of memory. However, next rejecting this explanation because 'my mind has not been moved / With any one conception of a thought / To such a purpose' (II.vi.31–3), Charlemont returns to this theory when he realizes that this self-analysis was incorrect:

> My actions daily conversant with war,
> The argument of blood and death, had left,
> Perhaps, th'imaginary presence of
> Some bloody accident upon my mind,
> Which, mixed confusedly with other thoughts,
> Whereof th'remembrance of my father might
> Be one, presented all together seem
> Incorporate, as if his body were
> The owner of that blood, the subject of
> That death, when he's at Paris and that blood
> Shed here.[54]

Again suggesting the dramatic import of the Siege of Ostend, Charlemont eventually decides that the 'ghost' was, among other thoughts, a memory of Ostend's dead superimposed upon a memory of his father. Crucially, however, Charlemont's favoured explanation of 'ghosts' is the memory of bloodied, often unburied, corpses.

Accompanying this scrutiny of memory is an equally close scrutiny of its natural or supernatural identity. As we have seen, Charlemont initially explains the apparition in terms of different kinds of illusions, rationalizing it as a natural phenomenon. His detailed explanations, however, are offset by what the audience know of the plot: that the ghost's claim that 'thy old father's dead / And thou by murder disinherited' (II.vi.19–20) is true. Moreover, the scene forces Charlemont to acknowledge the supernatural in memorial enactments. No sooner has he come to the end of his explanations than the ghostly Montferrers reappears, being put to the test by the Musketeer:

---

[53] *The Atheist's Tragedy*, II.vi.24–7.
[54] *The Atheist's Tragedy*, II.vi.49–59.

> Stand, stand I say. No? Why then, have at thee.
> Sir, if you will not stand, I'll make you fall.
> Nor stand, nor fall? Nay, then the Devil's dam
> Has broke her husband's head, for sure it is a spirit.
> I shot it through, and yet it will not fall.[55]

Continuing the scene's analytical mode, this speech emphasizes the formal developments of logic. Thus, *if* the apparition does not stand then it will be shot; but if it does not then fall, *then* it is a spirit. Repeating the point, the final line ensures we see the logic: 'I shot it through, and yet it will not fall.'

There is also irony here. Invoking the 'Devil's dam', the Musketeer implies he considers the apparition demonic, his naive behaviour also suggesting laughter. However, the scene insists the logical claims are not only of a simpleton: emphasizing a change in his thinking too, Charlemont is persuaded by the shooting that the apparition is a true remembrance:

> O pardon me. My doubtful heart was slow
> To credit that which I did fear to know.[56]

Pointedly, in this play about superstition, he also here implies people *fear* acknowledging the supernatural in remembrances.

Presenting the funeral of Montferrers and the mock-funeral of Charlemont in a 'church' (III.i.64), act III, scene i continues its ambiguous remembrances in an explicitly religious setting in which – not for the first time in this study – church and theatre overlap. The performances of remembrance are noteworthy.

Montferrers is given 'the rites that do belong / To soldiers' because he 'held open war with sin', while both father and son are proclaimed Christian heroes, 'two Herculean pillars':

> His life's example was so true
> A pratique of religion's theory
> That her divinity seemed rather the
> Description than th'instruction of his life.
> And of his goodness was his virtuous son
> A worthy imitator.[57]

As D'Amville speaks these lines, there is irony in the performance; however, like Borachio's fake remembrance of Charlemont at Ostend,[58] the speech cannot be reduced to a parody. Being performed for those at the funeral, these lines too contain the 'sweet eloquence' D'Amville earlier commended in Borachio, being thus affective despite the speaker. Thus, the audience can see the irony, but it hears the mourning.

---

[55] *The Atheist's Tragedy*, II.vi.62–6.
[56] *The Atheist's Tragedy*, II.vi.67–8.
[57] *The Atheist's Tragedy*, III.i.44; 38–43.
[58] See above, p. 109–10.

The scene also presents two lengthy epitaphs as part of what D'Amville calls 'a living monument / To let succeeding ages truly know' the histories of the dead (III.i.2–3). Here, then, the irony evoked by the person of the speaker contrasts with the allegedly 'true' use of monuments. Containing much religious suggestiveness, Montferrers's epitaph is as follows:

> *The Epitaph of* Montferrers
> *Here lie the ashes of that earth and fire*
> *Whose heat and fruit did feed and warm the poor.*
> *And they, as if they would in sighs expire*
> *And into tears dissolve, his death deplore.*
> *He did that good freely, for goodness sake,*
> *Unforced, for generousness he held so dear*
> *That he feared none but Him that did him make,*
> *And yet he served Him more for love than fear.*
>   *So life provided that though he did die*
>   *A sudden death, yet died not suddenly.*[59]

This epitaph not only offers the standard Christian consolation that the dead man 'died not suddenly';[60] it presents 'the poor' expiring in sighs and dissolving in tears for him, thus presenting not only traditionally performed remembrances, but also the traditional contract in which the poor were rewarded for praying for a wealthy benefactor.[61] That such traditional behaviour associates with the very 'pratique of religion's theory' (III.i.40) speaks loudly in Protestant England – despite the irony of the speaker – for Catholic remembrance.

By contrast, Charlemont's epitaph focuses on his early death in battle, but as 'a worthy imitator' of his father his traditional religion is implied. Bringing out Charlemont's martial death, moreover, presents a more specific link with Montferrers. D'Amville notes that 'The father / Held open war with sin, the son with blood' (III.i.10–11), uniting the father's spiritual war with the son's physical. Including occasions like the focal Siege of Ostend, military battle entails a spiritual struggle. In view of the contemporary concerns over dying a good death, the end of the epitaph is notable:

> *He did not suffer an untimely death,*
> *But we may say of his blest decease:*
> *He died in war, and yet he died in peace.*[62]

---

[59] *The Atheist's Tragedy*, III.i.44; 38–43.

[60] For my discussion of the significance of deathbed performances in the contemporary Christian thinking, see the Introduction, p. 4, note 13. For further discussion, see Gittings, 'Sacred and Secular', pp. 154–6.

[61] As Greenblatt observes, 'masses for the dead were closely linked to almsgiving'. See *Hamlet in Purgatory*, p. 148. The link is visible in my citation of the *View of Popish Abuses* in the Introduction, p. 7.

[62] *The Atheist's Tragedy*, III.i.33–5.

Though there is always the unstable irony of D'Amville speaking, death at Ostend is remembered as a 'blest' decease. Thus, if Montferrers is a warrior against sin, Charlemont is a crusader for religious truth.

The end of the funeral is not the end of the memorial: stage directions remove the characters on stage and present Castabella 'mourning, to the monument of CHARLEMONT'. Thus, the emotional remembrances she will perform no longer entail irony by depending on D'Amville, though the further irony that Charlemont is alive remains.

Castabella begins with a performed prayer that the 'sacrifice' of her 'tears' for Charlemont be acceptable to God:

> O Thou that know'st me justly Charlemont's,
> Though in the forced possession of another,
> Since from thine own free spirit we receive it
> That our affections cannot be compelled
> Though our actions may, be not displeased if on
> The altar of his tomb I sacrifice
> My tears.[63]

Besides displaying overtly emotional remembrance, this speech also implies there is an 'altar' above Charlemont's tomb, highlighting contemporary controversy as altars had been replaced with 'communion tables' by Reformers keen to play down the massing associations of 'sacrifice'.[64] Especially as Castabella prays her 'sacrifice' will not 'displease', in a generic tradition taking in *Titus Andronicus*, *Antonio's Revenge* and now *The Atheist's Tragedy*, revenge tragedy makes dramatic capital of the contemporary controversy associating the remembrances of the dead and the Eucharist.[65]

The entrance of Charlemont to discover 'the fatal monument / Of my dead father' (III.i.65–6), as well as 'My Castabella mourning o'er my hearse' (III.i.71), not only ironizes but also extends the performance of mourning. For Charlemont ends the scene by highlighting his overpowering grief before the tomb:

> Of all men's griefs, must mine be singular?
> Without example? Here I met my grave,
> And all men's woes are buried in their graves
> But mine. In mine my miseries are born.
> I prithee sorrow, leave a little room
> In my confounded and tormented mind
> For understanding to deliberate
> The cause or author of this accident –[66]

---

[63] *The Atheist's Tragedy*, III.i.53–9.
[64] For an example of such Reformed action, see the alterations to Paul's Cathedral in Chapter 2, p. 79.
[65] For my discussion of this contemporary association, see the Introduction, p. 3–4.
[66] *The Atheist's Tragedy*, III.i.130–7.

That Charlemont should mourn at his own tomb suggests irony; however, that his emotional display contrasts explicitly with those whose woes die with them, and that his mourning is for his father, makes it authentic.

Entailing a complex dramatic response, however, irony is also present in Castabella's reaction to Charlemont's appearance. Initially considering him a ghost, Castabella swoons; defying irony, however, Charlemont persuades her to accept his reality in a complex argument:

> Reduce thy understanding to thine eye.
> Within this habit which thy misinformed
> Conceit takes only for a shape live both
> The soul and body of thy Charlemont.[67]

Even as he persuades Castabella to see him as 'thy Charlemont', Charlemont urges an epistemology based exclusively on visual perception: '*Reduce* thy understanding to thine eye'. With inevitably controversial implication in this funerary setting, thus, Charlemont persuades Castabella to take performances for truth.

Testing funerary performances for their truthfulness continues in the following scene, in which D'Amville, Sebastian and the Puritan, Languebeau Snuff, each briefly take Charlemont for a figure from the grave. The complicated passage opens as follows:

> *Enter* CHARLEMONT; D'AMVILLE *counterfeits to take him for a ghost*
> D'AMVILLE What art thou! Stay! Assist me troubled sense.
> My apprehension will distract me. Stay!
> LANGUEBEAU SNUFF *avoids him fearfully*
> SEBASTIAN What art thou? Speak!
> CHARLEMONT   The spirit of Charlemont.
> D'AMVILLE O stay. Compose me. I dissolve.
> LANGUEBEAU No, 'tis profane. Spirits are invisible. 'Tis the fiend i' th' likeness of Charlemont. I will have no conversation with Satan.
> *Exit* [Languebeau] SNUFF
> SEBASTIAN The spirit of Charlemont? I'll try that.
> *Strike[s], and the blow[s] returned*
> 'For God, thou sayest true; th'art all spirit.'[68]

Reactions to this 'ghostly' remembrance of Charlemont run on characteristically religious lines. The atheist, Charlemont, only pretends fearful belief. The Puritan, Languebeau – who proclaims spirits 'invisible' – thinks he has met the devil.[69] Sebastian's pragmatic response is to 'try' the figure, but the trial leads to a comic paradox: Charlemont is human but also 'all spirit'. Proclaiming such spirituality a 'lie' (III.ii.29), Sebastian next tries killing Charlemont, but just as the clash of their weapons suggests a *material* Charlemont, the Ghost of Montferrers enters. Thus, the

---

[67] *The Atheist's Tragedy*, III.i.78–81.
[68] *The Atheist's Tragedy*, III.ii.18–26.
[69] Marshall notes the historical and religio–political aspect of this claim by the Puritan on p. 257 of *Beliefs and the Dead*.

scene concludes its trial on contradictory notes: apparently, there are both fraudulent *and* real memorials seen as ghosts – or, at least, more and less real representations of the dead. Crucially in this finally inconclusive trial, however, beliefs about the dead – here indistinguishable from beliefs about *performances* of remembrance – run according to religious viewpoint. Being 'between the passion of / My blood and the religion of my soul' (III.ii.35–6), in Charlemont's phrase, there is a contrast of felt remembrance and religious doubt.

Opening in a churchyard as the clock strikes twelve, act IV, scene iii heightens the emphasis on religion and its supernatural beliefs. Arriving for a sexual encounter with Soquette under cover of night, the Puritan Languebeau Snuff implies the religious dilemmas: the church is, he says, 'the house which *the superstitious* call St Winifred's church' (IV.iii.53–4; my emphasis); moreover, 'There's a talk ... that the ghost of old Montferrers walks' as 'In this church he was buried' (IV.iii.59–61). Unreformed rumour and belief, of which Snuff is contemptuous, seems rife.

In a passage thick with irony, however, the scene contrasts Snuff's comically sexual encounter with Soquette with the ghastly attempted rape of Castabella by D'Amville. The atheist's motives are themselves to do with remembrance, suggesting Christian parody: with his lineage in 'ruins' (IV.iii.117; 122), D'Amville hopes to 'Raise his eternal monument' (IV.iii.121) through Castabella. Moreover, as we shall see, both of the scene's botched versions of sexuality are ironically performed over the highly visible 'bones' of the dead, Charlemont's to-ing and fro-ing between the two pairs also linking Snuffe's farcical sexuality with D'Amville's ghastly equivalent. The scene is fraught with unstable irony and, as I suggested earlier, *trompes l'émotions*. To make sense of its meanings, I consider the elements separately, beginning with Languebeau and farce.

Languebeau's plan in coming to the churchyard is to disguise his sexual hypocrisy. Suggesting contemporary religious beliefs, however, he tells Soquette that 'if any stranger fall upon us before our business be ended, in this disguise I shall be taken for that ghost [of Montferrers] and never be called to examination' (V.iii.61–3). When Charlemont enters, he disturbs the 'business' of the pair, who exit separately. When Languebeau returns, looking for Soquette, he mistakes the corpse of Borachio – earlier killed by Charlemont – for that of Soquette:

Soquette! Soquette! O art thou there?
   He mistakes the body of BORACHIO *for* SOQUETTE
Verily, thou liest in a fine premeditate readiness for the purpose. Come, kiss me, sweet Soquette. – Now purity defend me from the sin of Sodom! This is a creature of the masculine gender, – Verily the man is blasted. – Yea, cold and stiff! – Murder, murder, murder.[70]

As the hypocritical Puritan gets his comic come-uppance, such ironies as 'cold *and stiff*' bear notice. Remembering them, however, the corpse of Borachio forces Snuff to call the dead to mind.

The dead are remembered in the scene in other ways too. Stage directions state of Charlemont that 'To get into the charnel house he takes hold of a death's head; it

---

[70] *The Atheist's Tragedy*, IV.iii.206–11.

slips and staggers him'; later, he 'Hides himself in a charnel house'. Thus, there is clowning in the scene, but it is clowning which foregrounds reminders of the dead. There is also, amid this funerary paraphernalia, the other ghastliness: the attempted rape of Castabella.

When Castabella discovers D'Amville's intention, she initially laments her 'prayers and tears in vain', but she then addresses the 'patient Heaven' (IV.iii.162; 163) in further prayer. Revealingly, D'Amville mocks her emotional prayer, assuming its plea is to a dead who might listen:

> cry to the graves
> The dead can hear thee invoke thy help.[71]

This ironic and demystifying mockery, however, is offset by D'Amville's now ghastly persona – what Castabella calls a soul infecting the air

> *more than* the damps that rise
> From bodies but half rotten in their graves.[72]

And D'Amville's irony is further offset by the intervention of Charlemont from – inevitably – the memorial charnel house. For in this dramatic construction, the charnel house seemingly responds to Castabella's prayers, the dead thus seemingly remembering the living, especially as Charlemont enters wearing Snuff's cast-off ghost costume. Castabella's prayer that to escape D'Amville the 'grave might open, and my body' be 'bound to the dead carcass of a man / Forever…' (IV.iii.171–3) also turns out to be ironically answered: she is to be 'bound' to Charlemont (returning from the grave) in marriage.

There are still further ironies. Stage directions indicate that the ghostly Charlemont 'frights D'Amville away', but the atheist is so terrified that when we next meet him he has seemingly developed a conscience; he believes in ghosts (for mistaken reasons) and endlessly and extravagantly remembers the dead:

> Enter D'AMVILLE *distractedly; he starts at the sight of a death's head*
> D'AMVILLE   Why dost thou stare upon me? Thou art not
> The skull of him I murdered. What has thou
> To do to vex my conscience. Sure thou were't
> The head of a most dogged usurer,
> The sky there, the sky there, she could shut her windows and
> The doors of this great chamber of the world,
> And draw the curtains of the clouds between
> Those lights and me about this bed of earth,
> When that same strumpet, Murder, and myself,
> Committed sin together. Then she could
> Leave us i' th' dark till the close deed
> Was done, but now that I begin to feel
> The loathsome horror of my sin and, like

---

[71] *The Atheist's Tragedy*, IV.iii.169–70.
[72] *The Atheist's Tragedy*, IV.iii.153–4; my emphasis.

> A lecher emptied of his lust, desire
> To bury my face under my eyebrows and
> Would steal from my shame unseen, she meets me
> I' th' face with all her light corrupted eyes
> To challenge payment of me. O behold!
> Yonder's the ghost of old Montferrers in
> A long white sheet, climbing yond' lofty mountain
> To complain to Heav'n of me. Montferrers!
> 'Pox o' fearfulness. 'Tis nothing but
> A fair white cloud...[73]

Amid this extended expression of the 'feel' of remembrances, the atheist even comes to believe in Montferrers's ghost – with further irony as at this point he is not on stage. Mistaking Snuff for a ghost soon after, D'Amville will again see ghosts where there are none – for which he will be chastised in the Lucretian style noticed previously: 'their walking spirits are but imaginary fables. There's no such thing in *rerum natura*' (IV.iii.275). By this point, however, Languebeau's opinion – or any other – has become so mired in competing ironies that true remembrance of the dead seems undistinguishable from false. The complex accumulation of implicitly performed but unanswered questions (What is a true remembrance as opposed to a parody? Is parodying a Catholic remembrance immoral? Which religious styles of remembrance are correct? Are ghosts illusory remembrances because performed? Do the dead hear and answer the living?) makes any clear perspective on the matter impossible.

Uncertainty is D'Amville's closing note. Seeking contentment in 'philosophy', he tries to spare Charlemont from the course of law:

> Thou shalt read
> Philosophy to me. I will find out
> Th'efficient cause of a contented mind;
> But if I cannot profit in't, then 'tis
> No more, being my physician, but infuse
> A little poison in a potion when
> Thou giv'st me physic, unawares to me.
> So I shall steal into my grave without
> The understanding or the fear of death,
> And that's the end I aim at, for the thought
> Of death is a most fearful torment; is't not?[74]

Notably, to one who initially (and philosophically) held no fear of it, death has become a 'fearful torment': the remembrances of Montferrers and the churchyard overwhelm the atheist who therefore prefers death to the *thought* of death. Recalling the skull that ironically struck Charlemont on the head in the charnel house – a most forceful reminder – a final irony will present the madman braining himself.

Thus, Charlemont is left with the dramatic burden of memory; for inevitably,

---

[73] *The Atheist's Tragedy*, IV.iii.212–35.
[74] *The Atheist's Tragedy*, V.ii.165–75.

> When those nuptual rites are done
> I will perform my kinsmen's funerals.[75]

Yet with what rite for the dead? The closing lines present a muted mourning, but one repaying attention:

> Thus by the work of Heaven the men that thought
> To follow our dead bodies without tears
> Are dead themselves, and now we follow theirs.[76]

Charlemont implies a providential end, but as 'we' follow the burials of persons who themselves meant to follow the dead, he suggestively piles funerals one on the other much as the play has piled corpse upon corpse. The result is an image of life composed of funeral, in which mourners are little different from the corpses that, ironically, they 'follow'. Yet this last assertion of ironic *and* extensive remembrance is accompanied by a deliberate comment on emotional mourning: for who are those finally unnamed but mistaken men 'that thought / To follow our dead bodies without tears'? The play's resounding answer is the atheist D'Amville and the Puritan Languebeau Snuff, traditional mournings being thus delicately affirmed.

The White Devil, c.1613

Suggesting the conquest of death through remembrance even before one opens the play, the valediction of Webster's address 'To the Reader' is 'non norunt, haec monumenta mori': 'These monuments know not death' (Martial x.2).[77] Driven by a feud between the Duke of Brachiano and the Medici Duke of Florence, Francisco, and presenting the rise of Pope Paul IV, *The White Devil* follows the destruction of the family of Cornelia: despite her warning, her children Flamineo, Vittoria and Marcello are each caught up in the feud and – like Isabella and later Brachiano – destroyed by it, the play presenting many opportunities to perform remembrances. Cornelia's pivotal role in these performances, however, needs immediate attention: besides mothering the central family, she openly condemns her children's activities and later mourns them, thus presenting not just the one substantial, moral voice of the play, but also a mournfulness resonating through the various remembrances in defiance of Reform.[78] As we shall see, other features of the play support her moral *and* mournful outlook.

---

[75] *The Atheist's Tragedy*, V.ii.294–5.
[76] *The Atheist's Tragedy*, V.ii.299–301.
[77] The quotation from Martial occurs at the very end of the letter 'To the Reader' which Webster added to the play for publication. This citation, and each further citation from the play, is from John Webster, *The White Devil*, ed. by Christina Luckyja (London: A. & C. Black; New York: Norton, 1996).
[78] My emphasis thus differs from that of Shell who (following the flawed, Broudian view that the Whore of Babylon is the genre's central, religious motif) considers *The White Devil* to expose the 'hypocrisy and dazzling corruption of the Romish Church', though doing so only 'among the complex associations which it [the play] invites'. See Shell, 'The Livid

Thus, giving rise to the feud with Francisco, *The White Devil*'s opening tale of adultery is constructed on a remembrance. In act I, scene ii, Vittoria carefully negotiates becoming Brachiano's mistress by retelling a story that she claims she dreamt. The play makes plain her tale requires interpretation:

> FLAMINEO　　She hath taught him in a dream
> 　　　　　　　To make away the duchess and her husband.
> BRACHIANO [*Embracing* VITTORIA]　　Sweetly shall I interpret this your dream, –
> 　　　　　　　You are lodged within his arms who shall protect you,
> 　　　　　　　From all the fevers of a jealous husband,
> 　　　　　　　From the poor envy of our phlegmatic duchess…[79]

Flamineo and Brachiano get the gist of Vittoria's story, but a closer look at it reveals a second and less 'sweet' meaning. Here is the passage:

> VITTORIA　　Methought I walked about the mid of night,
> 　　　　　　Into a church-yard, where a goodly yew-tree
> 　　　　　　Spread her large root in ground, – under that yew,
> 　　　　　　As I sat leaning on a grave,
> 　　　　　　Checkered with cross-sticks, there came stealing in
> 　　　　　　Your duchess and her husband, one of them
> 　　　　　　A pick-axe bore, th'other a rusty spade,
> 　　　　　　And in rough terms they gan to challenge me
> 　　　　　　About this yew.
> BRACHIANO　　　　　　　　That tree.
> VITTORIA　　　　　　　　　　　　　This harmless yew.
> 　　　　　　They told me my intent was to root up
> 　　　　　　That well-grown yew, and plant i' th' stead of it
> 　　　　　　A withered blackthorn, and for that they vow'd
> 　　　　　　To bury me alive: my husband straight
> 　　　　　　With pick-axe gan to dig, and your fell duchess
> 　　　　　　With shovel, like a Fury, voided out
> 　　　　　　The earth and scattered bones. Lord, how methought
> 　　　　　　I trembled, and yet for all this terror
> 　　　　　　I could not pray.[80]

The meanings Flamineo and Brachiano decipher depend on a punning association of the yew with Brachiano ('you').[81] However, this 'sweet' interpretation does little justice to the embellished detail and extensiveness of Vittoria's story, glossing

---

Flash: Anti-Catholicism, Revenge Tragedy and the Dehistoricised Critic', in *Catholicism, Controversy and the English Literary Imagination*, pp. 23–55 (48). For another anti-Catholic view of Webster, see Nicholas de Jongh's MPhil thesis 'The Role of Death and Dying in Webster's *The Duchess of Malfi* and *The White Devil*' (University of London, 1984).

[79]　*The White Devil*, I.ii.255–60.
[80]　*The White Devil*, I.ii.230–48.
[81]　Thus, the drama expands a moment in *Titus Andronicus* in which Tamora tells her sons, 'But straight they told me they would bind me here / Unto the body of a dismal yew / And leave me to this miserable death' (*Titus Andronicus*, II.iii.105–7).

over the sustained nightmare of her imagery and, especially, the dependence of her 'dream' on ideas of funeral.[82]

As so often in revenge tragedy, the setting is a churchyard. This one being complete with traditional 'yews', Vittoria imagines herself leaning over a tomb in an attitude of contemplation; when Camillo and the Duchess dig the yard, they reveal a plausible 'terror' of 'earth and scattered bones'.

This detailed presentation of a Christian churchyard is compounded by two further contemporary terrors. First, in imagining herself buried alive, Vittoria fearfully imagines her burial without formal funeral; second, this funerary deprivation means a burial without prayer: all alone, she 'could not pray'. Ironically, thus, just as Vittoria enters a relationship traditionally sinful, she exposes the death to which her relationship will lead, expressing that negative as a riteless and prayerless funeral.

The horror of dying without proper rite is brought out by Cornelia, who considers Vittoria's (and Flamineo's) amatory plot 'a burial plot / For both your honours' (I.ii.275–6). Speaking of a 'fair garden' (I.ii.272) become this 'burial plot', she will also locate the dishonour in a transformed graveyard, linking the adulterous and the funerary plots directly. Indeed, *as* a buried woman, Vittoria thus becomes a metaphorically unmarked ground above which the 'yew' of Brachiano leans darkly. Cornelia presents their love as a funerary *curse*:

If thou dishonour thus thy husband's bed,
Be thy life short as are the funeral tears
In great men's, –[83]

Although she is interrupted, notice that her cursed funeral implies one *without* tears.

Also implying adultery means a dishonoured death, Isabella too speaks up for mournful funerals. Thus, as this second senior woman of the play is abandoned by Brachiano, she thinks of her 'winding sheet' (II.i.205). She then asks, 'in my death / Turn to your ancient pity, though not love' (II.i.178–9), thereafter adding she will 'pray for' Brachiano as if 'upon a woeful widowed bed' (II.i.210–10). Thus, Vittoria *and* Brachiano are dishonoured by their love; the dishonour of each emerges through a funerary language in which ritual mourning is vital.

However, unremittingly linking reduced memorial rites with actions of dishonour, remembrances of the dead suffuse the play. Thus, whores are 'those flattering bells that have all one tune / At weddings and at funerals' and are 'Worse than dead bodies, which are begg'd at gallows / And wrought upon by surgeons' (III.ii.93–4; 97–8); sinister friends 'shake hands / In a friend's grave together' (III.ii.295–6); the unjust man is discovered 'in his grave' (IV.i.11). As Flamineo puts it to Brachiano, the corrupting Duke 'digs turves out of my [Flamineo's] grave to feed your [Brachiano's] larks' (IV.ii.64), all such phrases negatively presenting reduced funerary ritual.

---

[82] Historical resonance for this funerary 'dream' is observed by Martin Wiggins, in 'As I sat leaning on a grave / Checkered with cross-sticks', in *Notes & Queries* 240 (1995), pp. 369–70.

[83] *The White Devil*, I.ii.293–5.

The Catholicism of mournfulness emerges especially in the trial of Vittoria for the murder of her husband. Presenting a contest between Cardinal Monticelso and Vittoria, the scene has been viewed as a 'fusion of whore and churchman' in the anti-Catholic style,[84] but mourning itself is put on trial in the scene, complicating such perspective. Linking Catholicism with performances of mourning to discredit her character, Monticelso condemns Vittoria for her everyday dress: 'is this', he demands, 'a mourning habit?' (III.ii.122). In response, Vittoria defends herself by agreeing her dress is inappropriate but arguing the mistake was accidental:

> Had I foreknown his [Camillo's] death as you suggest,
> I would have bespoke my mourning.[85]

Thus, both characters acknowledge that performing mourning is a valuable activity; and thus, since the play has previously presented mournfulness as a central value, we cannot write them off as Catholics.

Other characters in the scene support mourning. Telling Francisco of the death of Isabella (his mother and Francisco's sister), the touchingly young Giovanni is consumed with grief. In a passage soused with tearful language, the boy confesses he has 'not slept these six nights' (III.ii.327); valuing his performance, however, he tells Francisco he too should dress in black, his own black garb and broken phrases expressing his mourning:

> FRANCISCO   How now, my noble cousin, what in black?
> GIOVANNI   Yes, uncle, I was taught to imitate you
>   In virtue, and you must imitate me
>   In colours for your garments – my sweet mother
>   Is …
> FRANCISCO   How? Where?
> GIOVANNI   Is there – is yonder, – indeed sir, I will not tell you,
>   For I shall make you weep.
> FRANCISCO   Is dead.
> GIOVANNI   Do not blame me now,
>   I did not tell you so.[86]

Notably, moreover, in what we have now established as a norm of revenge tragedy, Giovanni's emotion – which will affect even the hardened Francisco – is due not only to his mother's death, but also, as he tells Francisco, to the style of her funeral:

> I am to complain to you, sir.
> I'll tell you how they used her now she's dead:
> They wrapp'd her in a cruel fold of lead,
> And would not let me kiss her.[87]

---

[84] Shell, p. 48.
[85] *The White Devil*, III.ii.123–4.
[86] *The White Devil*, III.ii.311–19.
[87] *The White Devil*, III.ii.332–5.

The child's mourning over the corpse – recognized by Francisco as 'love' (III.ii.335) – has been cut off. We shall observe his complaint against such reduction being picked up by Cornelia, but notice here the pathetically highlighted repressions of mourning: 'I will not tell you, / For I shall make you weep'; and 'Do not blame me now / I did not tell you so'.

Demanding his entourage 'Take him away for God's sake' (III.ii.339), Francisco restrains his grief for his sister until Giovanni is gone. His acknowledgement of that grief, however, is deliberate, especially as the second half of the play – Francisco's revenge – turns on it:

Believe me I am nothing but her grave,
And I shall keep her blessed memory
Longer than thousand epitaphs.[88]

Thus, Francisco will commemorate Isabella in the revenge he unleashes – here presented not only in analogy to commemorative activity (grave, blessed memory, epitaphs), but as a maximal revenge: one that lasts *longer* than a thousand epitaphs. And, recalling the model of Hieronimo in *The Spanish Tragedy*, the ensuing revenge tragedy that he plots is a remembrance of the dead, the very theatre being a monument. Implying the value he attaches to funeral, Francisco will go on to express a view encountered repeatedly in this study – that he will be revenged on his enemy by *depriving* him of funeral's rituals:

Like the wild Irish I'll ne'er think thee dead
Till I can play at football with thy head.[89]

Rituals for corpses are – despite active Reformers – valuable.

Yet the dramatic vengeance unleashed by Francisco contains various ironies. Thus, unlike Hieronimo, Francisco is not so distraught as to carry out his vengeance himself, allowing the responsibility to fall on others and thus making revenge seem as much to do with Machiavellianism as 'outrage'. A note of falsehood is already audible at the outset:

To fashion my revenge more seriously,
Let me remember my dead sister's face:
Call for her picture: no, I'll close mine eyes,
And in a melancholic thought I'll frame
Her figure 'fore me.
Enter ISABELLA's *Ghost*
          Now I ha't – how strong
Imagination works! how she can frame
Things which are not! methinks she stands afore me;
And by the quick idea of my mind,
Were my skill pregnant, I could draw her picture.
Thought, as a subtle juggler, makes us deem

---

[88] *The White Devil*, III.ii.340–2.
[89] *The White Devil*, IV.i.136–7.

>   Things supernatural, which have cause
>   Common as sickness. 'Tis my melancholy. –
>   How cam'st thou by thy death? – how idle am I
>   To question mine own idleness? did ever
>   Man dream awake till now? – remove the object –
>   Out of my brain with 't; what have I to do
>   With tombs or death-beds, funerals or tears,
>   That have to meditate upon revenge?
>   So now 'tis ended, like an old wives' story.
>   Statesmen think often they see stranger sights
>   Than madmen. Come, to this weighty business.
>   My tragedy must have some idle mirth in't...[90]

In deriving both 'tragedy' and 'revenge' from a remembrance of the dead, the soliloquy paradigmatically acknowledges the genre's funerary origins. Yet in moving from a tragic revenge conceived 'more seriously' to one with 'some idle mirth in't', Francisco implies *his* remembrance is a game. Indeed, rejecting interest in 'tombs or death-beds, funerals or tears', and dismissing ghostly visitations as 'old wives' stories', Francisco rejects the traditional causes of revenge; in ludicrously alleging in what follows that his motive is 'love' for Vittoria (IV.i.20), he even turns the generic remembrance into a game. Thus, Francisco opens an ironic seam in the remembrances of the play's latter stages; further contrasting with a series of traditional remembrances, as we shall see, that irony is never allowed to dominate the drama, but an instability creeps in.

Limitations to Francisco's perspective are already clear at the outset: though he dismisses her image from his mind as 'my melancholy', it is clear to the audience (seeing the image too) that Isabella has a life beyond Francisco. The limitations emerge more fully after Brachiano's death, when Flamineo decides to 'speak with this duke yet' (V.iii.206). Francisco's response is doubtful: 'Now he's dead?' (V.iii.207). Yet according to Flamineo, speech with the dead is a religious option:

>   if prayers or oaths
>   Will get to th' speech of him, though forty devils
>   Wait on him in his livery of flames,
>   I'll speak to him.[91]

Moreover, seeing Brachiano's ghost, he will flatly contradict Francisco's view that ghosts are products of melancholy. 'This is *beyond* melancholy', he tells us (V.iv.144; my emphasis). Finally, notice that Flamineo's religion is specifically Catholic: 'our Italian churchmen', he observes, 'Make us believe dead men hold conference with their familiars' (V.iv.138–9). Here as elsewhere, there are suggestions of demonic activity, but they remain only suggestions. Flamineo's pointedly controversial question 'what religion's best / For a man to die in?' (V.iv.129–30) brings out the scene's open-endedness.

---

[90] *The White Devil*, IV.i.98–118.
[91] *The White Devil*, V.iii.208–11.

Catholic remembrance was even more pointed at Brachiano's deathbed. Addressing the Duke in Latin, Lodovico and Gasparo arrive in Capuchin habits, carrying crucifix and 'hallowed candle'. Susan McLeod has observed the scene's 'careful verbal parallels' with the Roman-rite *Commendatio Animae* or 'Recommendation of a Departing Soul':[92]

> The rubrics for the rite of commendation call for a candle to be lit, and for the priest to place a crucifix within sight of the dying person, "so that he might take comfort from the hope it symbolises". The stage directions for Brachiano's death scene say that the Duke "seems here near his end. Lodovico and Gasparo in the habit of Capuchins present him in bed with a crucifix and hallowed candle" (V.iii.129 s.d.). The comforting powers of the crucifix are then called to our attention:
>
> *Flam.* See, see, how firmly he doth fix his eye
> Upon the crucifix.
> *Vit.* O hold it constant.
> It settles his wild spirits; and so his eyes
> Melt into tears.
>
> After the lighting of the candle and the presentation of the crucifix the commendation ceremony calls for a litany, shared between the priest and the bystanders, where they pray for the departing soul to be spared on the day of judgement. Following the presentation of Brachiano flanked by a hallowed candle and crucifix, there is a litany shared between Lodovico and Gasparo which suggests that Brachiano's spear and shield (probably still on stage from the fight at the barriers) symbolize his spiritual armour on the day he will have to fight the devil (135–139) ...
>
> After the litany is prayed, the *Commendatio Animae* calls for a series of prayers for the deliverance of the soul from the devil and its acceptance into heaven. The rubrics then state:
>
> At the moment a person is departing this life ... the following aspirations may be whispered into his ear...: 'Into thy hands, O Lord, I commend my spirit. O Lord, Jesus Christ, receive my soul ... O Mary, Mother of grace, Mother of mercy, shield me from the enemy, and receive me at the hour of my death ... Jesus, Mary, Joseph– with you in peace will I sleep and take my rest.'[93]

'It is at this point in the play', McLeod adds, 'that the inversion [by Webster] of the ceremony begins'.

McLeod explains how 'inverted rituals' function as 'symbols of the disorder of the world of the play': her interest is not primarily religious.[94] Yet having established the

---

[92] McLeod's recognition of the scene's origin is noted in detailed footnotes in *The White Devil*, ed. Luckyja, pp. 122–3. I quote McLeod, however, because her discussion more fully suggests the detailed association between Webster's dramatic scene and the Roman ritual, and because her discussion is less widely noticed than it should be.

[93] Susan H. McLeod, *Dramatic Imagery in the Plays of John Webster*, Salzburg Studies in English Literature: Jacobean Drama Studies (Salzburg: University of Salzburg, 1977), pp. 65–6.

[94] McLeod, p. 65. See also James R. Hurt, 'Inverted Rituals in Webster's *The White Devil*', *Journal of English and Germanic Philology* 61 (1962), pp. 42–7, though Hurt's

close derivation of the scene from the *Commendatio*, she also observes its dramatic departures, illustrating Webster's complex use of the Catholic rite. Thus, where the *Commendatio* invokes prayers whispered in the dying person's ear, Lodovico and Gasparo's ask for privacy to 'whisper in his ears / Some private meditations' – which turn out to be curses; where the soul is commended to God in the rite, Lodovico and Gasparo commend Brachiano to the devil; where the dying man should call on 'Jesus, Jesus, Jesus,' Brachiano calls on 'Vittoria, Vittoria'. Even the request that everyone leave the room 'is a further perversion of the rite: all those present should have stayed since participation in the ceremony was an important act of charity'.[95] Amid all this, however, McLeod fails to note what is perhaps most striking: the 'savage parody of religious ritual'[96] she observes is a parody of *Roman Catholic* ritual; thus, the *deviation* from the rite to imply 'disorder' associates the Catholic rite with order. The scene's identification of 'hell' (V.iii.181) makes the same point: taunting their enemy as 'damned ... Perpetually' (V.iii.153), Lodovico and Gasparo tell Brachiano his funeral will be beggarly:

> LODOVICO: And thou shalt die like a poor rogue.
> GASPARO   And stink
>   Like a dead fly-blown dog.
> LODOVICO   And be forgotten
>   Before thy funeral sermon.[97]

Whether or not it applies to Brachiano, damnation is here an impoverished funeral and, defying Reformers, a briefly performed remembrance.

Cornelia's mourning for Marcello is a completely contrasting performance. Her sustained mourning emphasizes 'perpetual sorrow':

> CORNELIA   O my perpetual sorrow!
> HORTENSIO   Virtuous Marcello.
>   He's dead: pray leave him lady: come, you shall.
> CORNELIA   Alas, he is not dead: he's in a trance.
>   Why here's nobody shall get anything by his death. Let
>   me call him again for God's sake.
> CARLO   I would you were deceiv'd.
> CORNELIA   O you abuse me, you abuse me, you abuse me.
>   How many have gone away thus for lack of tendance;
>   rear up his head, rear up his head; his bleeding inward will
>   kill him
> HORTENSIO You see he is departed.
> CORNELIA   Let me come to him; give me him as he is, if he
>   be turn'd to earth; let me but give him one hearty kiss, and
>   you shall put us both in one coffin: fetch a looking-glass,

---

association of the rite with 'hell' is too general. For my consideration of 'hell' regarding *funerary ritual*, see p.128.

[95] See McLeod, pp. 67–8.
[96] McLeod, pp. 68–9.
[97] *The White Devil*, V.iii.168–70.

	see if his breath will not stain it; or pull out some feathers from my pillow, and lay them to his lips, – you will lose him for a little pains-taking?
HORTENSIO	Your kindest office is to pray for him
CORNELIA	Alas! I would not pray for him yet. He may live to lay me i' th' ground, and pray for me, if you'll let me come to him.[98]

Complaining hysterically of the 'abuse' of her friends, repeating exclamations and punctuating them with 'Alas' and 'O', Cornelia performs an extreme mournfulness. Exacerbating the traditionalism of the scene, Hortensio tells her to pray for Marcello's soul, while Cornelia herself hopes Marcello may yet 'pray for me' after she is dead.

Two scenes later, in the last we see of her, Cornelia is still mourning. Revealingly addressing Flamineo, Francisco introduces the action:

> Your reverend mother
> Is grown a very old woman in two hours.
> I found them winding of Marcello's corse;
> And there is such a solemn melody
> 'Tween doleful songs, tears, and sad elegies: –
> Such, as old grandames, watching by the dead,
> Were wont t'outwear the nights with, that believe me
> I had no eyes to guide me forth the room,
> They were so o'ercharged with water.[99]

Francisco's 'old grandames' sitting through nights of vigils evoke a former society – as will Cornelia's allusion to a 'grandmother' who

> Was wont, when she heard the bell toll, to sing
> O'er unto her lute.[100]

Thus, Cornelia is an old woman once again performing the rites of an older, pre-Reformation generation, 'oe'rcharging' even Francisco's eyes with the performed remembrances Reformers condemned.

Deciding to see Cornelia, Flamineo initially presents a Reformed perspective of it:

> I'll discover
> Their *superstitious* howling.[101]

Face to face with 'superstition', however, he is moved. Here is the moving scene.

A stage direction states that 'CORNELIA, [ZANCHE] *the moor and three other* LADIES [are] *discovered, winding* MARCELLO's *corse*'. There is then a 'doleful song' (in Francisco's phrase) and Cornelia's elaborate (and by any Reformed standard, superstitious) preparation of the corpse:

---

[98] *The White Devil*, V.ii.24–45.
[99] *The White Devil*, V.iv.51–9.
[100] *The White Devil*, V.iv.90–1.
[101] V.iv.62–3; my emphasis.

> This rosemary is witherd, pray get fresh:
> I would have these herbs grown up in his grave
> When I am dead and rotten. Reach the bays;
> I'll tie a garland here about his head:
> 'Twill keep my boy from lightning. This sheet
> I have kept this twenty year, and every day
> Hallow'd it with my prayers – I did not think
> He should have worn it.[102]

Keeping the corpse from lightning, ensuring the herbs at the graveside last: even as she performs the rite of remembrance, Cornelia highlights maintaining Marcello's memory. It even emerges 'twenty years' were spent hallowing the winding sheet with prayers, the 'superstition' of customary remembrances becoming the mark of a mother's care.

The performed remembrance of Cornelia is the scene's central act, but one or two moments bear special notice. Thus, Cornelia's claim that 'Cowslip water is good for the memory: pray buy me three ounces of't' (V.iv.87) emphasizes the popular context of her ritual. Remembering her grandmother singing 'when she heard the bell toll' (V.iv.90), similarly, Cornelia performs the much-anthologized song 'Call for the robin red-breast and the wren' also recalled in Eliot's *The Wasteland*:

> Call for the robin red breast and the wren,
> Since o'er shady groves they hover,
> And with leaves and flow'rs do cover
> The friendless bodies of unburied men.
> Call unto this funeral dole
> The ant, the field-mouse, and the mole
> To rear him hillocks, that shall keep him warm
> And (when gay tombs are robb'd) sustain no harm…[103]

This song over the dead fondly invokes each animal – robin, wren, ant, field-mouse and mole – because these 'cover' the unburied dead. Nature, in Cornelia's wishful imagination, performs tasks unsupplied by 'funeral dole', providing the unburied and 'friendless' dead with monuments and homes: 'hillocks, that shall keep him warm', even when the dwellings of the dead are desecrated ('when gay tombs are robb'd'). His briefly Reformist hostility dissolving in a poignant fellow-feeling, Flamineo says:

> I have a strange thing in me, to th' which
> I cannot give a name, without it be
> Compassion.[104]

It is in this new and emotional mood that he seeks out Brachiano's ghost.

Cornelia's song concludes with implied valuations of remembrance:

---

[102] *The White Devil*, V.iv.64–71.
[103] *The White Devil*, V.iv.92–9.
[104] *The White Devil*, V.iv.113–15.

But keep the wolf far hence that's friends to man
Or with his nails he'll dig them up again.
They would not bury him cause he died in a quarrel
But I have an answer for them.
Let holy church receive him duly
Since he payed the church tithes truly.[105]

In digging up rather than burying the dead, the wolf sinisterly contrasts with Cornelia's other, philanthropic animals. Bringing out the importance of funerary religion, however, Cornelia demands that *whatever* he may have done, 'holy church' must perform Marcello's burial.

It is in contrast with this and the previous, pious, funerary rituals that the deaths of Vittoria and Flamineo emerge. Neither comes close to the mother's piety, their mutual deceptions illustrating the 'burial plot / For both your honours' (I.ii.275–6) she foresaw at the start. Presenting a contrast with Cornelia in which remembrance remains focal, however, the end of the play still remembers the dead.

Thus, finding Vittoria reading, in act V, scene vi, Flamineo asks her if she is at 'prayers' (V.vi.1); and when Flamineo threatens suicide, she invokes the traditionalist argument that actions in this life have consequences in the next:

Are you grown an atheist? will you turn your body,
Which is the goodly palace of the soul
To the soul's slaughter-house?[106]

Presenting the Last Judgement as a corpse-strewn horror when that argument fails, she next tells Flamineo:

      yet remember,
Millions are now in graves, which at last day
Like mandrakes shall rise shrieking.[107]

Still not dissuading Flamineo, Vittoria ironically promises to join him 'Most religiously' in suicide (V.vi.97); piling irony on irony as Flamineo pretends to die, she justifies breaking her word with the Christian claim (dependent on a view of free will at odds with Calvinism) that suicide means damnation. Bringing out the funerary in this theological discussion, Zanche gloats that Flamineo's rite of remembrance will be impoverished: 'we'll give it out / Thou didst this violence upon thyself' and 'drive a stake / Through thy body' (V.vi.143–5).

Highlighting the religion of death, Flamineo also mocks both the Roman Catholic Purgatory *and* a Reformed Eucharist. Here he is on Purgatory:

Whither shall I go? O Lucian, thy ridiculous purgatory!
to find Alexander the Great cobbling shoes,
Pompey tagging points, and Julius Caesar making

---

[105] *The White Devil*, V.iv.100–5.
[106] *The White Devil*, V.vi.54–6.
[107] *The White Devil*, V.iv.63–5.

hair buttons; Hannibal selling blacking, and Augustus crying
garlic, Charlemagne selling lists by the dozen, and King
Pippin crying apples in a cart drawn with one horse.[108]

This suggests anti-Catholicism, but the parodied Eucharist of the Reformed that follows forbids any such clear response. Imagining a burning and sooty hell, thus, Flamineo says, 'My liver's parboiled like Scotch holy bread; There's a plumber laying pipes in my guts; it scalds' (V.vi.141–2): if Purgatory is ridiculous, the Reformed 'holy bread' here topically associated with Scotland is an ingested hell.[109] Notice, however, the implicit irony in each and every such claim: since Flamineo is *pretending* death, nothing he says is of face value.

Religious ambivalence characterizes Vittoria's actions in the scene. Having learnt in the play to 'personate masculine virtue' (III.ii.136), she now shows her steel, Flamineo therefore praising her as among

> many glorious women that are famed
> For masculine virtue.[110]

In her 'masculine' toughness, however, Vittoria especially contrasts with Cornelia's mournfulness, and religious contrasts are therefore implicit. As Patricia Phillippy observes, considering it 'an imperfect version of men's stoic sorrow', a 'uniquely Protestant assault on wivish mourning' conflated 'excessive feminine grief which unduly laments the body's demise with Catholic mourning'.[111] Thus, Vittoria's 'masculine virtue' presents a Reformed perspective; yet the condemnation of wives who forget husbands 'Ere the worm pierce your winding sheet, ere the spider / Make a thin curtain for your epitaphs' (V.vi.155–6) condemns her masculine virtue.

Approaching death, Vittoria continues to reject any mournful disposition, claiming to be 'too true a woman' to show emotion and emphasizing that 'I will not in my death shed one base tear' (V.vi.221; 223). Yet despite the defiance, her final phrases are marked by emotional and religious language and show contrition and uncertainty:

---

[108] *The White Devil*, V.vi.105–10.

[109] 'Scotch holy bread' has the contemporary sense of 'a sodden sheep's liver', but a play on words denoting the Reformed Eucharist is inevitable. Matters of Scottish religion gained in topicality in England with the ascent of James VI of Scotland to the English throne in 1603; in the 1605 Assembly, James called Scottish clerics to London to demonstrate his 'resolution to make the Kirk conform more closely to its English counter-part', pursuing such controversial policy in a series of further encounters until his death in 1625. 'Popish' ceremonies, such as kneeling at the administering of communion, were among the issues on which James clashed with the Scottish ministers. For details, see Alan R. MacDonald, *The Jacobean Kirk, 1567–1625: Sovereignty, Polity and Liturgy*, St Andrews Studies in Reformation History (Aldershot and Brookfield, VT: Ashgate, 1998), especially pp. 101–70; my quotation is from p. 125.

[110] *The White Devil*, V.vi.242–3.

[111] Patricia Phillippy, *Women, Death and Literature in Post-Reformation England* (Cambridge: Cambridge University Press, 2002), p. 8. Phillippy uses the term 'stoic' generally rather than in a more technical sense.

> *O* my greatest *sin* lay in my blood.
> Now my blood pays for't.[112]

> My *soul* like to a ship in a black storm
> Is driven I know not whither.[113]

Thus, defying emotionalism in a Christian setting while nevertheless presenting it, Vittoria's death is a seventeenth-century paradox.

Flamineo's death *seems* more straightforward. Advised by Lodovico to commend himself to heaven, his response is defiant: 'No, I will carry mine own commendations thither' (V.vi.195). In further defiance, he adds:

> at myself I will begin and end:
> While we look up to heaven we confound
> Knowledge with knowledge.[114]

His final words reject the tolling remembrance of church bells, though not remembrance itself:

> Let no harsh flattering bell resound my knell,
> Strike thunder, and strike loud to my farewell.[115]

There remain Christian ambiguities too. Between life and death, Flamineo claims to

> recover like a spent taper, for a flash
> And instantly go out.[116]

Entailing a Catholic remembrance, this most self-conscious line presents Flamineo – the literal flame – as holding a candle before death. His following lines bring out the Catholic image:

> Let all that belong to great men remember th' old wives'
> tradition, to be like the lions i' th Tower on Candlemas day,
> to mourn if the sun shine for fear of the pitiful remainder of
> winter to come.[117]

These gnomic phrases develop a proverb: 'If Candlemas day be fair and bright, winter will have another flight.'[118] However, in view of Flamineo's previous likening of himself to a 'spent taper', 'Candlemas' is especially resonant. Deriving from Jewish ceremonies of purity, the feast was developed by Latin-rite Christians into a

---

[112] *The White Devil*, V.vi.238–9; my emphasis.
[113] *The White Devil*, V.vi.246–7; my emphasis.
[114] *The White Devil*, V.vi.256–8.
[115] *The White Devil*, V.vi.273–4.
[116] *The White Devil*, V.vi.261–2.
[117] *The White Devil*, V.vi.263–6.
[118] For discussion, see Luckyja (ed.), p. 150.

mass and candle-lit procession from a central church to its surrounding cemetery.[119] Thus, even in Flamineo's defiance of a religious death, there is an ironically contrasting, Catholic performance of remembrance. Although Giovanni – supported by an English Ambassador – will shortly clean up with a simple 'Remove the bodies' (V.vi.288), an irony of lost rites – made much of throughout – persists.

The Duchess of Malfi, c.1613[120]

Following the address 'To the Reader' of *The White Devil*, Webster's letter dedicating *The Duchess of Malfi* 'To the right honourable George Harding' presents a second authorial interest in remembrances of the dead. In particular, the dedication's allusion to 'relics' emphasizes a dramatic theme: 'I do not altogether look up to your title', Webster states, 'the ancientest nobility being but a relic of time past, and the truest honour indeed being for a man to confer honour on himself'.[121] Implicit in this anti-hierarchical statement is contempt for relics also visible in *The Duchess of Malfi*; however, as there is paradox in dedications presenting contempt for their dedicatees, so the extent of Webster's contempt for relics in this dedication, and his related view of 'honour', is uncertain, unstable irony being visible already.

A second, contemporary observation of relevance comes from the Venetian Ambassador, Orazio Busino. Seeing the play in 1618, this Roman Catholic proclaimed it 'acted in condemnation of the grandeur of the church which they [the English] despise and which in this kingdom they hate to the death'.[122] However, implying that in fact the play's religion was performed with some reverence, he also observed in the 1618 production a 'great ceremoniousness' in the Cardinal and 'his chaplains' before an 'altar'.[123] Thus, despite claims to the contrary, even a religiously partisan observer like Busino – whose view of England was clearly broad-brush – did *not* see a complete anti-Catholicism in Webster's drama. Looking beyond the self-evident corruptions of the Cardinal, and bearing in mind that all the major characters – worse *and* better – are Italians, what other views of Catholicism can we find? I begin with the opening, dramatic dilemma of the Duchess herself.

Making remembrance of the dead pivotal to the tragedy, the Duchess's dilemma at the beginning of the play – whether to obey her brothers by refraining from remarriage or not – is repeatedly a matter of widowhood, and so the remembrance of the dead. Advising her not to remarry, Ferdinand begins with the blunt observation 'You are a widow' (I.i.286), and widowhood has an important place in his and the

---

[119] See under 'Candlemas' in the *Catholic Encyclopedia* at www.newadvent.org/cathen/03245b.htm, last accessed 4 November 2007.

[120] Webster was 'working on *The Duchess of Malfi*, in 1612 ... [it] must have been performed before the end of 1614' – John Webster, *The Duchess of Malfi*, ed. by Brian Gibbons, 4th edn (London: A. & C. Black; New York: W.W. Norton, 2001), p. x. All textual citations are from this edition.

[121] See the 'Dedication: To the right honourable George Harding' in *The Duchess of Malfi*, p. 3.

[122] Gibbons (ed.), p. xxxix.

[123] Gibbons (ed.), p. xxxix.

Cardinal's ensuing warnings. Thus, 'They are most luxurious', says Ferdinand, 'That will wed twice' (I.i.290–1), his view being echoed by the Cardinal; for when the Duchess agrees not to marry, he too foregrounds the widow's theme:

> So most widows say,
> But commonly that motion lasts no longer
> Than the turning of an hourglass: the funeral sermon
> And it, end both together.[124]

Here, the Cardinal not only emphasizes the dilemma of widows, he also relates the alleged transgressions they perform to the funerals of their husbands, implying a correct widowhood is defined by the performance of remembrance.

It is, then, the sexuality of *widows* that is in focus in act I, scene i. Taking his leave, Ferdinand takes one, significant, parting shot: 'Farewell, *lusty widow*' (I.i.332; my emphasis). Thus, widowhood is not only the recurrent theme, it is both the opening and closing note of the discussion: the conflict between the Duchess and her brothers defining the drama turns on the sexual behaviour of *widows*, remembrance of the dead being therefore central. Angrily discovering the Duchess has married in act III, and responding to her question 'Why may I not marry?' (III.ii.109), Ferdinand highlights this:

> Thou art undone;
> And thou hast ta'en that massy sheet of lead
> That hid thy husband's bones, and folded it about
> My heart.[125]

Betraying, in Ferdinand's eyes, the memory of her husband, the Duchess has passed her obligation of remembrance to Ferdinand. It is, he thus claims, incumbent on him to be revenged. Although the drama will present his vengeance as semi-demonic, as we shall see, it also eventually implies a value in mourning, paradoxically supporting the Duke's defence of it.

Expanding the focus on remembrance, the sexual dilemma of the widow is explored in her courtship of Antonio. Finding Antonio initially hesitant in his embraces, the Duchess admonishes him:

> Sir, be confident,
> What is't distracts you? This is flesh and blood, sir,
> 'Tis not the figure cut in alabaster
> Kneels at my husband's tomb.[126]

Her defiance of her brothers distinguishes between two images of herself: as 'flesh and blood' and as 'the figure cut in alabaster' waiting endlessly at her husband's tomb. Further persuading Antonio of her sexuality, she presents herself as 'a *young* widow / That claims you for a husband' – one 'like a widow' using 'but

---

[124] *The Duchess of Malfi*, I.i.295–8.
[125] *The Duchess of Malfi*, III.ii.111–13.
[126] *The Duchess of Malfi*, I.i.444–7.

half a blush' in her seduction (I.i.449–51; my emphasis). Such persuasion ironically changes widowhood from a state of remembrance (as defined by her brothers) to one of sexual experience and availability.

The dilemma of remembrance or sexuality is thickened in a related treatment of honour. Beginning in act I, scene i with the Cardinal forbidding the Duchess '*anything* without the addition, honour' (I.i.19; my emphasis), the theme comes to a head when Ferdinand discovers the Duchess's defiance. He addresses the Duchess as follows:

> Dost thou know what reputation is?
> I'll tell thee – to small purpose, since th'instruction
> Comes now too late.
> Upon a time, Reputation, Love and Death
> Would travel o'er the world; and it was concluded
> That they should part, and take three separate ways:
> Death told them they should find him in great battles
> Or cities plagued with plagues; Love gave them counsel
> To enquire for him 'mongst unambitious shepherds,
> Where dowries were not talked of, and sometimes
> 'Mongst quiet kindred that had nothing left
> By their dead parents. 'Stay', quoth Reputation,
> 'Do not forsake me: for it is my nature
> If once I part from any man I meet
> I am never found again.'[127]

Presenting the contending forces of the play thus far, in Ferdinand's allegory love, death and reputation are the focal values. Emphasizing a financial aspect of marriage also already visible in act I, scene i, according to Ferdinand love ought only to grow where 'dowries' are 'not talked of'. However, according to Ferdinand, financial concerns are secondary to 'reputation' since this is irretrievable. Instructing the Duchess in this lesson, Ferdinand thus implies that the real cause of his anger is not money but the perception of honour. Thus, Ferdinand's message is that by sexually betraying her widowhood, the honour of the Duchess was lost. The significance of the Duchess's honour also emerges with Ferdinand questioning her very essence:

> is it true thou art but a bare name
> And no essential thing?[128]

Asking 'Why should only I / Of all the other princes in the world / Be cased up like a holy relic?' (III.ii.136–8), the Duchess especially brings out a Catholic aspect of her dilemma: being 'cased up' in widowhood by her brothers, her implicitly anti-Catholic objection is to her treatment as the venerated corpse of a saint instead of a woman. This cuts no ice with Ferdinand, who maintains the traditional role of widows until the end, but their difference of outlook is thematically amplified when Bosola proposes to 'feign a pilgrimage / To our Lady of Loretto' (III.ii.303–4) to escape the

---

[127] *The Duchess of Malfi*, III.ii.119–33.
[128] *The Duchess of Malfi*, III.ii.73–4.

Duke. The controversy within the drama emerges especially in an exchange between the Duchess and Cariola:

> CARIOLA   I do not like this jesting with religion
> This feigned pilgrimage.
> DUCHESS   Thou art a superstitious fool.[129]

Suggesting also her view of strict widowhood – as her brothers wish, an *endless* remembrance of her husband – the Duchess's Reformist contempt for venerating the dead is unambiguous: to her, jesting with Loretto's saint is irrelevant. However, Cariola's defence of the Virgin Mary's emphatically Catholic reliquary presents an alternative and so ambiguous view of the matter. Presenting unstable ironies, as we shall see, in the remainder of the play such contrast between traditional and Reformed expands. Staging the shrine of Loretto itself in act III, scene iv is only a beginning: the scene presents an overt condemnation of the Cardinal as 'much too cruel' (III.iv.26), but as Brian Gibbons observes, Webster seemingly intended 'an elaborate imitation' of the Loretto shrine and the Cardinal's Catholic rites.[130]

Presenting such ambiguous religion, further thematic amplifications recur through the course of the play. First, there is a thematic treatment of the afterlife and Purgatory; second, there are Antonio's remembrances in the 'ruined abbey'; and last, there are the closing remembrances. I take each in turn, beginning with 'Purgatory'.

Leading Antonio in act I, scene i, the Duchess asks him: 'What do you think of marriage? (I.i.384). In the course of the play, Antonio is called a 'precise fellow' (II.iii.67) *and* one considering 'religion / But a school-name, for fashion of the world' (V.ii.129–30), but whether a proto-Puritan or an atheist,[131] this Italian is certainly only Roman Catholic by birth; his answer to the Duchess reflects this:

> I take't as those that deny purgatory,
> It locally contains or heaven or hell;
> There's no third place in't.[132]

The anti-Catholic joke about Purgatory overtly presents a Reformed view of remembrance; metaphorically, however, Antonio here introduces the idea that marriage is a kind of afterlife – a foreboding idea eventually becoming reality when the Duchess is captured by Ferdinand and imprisoned. For Ferdinand's prison is a liminal world of the dead. Approaching it, the Duchess observes:

---

[129] *The Duchess of Malfi*, III.ii.313–14.

[130] See Gibbons (ed.), p. 76. Loretto being *the* Marian shrine of sixteenth- and seventeenth-century Europe, the significance of Webster's dramatic location would have been well known. The place of the Virgin Mary in Renaissance drama is increasingly recognized. For recent discussion, see *Marian Moments in Renaissance Drama*, ed. by Regina Buccola and Lisa Hopkins (Aldershot and Burlington, VT: Ashgate, 2007).

[131] Notice, however, the implied overlap between the two outlooks: it recalls *The Atheist's Tragedy*.

[132] *The Duchess of Malfi*, I.i.385–7.

I have heard that Charon's boat serves to convey
All o'er the dismal lake, but brings none back again.[133]

Once within the prison, Bosola tells the Duchess he has 'come to make thy tomb' (IV.ii.110), thereby eerily suggesting she is dead already. The dead man's hand that she is passed in the dark, and the figures of Antonio and his children seemingly dead, all further serve to convey an underworld summarized simply as 'O horrible!' (IV. i.52).

Suggesting the torments for the damned, the play sustains the idea that the vengeance of Ferdinand (the tormentor of the Duchess in this liminal afterlife) is a vengeance of *fire*. Thus, Pescara notes: 'A very salamander lives in's [Ferdinand's] eye / To mock the eager violence of fire' (III.iii.48–9); and the Doctor tells Ferdinand: 'I have brought your grace a salamander's skin, to keep you from sun-burning' (V.ii.60–1). Specifically linking his 'fire' with his vengefulness, Ferdinand uses Bosola as an instrument 'To feed a fire as great as my revenge' (IV.ii.136), also informing the Cardinal they must

> Apply desperate physic!
> We must not now use balsamum, but fire
> ...
> To purge infected blood, such blood as hers.[134]

The 'desperate' nature of his physic becomes explicit when Bosola asks why he tortures the imprisoned Duchess:

BOSOLA   Why do you do this?
FERDINAND   To bring her to despair.[135]

Ferdinand's fiery torment of the Duchess among the dead is not to cure her, as his metaphors of 'physic' might imply, but to damn her: drawing on the dramatic tradition of the moralities still prominent in plays following *Dr Faustus*, 'despair' implies a theology of damnation, associating the tormenting Ferdinand with theatrical devils.[136]

Resounding in anti-Catholicism, all this substantiates Antonio's view that marriage can 'locally contain' hell. However, Webster also substantiates the second part of Antonio's proposition: that there is no Purgatory. Presenting himself as the 'tomb-maker' (IV.ii.140), Bosola tells the Duchess: 'My trade is to *flatter* the dead' (IV.ii.139; my emphasis). Thus, on Ferdinand's orders, he implies that tombs are *empty* monuments: that their remembrance of the dead is to no purpose. When the Duchess asks about her tomb, the point re-emerges:

---

[133] *The Duchess of Malfi*, III.v.106–7.
[134] *The Duchess of Malfi*, II.v.21–6.
[135] *The Duchess of Malfi*, IV.i.112–13.
[136] For a complete history of stage devils, see Cox, *The Devil and the Sacred*.

DUCHESS   Let me be a little merry. Of what stuff will you make it?
BOSOLA   Nay, resolve me first, of what fashion?
DUCHESS   Why, do we grow fantastical in our death-bed, do we affect fashion in the grave?
BOSOLA   Most ambitiously.[137]

The grandeur of monuments for the dead becomes here mere fantasy, fashion and ambition. Implicitly, thus, the monuments themselves are worthless.

However, in act IV, scene i, substantial ambiguities begin to creep into the drama, muddying this Reformist perspective with unstable ironies. The first direct suggestion of a challenge emerges from Bosola as he pleads that Ferdinand stop tormenting the Duchess:

> Faith, end here.
> And go no further in your cruelty.
> Send her a penitential garment to put on
> Next to her delicate skin, and furnish her
> With beads and prayer books.[138]

Besides the anti-Calvinism in which the Duchess might be saved through prayers and penitence – especially in this place of the dead – this presentation of rosary beads as instruments of mercy is resoundingly Catholic. Rosary beads suggesting prayers to the Virgin, indeed, the remembrance of a saint already prominent in the play is implicit.

Yet it is in remembrances of the Duchess that the Reformed perspective suffers its first reversal. Associating her dislike of strict widowhood with a Reformed view of mourning, the Duchess had earlier argued: 'Past sorrows, let us *moderately* lament them' (III.ii.316; my emphasis). Arrested by Bosola only two scenes later, however, her fortitude is already collapsing – as her farewell to Antonio implies:

DUCHESS   I know not which is best,
          To see you dead, or part with you; farewell, boy,
          Thou art happy, that thou hast not understanding
          To know thy misery; for all our wit
          And reading brings us to a truer sense
          Of sorrow. In the eternal Church, sir,
          I do hope we shall not be parted thus.[139]

Thus, as death approaches, the Duchess begins to express a 'truer sense' of sorrow than hitherto. Antonio's response is to enjoin her to 'be of comfort / Make patience a noble fortitude' (III.v.70–1) and 'Do not weep' (III.v.79), but rather than reassuring the Duchess, what emerges as they separate is a division between their views of grief. Explaining her emotion, the relics of the grave are newly tangible to the Duchess as they kiss goodbye:

---

[137] *The Duchess of Malfi*, IV.iii.143–7.
[138] *The Duchess of Malfi*, IV.i.113–17.
[139] *The Duchess of Malfi*, III.v.64–70.

> Your kiss is colder
> Than that I have seen an holy anchorite
> Give to a dead man's skull.[140]

Contrasting her erotic devotion with a Catholic devotion to the dead, the phrase pointedly suggests the erotic being overwhelmed and displaced by the religious.

Claiming, near the end of her ordeal, that the 'sad spectacle' (IV.i.56) of her dead family 'wastes me' (IV.i.61), the Duchess's fortitude is eventually broken; although she is subject to a deception and will yet die bravely, she finds the mournfulness of death inevitable. Thus, having risked and given her life to avoid a widowhood, the Duchess ironically ends up a mourner: 'acquainted with sad misery, / As the tanned galley-slave is with his oar' (IV.ii.27–8); and, more notably still, 'like some reverend *monument* / Whose ruins are ever pitied' (IV.ii.33–4; my emphasis).

The death of the Duchess also gives rise to other mournful developments. Confronting her with the spectacle of her family, Bosola had presented in the prison a Reformed mourning:

> Hereafter you may *wisely* cease to grieve
> For that which cannot be recovered.[141]

However, showing the Duchess's corpse to Ferdinand, Bosola tells him to 'here begin your pity' (IV.ii.247), implying emotion for the dead is appropriate. Having previously wavered between admiration of the Duchess and obedience to Ferdinand, by the end of the scene Bosola is acknowledging an extravagant grief and reprimanding himself for not having wept earlier. First, there is his surprise: 'This is manly sorrow: / These tears, I am certain, never grew / In my mother's milk' (IV.ii.351–3); then there is his regret: 'where were / These penitent fountains while she was living?' (IV.ii.354–5). Guilt combining with mourning, Bosola's tears are 'penitent', but they are also for the Duchess.

Significantly, Bosola ends by anticipating a 'reverend' burial of the Duchess despite Ferdinand:

> Come, I'll bear thee hence
> And execute thy last will: that's deliver
> Thy body to the reverend dispose
> Of some good women; that the cruel tyrant
> Shall not deny me…[142]

Thus, there is a second reversal. Having previously condemned monuments to the dead, Bosola ends the scene commending the ritual 'dispose' of the corpse of the Duchess as well as the mourning of women.

The third reversal of the scene concerns Ferdinand, who also gives way to a performance of emotional remembrance. Initially restraining his emotion, he looks coldly at the corpse; under instruction from Bosola, however, he finds his tears:

---

[140] *The Duchess of Malfi*, III.v.86–8.
[141] *The Duchess of Malfi*, IV.i.58–9; my emphasis.
[142] *The Duchess of Malfi*, IV.ii.359–63.

BOSOLA	Fix your eye here.
FERDINAND	Constantly.
BOSOLA	Do you not weep?
	Other sins only speak; murder shrieks out.
	The element of water moistens the earth,
	But blood flies upward and bedews the heavens.
FERDINAND	Cover her face. Mine eyes dazzle. She died young.[143]

After the series of mournful prompts from Bosola, Ferdinand's initially 'constant' gaze re-emerges as 'eyes' in a 'dazzle' of tears,[144] his abrupt and brief phrases also revealing his grief. Thus, for the third time in the scene, grief for the dead seems inevitable, the action presenting a sustained traditionalism that transforms the play's religious emphasis.

However, the following drama subjects this transformed view to irony in two different ways. First, there is the extreme grief of Ferdinand, which the doctor diagnoses as 'lycanthropia':

DOCTOR	A very pestilent disease, my lord,
	They call lycanthropia.
PESCARA	What's that?
	I need a dictionary to't.
DOCTOR	I'll tell you.
	In those that are possessed with't there o'er-flows
	Such melancholy humour they imagine
	Themselves to be transformed into wolves:
	Steal forth to chuch-yards in the dead o' th' night
	And dig dead bodies up…[145]

Presenting Reformed hostility to extensive sorrow for the dead, Ferdinand's alleged excess of melancholy leads to 'madness' (V.ii.26). Pointedly, moreover, the symptom of this madness is an inappropriate obsession with the dead, thus 'over-remembrance'.

After the Duchess's death, melancholy remembrance also disturbs Antonio. However, in contrast to Ferdinand, Antonio's sorrow is by no means clearly a perversion. Set in the 'ruins of an ancient abbey' (V.iii.2), the scene suggests a national sadness observed by Philip Schwyzer:

> For at least a century after the dissolution [of the monasteries in England], almost no one saw anything beautiful or sublime in the shattered husks of the religious houses … The immediate effect of the dissolution … was to make England appear a much uglier place.[146]

---

[143] *The Duchess of Malfi*, IV.ii.249–54.

[144] The tearful import of 'Mine eyes dazzle' is noted by Martin Wiggins, in 'Cover her face: Mine eyes dazzle. She died young', in *Notes & Queries* 240 (1995), p. 372; see also Gibbons (ed.), p. 102.

[145] *The Duchess of Malfi*, V.ii.5–12.

[146] Philip Schwyzer, 'The Beauties of the Land: Bale's Books, Aske's Abbeys, and the Aesthetics of Nationhood', in *Renaissance Quarterly* 57 (Spring 2004), pp. 99–125 (108).

Antonio brings out the sorrow of the scene in a nostalgic description stating he loves both it and the dead it recalls:

> I do love these ancient ruins:
> We never tread upon them but we set
> Our foot upon some reverend history,
> And questionless, here in this open court
> Which now lies naked to the injuries
> Of stormy weather, some men lie interred
> Loved the church so well, and gave so largely to't
> They thought it should have canopied their bones
> Till domesday…[147]

Antonio's nostalgia emerges especially in his presentation of the error of the dead, who eventually 'gave so largely' to the abbey for nothing.

The sorrow of the scene is further brought out in the sadness of the voice echoing from the Duchess's grave. For example:

> ANTONIO   My Duchess is asleep now,
>   And her little ones, I hope, sweetly. O heaven,
>   Shall I never see her more?
> ECHO   *Never see her more.*[148]

Presenting a refrain about the finality of death, this echo is mournful. Defying Reformist mourning, moreover, the Echo not only defines itself as 'A thing of sorrow', it defines *death* that way:

> DELIO   Now the echo hath caught you.
> ANTONIO   It groaned, methought, and gave
>   A very deadly accent!
> ECHO   *Deadly accent.*
> DELIO   I told you 'twas a pretty one. You may make it
>   A huntsman, or a falconer, a musician
>   Or a thing of sorrow.
> ECHO   *A thing of sorrow.*[149]

Bevington and Maus note the English association of act V, scene iii: 'the setting evokes not merely Catholic Italy, where ruined abbeys were presumably rare, but England, where after the Protestant Reformation, what Shakespeare called the "bare ruined choirs" of despoiled former monasteries and convents were a familiar sight. Indeed, one of the theaters where *The Duchess of Malfi* was first performed occupied land on which such a monastery had once stood'. See Katharine Eisaman Maus and David Bevington, 'General Introduction', in *English Renaissance Drama: A Norton Anthology*, ed. by David Bevington and Lars Engle (New York and London: Norton, 2002), p. xliv.

[147] *The Duchess of Malfi*, V.iii.9–17.
[148] *The Duchess of Malfi*, V.iii.39–41.
[149] *The Duchess of Malfi*, V.iii.20–4.

Although one may make other things of it, death is audibly a matter of groans: a thing of sorrow. Being moved enough directly to remember the Duchess's face, Antonio sees only sorrow:

> I marked not one repetition of the echo
> But that; and on a sudden, a clear light
> Presented me, a face folded in sorrow.[150]

Delio replies that this vision is 'Your fancy, merely' (V.iii.45), but this is beside the point: illustrating Antonio's mournfulness, the 'Echo' echoes Antonio's governing emotion. That Antonio with characteristic fortitude eventually shakes off the emotion as an 'abuse of life' (V.iii.47) is also irrelevant: although he thus defies his mournfulness in what Delio calls 'virtue' (V.iii.49), the scene's literally resounding mourning is too sustained and striking to be dismissed.

The persistence of the Echo emerges in two other ways. First, the Echo not only resounds and amplifies the mourning of Antonio for the Duchess, it also anticipates the death of Antonio himself in the next scene. For example, when Antonio refuses to answer the Echo because it is 'a dead thing' (V.iii.38), the Echo answers: 'Thou art a dead thing' (V.iii.38). Thus, the mournfulness of act V, scene iii looks *forward* to and resounds in Antonio's death, making Antonio's dismissal a failure.

Second, in the final moments of the play, as Ferdinand, the Cardinal and Bosola who has killed them, lie dying, Bosola's dying phrase cannot but recall the Echo in the ruined abbey:

> O, I am gone.
> We are only like dead walls, or vaulted graves,
> That, ruined, yields no echo.[151]

In view of act V, scene iii, this echo of a funerary 'ruin' and its very 'echo' are too self-conscious to be missed. In fact, in *echoing* the Echo, Bosola ironically remembers a mournful remembrance.

Emphasizing remembrances of the dead, the closing words are left to Delio:

> These wretched eminent things
> Leave no more fame behind 'em than should one
> Fall in a frost, and leave his print in snow;
> As soon as the sun shines, it ever melts,
> Both form and matter. I have ever thought
> Nature doth nothing so great for great men,
> As when she's pleased to make them lords of truth:
> Integrity of life is fame's best friend,
> Which nobly, beyond death, shall crown the end.[152]

---

[150] *The Duchess of Malfi*, V.iii.42–4.
[151] *The Duchess of Malfi*, V.v.95–7.
[152] *The Duchess of Malfi*, V.v.112–20.

There is nothing about mourning here *per se*, but an ideal of 'fame' and thus remembrance after death clearly underlies Delio's moral conclusion, the more so in that the final couplet echoes the *integer vitae* of Horace.[153] Moreover, though Delio says nothing about mourning, his view that villains are punished in death by being *forgotten* implies the traditional valuation of funerary memorial.

Emphasizing the Catholicism of that valuation, Delio's closing lines also echo the last sentiments of the *Cardinal*. Having proclaimed his 'sorrow' for his 'sin' (V.v.55), the Cardinal's last lines are:

> And now, I pray, let me
> Be laid by, and never thought of.[154]

Thus, the Cardinal too considers the punishment of a villain – such as himself – is to be forgotten in death. However, in asking to be 'laid by' and forgotten, he relates forgetting of the dead to the funereal laying out of his body. And thus, though Delio is not quite so overt, reduced remembrances *and* funerals turn out not as good in themselves, as Reformers contended, but as punishments for villains.

---

[153] For discussion of Delio's use of Horace, see Gibbons (ed.), p. 134.
[154] *The Duchess of Malfi*, V.v.88–9.

Conclusion

This book began with two claims: first, that revenge tragedy is not the anti-Catholic genre 'Broudian' critics have made out; and second, that the genre's persistent remembrances of the dead centre the genre in a traditionalism at odds with late sixteenth- and seventeenth-century Reform, suggesting a 'popery' contemporaries recognised less *as well as* more sympathetically. At the end of the study, we are now in the position to assert the validity of the second and so also the first claim: highlighting in a range of plays, the genre's traditional remembrances of the dead are now established, its sustained and traditional religious implication being thus established as well. Moreover, it has emerged that revenge tragedy normally defines its action in analogy to the contemporary performance of funeral. Thus, the very theatre it purports to present is inextricably bound in the era's funerary, and so religious, disputes.

A further point that has become clear is that the plays of Chapters 2 and 3, which are mostly chronologically later, subject their traditional remembrances to significant degrees of irony. Thus, although these later plays remain self-consciously rooted in the traditional performance of remembrance, to some extent the traditionalism emerges as a puzzle, the obscuring factor being either an overtly or implicitly Reformist doubt. In place of a 'grand narrative' of Reformed genre à la Broude, therefore, what emerges from this admittedly selective view of it is a genre that only gradually, and unevenly, took on Reformist traits.

Since the ruling Puritan faction which imposed the 'tantamount to secular' burial rites of 1644 was also the faction that closed the theatres in 1642, promising punishment and prison to those defying the law not to perform in 1647, and imposing further restrictive measures thereafter,[1] this conclusion – however selectively derived – should not be surprising. That Broudian critics have largely failed to notice, let alone respond to, the paradox of stricter Reformers destroying a generic expression allegedly sympathetic to Reform substantiates a worrying, recent claim: that literary research has too often been 'Protestantized in origin'.[2]

---

[1] For details see Henry Barton Baker, *English Actors from Shakespeare to Macready* (New York: Henry Holt & Co, 1879), pp. 27–35.

[2] See Shell, p. 3. Regarding revenge tragedy Shell herself does not go far enough in escaping Protestant, critical origins. However, her aim was to *begin* 'the task of reclamation' (p. 20). Exceptional critics have not ignored the paradox of a Reformist theatre. Margot Heinemann's *Puritanism and Theatre: Thomas Middleton and Opposition Drama under the Early Stuarts* (Cambridge: Cambridge University Press, 1980) famously attempted to confront the paradox by arguing that anti-theatricality had causes *other* than religion. Such other factors existed, but 'Puritan opponents of the theatre consistently reprocessed the more vitriolic attacks on actors of the church fathers such as Tertulian' to justify these attacks. See Hall, p. 424: Heinemann's view is reductive. Publishing her study in 1980, it lacked the

What, though, did happen to revenge tragedy after Webster? As Fredson Bowers long ago observed, the genre developed not only among the likes of Beaumont and Fletcher, Middleton and Ford, Massinger and D'Avenant, but also in a host of today still less known authors including Henry Chettle, Thomas Drue, Thomas Goff and James Shirley, among many others.[3] For our purposes, however, what is important is that right up until 1642, such theatre continued to be associated with performed remembrances and rituals of funeral. This, for example, is a response to Shirley's 1642 play *The Cardinal*, a play with clear anti-Laudian overtones:[4]

> As fate, which doth all human matters sway,
> Makes proudest things grow up into decay,
> And when they are to envied greatness grown,
> She wantonly falls off and throws them down:
> So, when our English drama was at height,
> And shined, and ruled with majesty and might,
> A sudden whirlwind threw it from its seat,
> Deflowered the groves, and quenched the Muses heat.
> Yet as in saints and martyred bodies, when
> They cannot call their blessed souls again
> To earth, relics and ashes men preserve,
> And think they do but what, blest, they deserve:
> So I, by my devotion led aspire
> To keep alive your noble vestal fire,
> Honour this piece, which shows, sir, you have been
> The last supporter of the dying scene;
> And though I do not tell you how you dress
> Virtue in glories, and bold vice depress;
> Nor celebrate your lovely Duchess' fall,
> Or the just ruin of your Cardinal;
> Yet this I dare assert, when men have named
> Jonson, the nation's laureate, the famed
> Beaumont and Fletcher, he that wo' not see
> Shirley the fourth, must forfeit his best eye.[5]

---

modern sense of seventeenth-century Protestants (such as Middleton) defyingly maintaining traditional religious outlooks.

[3] For Bowers's emphatic claim that revenge tragedy did not end with Webster, see *Elizabethan Revenge Tragedy, 1587–1642* (Gloucester, MA: Peter Smith, 1959), p. 62. Mainly because his too-formulaic approach excludes anything on the remembrance of the dead, Bowers has not figured in this study hitherto. However, for useful if ultimately simplistic introductions to these and many other writers influenced by and writing revenge tragedy until the close of the public theatres, see especially, pp. 100–258.

[4] For discussion of the play's treatment of Laud *and* 'popery', see James Shirley, *The Cardinal*, ed. by E.M. Yearling, Revels Editions (Manchester: Manchester University Press, 1986), pp. 5–6. Though we may dispute its exact nature, or even prefer the catch-all contemporary phrase 'tragedy of blood', Bowers considered *The Cardinal* 'as strict a revenge tragedy as *The Spanish Tragedy*'. See Bowers, p. 63.

[5] See the 'Commendatory Verses' in *The Cardinal*, pp. 45–6.

It is strongly speculated that Shirley was a Catholic and 'one Catholic addressing another' wrote these commendatory verses.[6] Yet whether or not, the 'whirlwind' that 'Deflowered the groves, and quenched the Muses heat' is presumably an allusion to the closing of the theatres in the same year as the play, implying anti-Puritanism and making the poem's repeated allusions to the dead especially pointed. For its allusions to 'saints', 'martyred bodies', 'blessed souls' and 'relics' come too thick and fast to suggest only the *historically* dying 'scene' of the theatres; in view of its sustained images of religious death, the poem's 'dying scene' wittily implies the performed scenes of death that are indeed also visible in *The Cardinal*. Thus, in the very year of the closing of the theatres, there is evidence that remembrances of the dead (here suggesting anti-Puritan veneration) continued as a dramatic preoccupation.

Nor is such audience-response unusual. The association of Massinger's *Roman Actor* (1626) with funerary 'idolatry' by the unknown *T.I.* has been observed previously,[7] but it is finally worth noting how many of the extant responses to the play link it more or less directly with funerary rituals. Thus, Thomas May claimed Massinger gave 'Paris, the best of Actors in his age' a fame 'In the *Flaminian* way, where people strow'd / His Grave with flowers, and *Martiall*'s wit bestow'd / A lasting Epitaph';[8] Robert Harvey claimed Caesar outlived his 'tragic Funeral' in the performance;[9] and May and John Ford both speak of Caesar's 'soul' as literally animating the performance of the actor, Paris.[10] Although there is hyperbole in these various compliments to the performance, the sustaining metaphors of remembrance in each of them – found also in reference to Shirley's *The Cardinal* – present us with audiences that kept on discovering funerary scenes in revenge tragedy until the shutting and shutting up of the theatres.

---

[6] See *The Cardinal*, p. 46, note 25.
[7] See the Introduction, p. 12. Bowers considered this play a looser kind of revenge tragedy: 'not in itself a revenge plot but ... set against a backdrop of revenges to which it [the plot] is eventually linked'. See Bowers, p. 206.
[8] See *The Roman Actor*, ed. Sanbridge, p. 48; spellings are modernized.
[9] See *The Roman Actor*, p. 49.
[10] See *The Roman Actor*, pp. 48–9. Relevantly, Ford has been seen as a Catholic. See Lisa Hopkins, *John Ford's Political Theatre* (Manchester and New York: Manchester University Press, 1994).

Select Bibliography

All citations from Shakespeare are from *The Norton Shakespeare: Based on the Oxford Edition*, ed. by Stephen Greenblatt et al. (New York and London: Norton, 1997).

Abrams, M.H. (ed.), *A Glossary of Literary Terms*, 5th edn (Fort Worth, TX: Holt, Rinehart and Winston, 1988).
Anonymous, *Great Britans Mourning Garment Given to all faithful subjects at the funeral of Prince Henry* (London, 1612) in the Henry E. Huntington Library and Art Gallery, http://eebo.chadwyck.com/search, last accessed 30 October 2007.
Ardolino, Frank, '"Now Shall I See the Fall of Babylon": *The Spanish Tragedy*', in *Shakespeare Yearbook* 1 (1990), pp. 106–13.
——, 'Hieronimo Agonistes: Kyd's Use of Hieronimo as Sanctified Revenger in *The Spanish Tragedy*', in *Journal of Evolutionary Psychology* 15 (1994), pp. 161–5.
Asquith, Claire, *Shadowplay: The Hidden Beliefs and Coded Politics of William Shakespeare* (New York: Public Affairs, 2005).
Aubrey, John, *Remaines of Gentilisme and Judaisme*, ed. by James Britten, Publications of the Folklore Society (London: W. Satchell, Peyton and Co., 1881).
Baker, Henry Barton, *English Actors from Shakespeare to Macready* (New York: Henry Holt & Co, 1879).
Barber, C.L., *Creating Elizabethan Tragedy: The Theatre of Marlowe and Kyd*, ed. by Richard P. Wheeler (Chicago and London: University of Chicago Press, 1988).
Bate, Jonathan, 'Lucius, The Severely Flawed Redeemer of *Titus Andronicus*: A Reply', in *Connotations* 6/3 (1996–1997), pp. 330–33.
——, (ed.), *Titus Andronicus* (London: The Arden Shakespeare, 1995; 2002).
Battenhouse, Roy, 'The Ghost in *Hamlet*: A Catholic "Linchpin"?', *Studies in Philology* 68 (1951), pp. 161–92.
Beauregard, David, 'Shakespeare against the Homilies: The Theology of Penance in the Comedies', in *The Ben Jonson Journal* 7 (2000), pp. 27–54.
Bevington, David (ed.), *The Spanish Tragedy: Thomas Kyd*, Revels Student Editions (Manchester: Manchester University Press, 1996).
Bowers, Fredson, *Elizabethan Revenge Tragedy, 1587–1642* (Gloucester, MA: Peter Smith, 1959).
Braden, Gordon, *Renaissance Tragedy and the Senecan Tradition: Anger's Privilege* (New Haven, CT: Yale University Press, 1985).
Broude, Ronald, 'Roman and Goth in *Titus Andronicus*', in *Shakespeare Studies* 6 (1970), pp. 27–34.
——, 'Truth, Time and Right in *The Spanish Tragedy*', in *Studies in Philology* 68 (1971), pp. 130–45.
——, '*Vindicta Filia Temporis*: Three English Forerunners of the Elizabethan Revenge Play', in *Journal of English and Germanic Philology* 72 (1973), pp. 489–502.

——, 'Revenge and Revenge Tragedy in Renaissance England', in *Renaissance Quarterly* 28 (1975), pp. 38–58.

——, 'Four Forms of Vengeance in *Titus Andronicus*', in *Journal of English and Germanic Philology* 78 (1979), pp. 494–507.

Browne, Thomas, *Religio Medici and Other Writings* (London: Dent, 1965).

Buccola, Regina, and Lisa Hopkins (eds), *Marian Moments in Renaissance Drama* (Aldershot and Burlington, VT: Ashgate, 2007).

Burgess, Clive, '"Longing to be Prayed for": Death and Commemoration in an English Parish in the Later Middle Ages', in *The Place of the Dead: Death and Remembrance in Late Medieval and Early Modern Europe*, ed. by Bruce Gordon and Peter Marshall (Cambridge: Cambridge University Press, 2000), pp. 44–65.

Claire, Janet, *'Art Made Tongue-Tied by Authority': Elizabethan and Jacobean Censorship* (Manchester and New York: Manchester University Press, 1990).

Collinson, Patrick, 'John Stow and Nostalgic Antiquarianism', in *Imagining Early Modern London: Perceptions and Portrayals of the City from Stow to Strype, 1598–1720*, ed. by J.F. Merritt (Cambridge: Cambridge University Press, 2001), pp. 27–51.

Cook, G.H., *Old Saint Paul's Cathedral* (London: Phoenix House, 1955).

Cooper, W.R. (ed.), *The New Testament: Translated by William Tyndale: The Text of the Worms Edition of 1526 in Original Spelling* (London: The British Library, 2000).

Cox, John, *The Devil and the Sacred in English Drama, 1350–1642* (Cambridge: Cambridge University Press, 2000).

Cressy, David, *Birth, Marriage and Death: Ritual, Religion and the Life-Cycle in Tudor and Stuart England* (Oxford: Oxford University Press, 1997).

——, Review of Peter Marshall's *Beliefs and the Dead in Reformation England*, in *Renaissance Quarterly* 57 (Spring 2004), p. 358.

De Jongh, Nicholas, 'The Role of Death and Dying in Webster's *The Duchess of Malfi* and *The White Devil*' (University of London, MPhil thesis, 1984).

Devlin, Christopher, *Hamlet's Divinity* (Carbondale, IL: Southern Illinois University Press, 1963).

Diehl, Huston, *Staging Reform, Reforming the Stage: Protestantism and Popular Theatre in Early Modern England* (Ithaca, NY: Cornell University Press, 1997).

Dillon, Janette, '*The Spanish Tragedy* and Staging Languages in Renaissance Drama', *Research Opportunities in Renaissance Drama* 34 (1995), pp. 15–40.

Döring, Tobias, *Performances of Mourning in Shakespearean Theatre and Early Modern Culture*, Early Modern Literature in History (Basingstoke and New York: Palgrave Macmillan, 2006).

Douglas, Audrey, and Peter Greenfield (eds), *Records of Early English Drama: Cumberland, Westmorland, Gloucestershire* (Toronto; Buffalo; London: University of Toronto Press, 1986).

Drabble, Margaret (ed.), *The Oxford Companion to English Literature* (Oxford: Oxford University Press, 1985).

Duffy, Eamon, *The Stripping of the Altars: Traditional Religion in England, 1400–1580* (New Haven, CT, and London: Yale University Press, 1992).

——, *The Voices of Morebath: Reformation and Rebellion in an English Village* (New Haven, CT, and London: Yale University Press, 2001).

Dutton, Richard, *Licensing, Censorship, and Authorship in Early Modern England* (Basingstoke and New York: Palgrave, 2000).

——, *Mastering the Revels: The Regulation and Censorship of English Renaissance Drama* (Basingstoke and London: Macmillan, 1991).

Eliot, T.S., 'Hamlet', in *Selected Prose* (Harmondsworth: Penguin, 1953; 1958).

Engel, William E., *Mapping Mortality: The Persistence of Memory and Melancholy in Early Modern England* (Amherst, MA: University of Massachusetts Press, 1995).

——, *Death and Drama in Renaissance England* (Oxford: Oxford University Press, 2002).

Erne, Lukas, '"Enter the Ghost of Andrea": Recovering Thomas Kyd's Two-Part Play', in *English Literary Renaissance* 30 (2000), pp. 339–71.

——, '"Popish Tricks" and "a Ruinous Monastery": *Titus Andronicus* and the Question of Shakespeare's Catholicism', in *The Limits of Textuality*, ed. by Lukas Erne and Guillemette Bolens, Swiss Papers in English Language and Literature 13 (Tübingen: Narr, 2000), pp. 135–55.

Finnis, John, and Patrick Martin, 'Another Turn for the Turtle: Shakespeare's Intercession for Love's Martyr', in *The Times Literary Supplement* (18 April 2003), pp. 12–14.

Freud, Sigmund, 'Mourning and Melancholy', in *The Standard Edition of The Complete Psychological Works of Sigmund Freud*, vol. 14, trans. by James Strachey, ed. by Anna Freud, Alix Strachey and Alan Tyson (London: The Hogarth Press, 1957; repr. 1962; 1964).

Frye, Roland Mushat, *The Renaissance 'Hamlet': Issues and Responses in 1600* (Princeton, NJ: Princeton University Press, 1984).

Gair, W. Reaveley, *The Children of Paul's: The Story of a Theatre Company, 1553–1608* (Cambridge: Cambridge University Press, 1982).

—— (ed), *John Marston: Antonio's Revenge*, ed. by W. Reavley Gair (Manchester: Manchester University Press; Baltimore, MD: Johns Hopkins University Press, 1978; 1999).

Galloway, David (ed.), *Records of Early English Drama: Norwich, 1540–1642* (Toronto, Buffalo, London: University of Toronto Press, 1984).

Gassner, John, and William Green (eds), *Elizabethan Drama: Eight Plays* (New York: Applause, 1967; 1990).

Geyl, Pieter, *The Revolt of the Netherlands, 1555–1609* (London: Cassell, 1988).

Gibbons, Brian, *John Webster: The Duchess of Malfi*, 4th edn (London: A. & C. Black; New York: W.W. Norton, 2001).

Gittings, Clare, 'Urban Funerals in Late Medieval and Reformation England', in *Death in Towns: Urban Responses to the Dying and the Dead, 100–1600*, ed. by Steven Bassett (Leicester and New York: Leicester University Press; St Martin's Press, 1992).

——, 'Sacred and Secular: 1558–1660', in *Death in England: An Illustrated History*, ed. by Peter C. Jupp and Clare Gittings (Manchester: Manchester University Press, 1999), pp. 147–73.

Goodland, Katharine, *Female Mourning in Medieval and Renaissance English Drama: From the Raising of Lazarus to 'King Lear'*, Studies in Performance and Early Modern Drama (Aldershot, Ashgate, 2005).
Gordon, Andrew, 'The Act of Libel: Conscripting Civic Space in Early Modern England', in *Journal of Medieval and Early Modern Studies* 32/2 (Spring 2002), pp. 375–97.
Greenblatt, Stephen, *Shakespearean Negotiations: The Circulation of Social Energy in Renaissance England* (Oxford: Clarendon Press; Berkeley, CA, and Los Angeles: University of California Press, 1988).
——, *Hamlet in Purgatory* (Princeton, NJ, and Oxford: Princeton University Press, 2001).
——, et al. (ed.), *The Norton Shakespeare* (New York and London: Norton, 1997).
Gurr, Andrew, *The Shakespearean Stage, 1547–1642*, 2nd edn (Cambridge: Cambridge University Press, 1980).
Hadfield, Andrew, 'A Handkerchief Dipped in Blood in *The Spanish Tragedy*: An Anti-Catholic Reference?', in *Notes & Queries* 46 (1999), p. 197.
Haigh, Christopher, *English Reformations: Religion, Politics and Society under the Tudors* (Oxford: Clarendon Press, 1993).
Hall, Edith, 'The Ancient Actor's Presence since the Renaissance', in *Greek and Roman Actors: Aspects of an Ancient Profession*, ed. by Pat Easterling and Edith Hall (Cambridge: Cambridge University Press, 2003), pp. 419–34.
Hamlin, Hannibal, "Psalm Culture in the English Renaissance: Readings of Psalm 137 by Shakespeare, Spenser, Milton, and Others', in *Renaissance Quarterly* 55/1 (2002), pp. 224–57.
Hammersmith, James P., 'The Death of Castile in *The Spanish Tragedy*', in *Renaissance Drama* 16 (1985), pp. 1–16.
Hammond, Martin (ed. and trans.), *Homer: The Iliad: A New Prose Translation* (Harmondsworth: Penguin, 1987).
Harris, Duncan, 'Tombs, Guidebooks and Shakespearean Drama: Death in the Renaissance', in *Mosaic: A Journal for the Interdisciplinary Study of Literature* 15/1: 'Death and Dying' (1982), pp. 13–28.
Harrison, Robert Pogue, *The Dominion of the Dead* (Chicago and London: University of Chicago Press, 2003).
Heinemann, Margot, *Puritanism and Theatre: Thomas Middleton and Opposition Drama under the Early Stuarts* (Cambridge: Cambridge University Press, 1980).
Hill, Eugene D., 'Senecan and Vergilian [*sic*] Perspectives in *The Spanish Tragedy*', in *English Literary Renaissance* 15 (1985), pp. 143–65.
Hodgkins, Christopher, 'Plays out of Season: Puritanism, Antitheatricalism and Parliament's 1642 Closing of the Theaters', in *Centered on the Word: Literature, Scripture, and the Tudor-Stuart Middle Way*, ed. by Daniel W. Doerksen and Christopher Hodgkins (Newark, DE: Delaware University Press, 2005), pp. 298–318.
Hopkins, Lisa, *John Ford's Political Theatre* (Manchester and New York: Manchester University Press, 1994).

Horrox, Rosemary, 'Purgatory, Prayer and Plague, 1150–1380', in *Death in England: An Illustrated History*, ed. by Peter C. Jupp and Clare Gittings (Manchester: Manchester University Press, 1999).

Houlbrooke, Ralph, *Death, Religion and the Family in England, 1400–1750* (Oxford: Clarendon Press, 1998).

——, Review of Michael Neill's *Issues of Death: Mortality and Identity in the Drama of Shakespeare and His Contemporaries*, in *Renaissance Forum*, 4/1 (1999) at http://www.hull.ac.uk/renforum/v4no1/houlbroo.htm, last accessed 30 October 2007.

Hurt, James R., 'Inverted Rituals in Webster's *The White Devil*', *Journal of English and Germanic Philology* 61 (1962), pp. 42–7.

Jackson, MacDonald P. (ed.), *Thomas Middleton: The Revenger's Tragedy: A Facsimile of the 1607/8 Quarto* (Rutherford, NJ: Fairleigh Dickinson University Press, 1983).

Jenkins, Harold, '*Hamlet* Then till Now', in *Aspects of Hamlet: Articles Reprinted from 'Shakespeare Survey'*, ed. by Kenneth Muir and Stanley Wells (Cambridge: Cambridge University Press, 1979), pp. 16–27.

—— (ed.), *Hamlet*, The Arden Shakespeare (London and New York: Routledge, 1982; 1995).

Jensen, Ejner J., 'Kyd's *Spanish Tragedy*: The Play Explains Itself', in *Journal of English and Germanic Philology* 64 (1965), pp. 7–16.

Jensen, Kristian, 'Reform of Latin and Latin Teaching', in *The Cambridge Companion to Renaissance Humanism*, ed. by Jill Kraye (Cambridge: Cambridge University Press, 1996; repr. 1997; 1998; 2001; 2003), pp. 63–81.

Johnson, S.F., '*The Spanish Tragedy*, or Babylon Revisited', in *Essays on Shakespeare and Elizabethan Drama in Honour of Hardin Craig*, ed. by Richard Hosley (London: Routledge & Kegan Paul, 1963), pp. 23–36.

Joseph, Miriam, 'Discerning the Ghost in *Hamlet*', *Publications of the Modern Language Association of America* 76/5 (1961), pp. 493–502.

——, '*Hamlet*: A Christian Tragedy', *Studies in Philology* 59 (1962), pp. 119–40.

Kehler, Dorothea, '*Titus Andronicus*: From Limbo to Bliss', in *Shakespeare Jahrbuch* 128 (1992), pp. 125–31.

Kerrigan, John, *Revenge Tragedy: Aeschylus to Armageddon* (Oxford: Clarendon Press, 1996).

Kilroy, Gerrard, *Edmund Campion: Memory and Transcription* (Aldershot and Burlington, VT: Ashgate, 2005).

Klause, John, 'Politics, Heresy and Martyrdom in Shakespeare's Sonnet 124 and *Titus Andronicus*', in *Shakespeare's Sonnets: Critical Essays*, ed. by James Schiffer, Shakespeare Criticism 20, Garland Reference Library of the Humanities 1988 (New York: Garland, 2000), pp. 219–40.

Kliger, Samuel, 'The "Goths" in England: An Introduction to the Gothic Vogue in Eighteenth-Century Aesthetic Discussion', in *Modern Philology* 43 (1945), pp. 107–17.

——, 'The Gothic Revival and the German "Translatio"', in *Modern Philology* 45 (1947), pp. 73–103.

——, *The Goths in England: A Study in Seventeenth- and Eighteenth-Century Thought* (Cambridge, MA: Harvard University Press, 1952).

Lake, Peter, *The Antichrist's Lewd Hat: Protestants, Papists and Players in Post-Reformation England* (New Haven, CT, and London: Yale University Press, 2002).

Le Goff, Jacques, *The Birth of Purgatory*, trans. by Arthur Goldhammer (Chicago: University of Chicago Press, 1984).

Lesko, Diane, 'Ensor in his Milieu', *Artforum* 15/9 (May 1977), pp. 56–62.

Llewellyn, Nigel, *Funeral Monuments in Post-Reformation England* (Cambridge: Cambridge University Press, 2001).

Lomax, Marion, *Stage Images and Traditions: Shakespeare to Ford* (Cambridge: Cambridge University Press, 1978).

Loughrey, Bryan, and Neil Taylor (eds), *Thomas Middleton: Five Plays* (London: Penguin, 1988).

Luckyja, Christina (ed.), *John Webster: The White Devil* (London: A. & C. Black; New York: Norton, 1996).

McAlindon, Tom, *Shakespeare minus 'Theory'* (Aldershot and Burlington, VT: Ashgate, 2004).

McLeod, Susan H., *Dramatic Imagery in the Plays of John Webster*, Salzburg Studies in English Literature: Jacobean Drama Studies (Salzburg: University of Salzburg, 1977).

MacDonald, Alan R., *The Jacobean Kirk, 1567–1625: Sovereignty, Polity and Liturgy*, St Andrews Studies in Reformation History (Aldershot and Brookfield, VT: Ashgate, 1998).

Maltby, Judith, *Prayer Book and People in Elizabethan and Early Stuart England*, Cambridge Studies in Early Modern British History (Cambridge: Cambridge University Press, 1998).

Marshall, Peter, *Beliefs and the Dead in Reformation England* (Oxford and New York: Oxford University Press, 2002).

Matthews, W.R., and W.M. Atkins, *A History of St Paul's Cathedral and the Men Associated with It* (London: Phoenix House, 1957).

Maus, Katharine Eisaman (ed.), *Four Revenge Tragedies* (Oxford and New York: Oxford University Press, 1995).

Maus, Katharine Eisaman, and David Bevington, 'General Introduction', in *English Renaissance Drama: A Norton Anthology*, ed. by David Bevington and Lars Engle (New York and London: Norton, 2002).

Mayer, Jean-Christophe, *Shakespeare's Hybrid Faith: History, Religion and the Stage*, Early Modern Literature in History (Basingstoke: Palgrave Macmillan, 2006).

Merriam, Thomas, 'Indefinite Articles in *Titus Andronicus*, Peele and Shakespeare', in *Notes & Queries* 43/3 (1998), pp. 308–10.

Milward, Peter, *The Catholicism of Shakespeare's Plays* (Southampton: The Austen Press, 1997).

Morgan, Philip, 'Of Worms and War, 1380–1558', in *Death in England: An Illustrated History*, ed. by Peter C. Jupp and Clare Gittings (Manchester: Manchester University Press, 1999), pp. 119–46.

Morris, Brian, and Roma Gill (eds), *Cyril Tourneur: The Atheist's Tragedy* (London: A. & C. Black; New York: W.W. Norton, 1976; 1989).

Muir, Edward, *Ritual in Early Modern Europe: New Approaches to European History* (Cambridge: Cambridge University Press, 1997).

Mullaney, Stephen, 'Mourning and Misogyny: *Hamlet*, *The Revenger's Tragedy*, and the Final Progress of Elizabeth I', in *Shakespeare Quarterly* 45/2 (Summer 1994), pp. 139–62.

Mulryne, J.R., 'Nationality and Language in Kyd's *The Spanish Tragedy*', in *Travel and Drama in Shakespeare's Time*, ed. by Jean-Pierre Maquerlot and Michèle Willems (Cambridge: Cambridge University Press, 1996), pp. 87–105.

Neill, Michael, 'Feasts Put Down as Funeral', in *True Rites and Maimed Rites: Ritual and Anti-Ritual in Shakespeare and his Age*, ed. by Linda Woodbridge and Edward Berry (Urbana, IL, and Chicago: University of Illinois Press, 1992), pp. 47–74.

——, *Issues of Death: Mortality and Identity in English Renaissance Tragedy* (Oxford: Clarendon Press, 1997).

Orlin, Lena Cowen, 'Things with Little Social Life: Henslowe's Properties', in *Staged Properties in Early Modern English Drama*, ed. by Jonathan Gil Harris and Natasha Korda (Cambridge: Cambridge University Press, 2002), pp. 99–128.

Owens, Rebekah, 'Parody and *The Spanish Tragedy*', in *Cahiers Elisabéthains: A Biannual Journal of English Renaissance Studies* 71 (Spring 2007), pp. 27–36.

Phillippy, Patricia, *Women, Death and Literature in Post-Reformation England* (Cambridge: Cambridge University Press, 2002).

Pigman, G.W., III, *Grief and English Renaissance Elegy* (Cambridge: Cambridge University Press, 1985).

Prosseur, Eleanor, *Hamlet and Revenge* (Stanford, CA: Stanford University Press, 1967).

Puttenham, George, *The Arte of English Poesie*, Electronic Text Center, University of Virginia, http://etext.lib.virginia.edu/toc/modeng/public/PutPoes.html, last accessed 30 October 2007.

Rist, Thomas, *Shakespeare's Romances and the Politics of Counter-Reformation*, Renaissance Studies 3 (Queenston; Lewiston; Lampeter: Edwin Mellen, 1999).

——, 'Religion, Politics, Revenge: The Dead in Renaissance Drama', in *Early Modern Literary Studies* 9/1 (May 2003), at http://www.shu.ac.uk/emls/09-1/ristdead.html, last accessed 30 October 2007.

——, 'Memorial Revenge at the Reformations(s): Kyd's *The Spanish Tragedy*', in *Cahiers Elisabéthains: A Biannual Journal of English Renaissance Studies* 71 (Spring 2007), pp. 15–25.

——, 'Shakespeare Now and Then: Communities, Religion, Reception', in *Religion and Writing in England, 1558–1689: Studies in Community-Making and Cultural Memory*, ed. by Roger Sell and Anthony Johnson (Aldershot and Burlington, VT: Ashgate, 2008).

Rosalind, Ann, and Peter Stallybrass, *Renaissance Clothing and the Materiality of Memory* (Cambridge: Cambridge University Press, 2000).

Rouse, W.H.D (ed), *Lucretius: De Rerum Natura*, trans. by W.H.D. Rouse, rev. by Martin Ferguson Smith (Cambridge, MA: Harvard University Press; London: William Heinemann, 1975).

Rowell, Geoffrey, *The Liturgy of Christian Burial: An Introductory Survey of the Historical Development of Christian Burial Rites*, Alcuin Club Collections 59 (London: William Clowes & Sons, 1977).

Sanbridge, William Lee, Jr (ed.), *Massinger, Thomas: The Roman Actor*, Princeton Studies in English (Princeton, NJ: Princeton University Press, 1929).

Schiff, Gert, 'James Ensor: Skeletons in the Studio', in *Annual Bulletin* 4 (1980–1981), pp. 1–4.

Schwyzer, Philip, 'The Beauties of the Land: Bale's Books, Aske's Abbeys, and the Aesthetics of Nationhood', in *Renaissance Quarterly* 57 (Spring 2004), pp. 99–125.

——, *Literature, Nationalism and Memory in Early Modern England and Wales* (Cambridge: Cambridge University Press, 2004).

Scodel, Joshua, *The English Poetic Epitaph: Commemoration and Conflict from Jonson to Wordsworth* (Ithaca, NY, and London: Cornell University Press, 1991).

Shell, Alison, *Catholicism, Controversy and the English Literary Imagination, 1558–1660* (Cambridge: Cambridge University Press, 1999).

Sidney, Sir Philip, 'The Defense of Poesy', in *Renaissance Literature: An Anthology*, ed. by Michael Payne and John Hunter (Oxford: Blackwell, 2003), pp. 501–27.

Spicer, Andrew, '"Rest of their Bones": Fear of Death and Reformed Burial Practices', in *Fear in Early-Modern Society*, ed. by William Naphy and Penny Roberts (Manchester and New York: Manchester University Press, 1997), pp. 167–83.

Stymeist, David, 'John Marston', in *Literary Encyclopedia*, http://www.litencyc.com/php/speople.php?rec=true&UID=4987, last accessed 31 October 2007.

Summerville, C. John, *The Secularization of Early Modern England: From Religious Culture to Religious Faith* (New York and Oxford: Oxford University Press, 1992).

Swärdh, Anna, *Rape and Religion in English Renaissance Literature: A Topical Study of Four Texts by Shakespeare, Drayton and Middleton* (Uppsala: University of Uppsala Press, 2003).

Thomas, Keith, *Religion and the Decline of Magic* (London: Weidenfeld and Nicholson, 1973).

Tyacke, Nicholas, *Anti-Calvinists: The Rise of English Arminianism c.1590–1640* (Oxford: Clarendon Press, 1990).

Veevers, Erica, *Images of Love and Religion: Queen Henrietta and Court Entertainments* (Cambridge: Cambridge University Press, 1989).

Vickers, Brian, *Shakespeare, Co-Author: A Historical Study of Five Collaborative Plays* (Oxford and New York: Oxford University Press, 2002).

Voss, Paul, 'The Catholic Presence in English Renaissance Literature', in *The Ben Jonson Journal* 7 (2000), pp. 1–26.

Wells, Stanley, and Gary Taylor (eds), *The Oxford Shakespeare: The Complete Works* (Oxford: Oxford University Press, 1988).

Wickham, Glynn, *Early English Stages, 1300–1660*, vol. 2.1 (Routledge & Kegan Paul, 1963).

Wiggins, Martin, 'As I sat leaning on a grave / Checkered with cross-sticks', in *Notes & Queries* 240 (1995), pp. 369–70.

——, 'Cover her face: Mine eyes dazzle. She died young', in *Notes & Queries* 240 (1995), p. 372.

Wilson, Richard, *Secret Shakespeare: Studies in Theatre, Religion and Resistance* (Manchester and New York: Manchester University Press, 2004).

Woodward, Jennifer, *The Theatre of Death: The Ritual Management of Royal Funerals in Renaissance England, 1570–1625* (Woodbridge: The Boydell Press, 1997).

Yates, Frances, *The Art of Memory* (Harmondsworth: Penguin, 1966).

Yearling, E.M. (ed.), *James Shirley: The Cardinal*, Revels Editions (Manchester: Manchester University Press, 1986).

Young, R.V., 'Shakespeare's History Play and the Erasmian Catholic Prince', in *The Ben Jonson Journal* 7 (2000), pp. 89–114.

Zimmerman, Susan, *The Early Modern Corpse and Shakespeare's Theatre* (Edinburgh: Edinburgh University Press, 2005).

Index

Aaron (Shakespeare) 44, 45, 46, 47, 48, 53, 54, 55, 56
Abbot, Robert 8
Abrams, M. H. 107, 149
Achilles 31, 62
Acts and Monuments 20, 21
Admonition to the Parliament, 6, 22
Aeschylus 11, 30, 153
aesthetic 15, 18, 19, 20, 25, 40, 43, 44, 141, 153, 156
aides-mémoires 5, 11, 79
Alarbus (Shakespeare) 48, 55, 60, 88
All Saints, Bristol 4
altar 3, 5, 11, 15, 79, 85, 108, 116, 134, 150
Andrea (Kyd) 29, 30, 31, 32, 33, 34, 35, 36, 37, 40, 41, 43, 151
Andrugio, Ghost of (Marston) 81, 82, 83, 86, 87, 92
Antonio (Marston) 81, 82, 83, 84, 85, 86, 87, 88, 89, 90, 91, 92, 93, 95
Antonio's Revenge 1, 12, 26, 74, 75–95, 97, 116, 151
Antonio (Webster) 135, 137, 138, 139, 141, 142, 143
Ardolino, Frank 29, 30, 149
Aristotelian 12, 20
Armada, Spanish 2, 27, 28
Arte of Rhetorique 22, 23
Art of English Poesie, The 12, 25, 155
Asquith, Claire 2, 28, 45, 46, 149
atheist 22, 26, 97, 107, 112, 118, 119, 120, 121, 131, 137
Atheist's Tragedy, The vii, 26, 97, 107–121, 137, 155
Aubrey, John 6, 8, 149

Babington, Bishop Gervase 20
Babylon, 1, 2, 26, 28, 29, 38, 40, 41, 84, 105, 121, 149, 153
Baker, Thomas 4
Bancroft, Bishop Richard 75, 77, 78,
Barber, C. L. 35, 37, 149
Barrow, Henry 7
Bassianus (Shakespeare) 51, 52, 54

Bate, Jonathan 46, 47, 53, 149
Battenhouse, Roy 14, 149
Bazardo (*The Spanish Tragedy*) 43, 44, 64
Beauregard, David 94, 149
bede-role 4, 84, 93
Belforest (Tourneur) 111, 112
Bel-Imperia (Kyd) 34, 35, 41
Bell, Thomas 6
Bevington, David 33 142, 149, 154
Bible, 3, 24, 35, 41
Blackfriars, The 11, 76, 77, 81
blood 3, 25, 36, 39, 40, 42, 44, 51, 52, 53, 59, 62, 68, 70, 74, 81, 86, 88, 89, 91, 92, 102, 106, 108, 113, 115, 118, 133, 135, 138, 141, 146, 152
body 4, 7, 9, 20, 33, 34, 36, 37, 39, 40, 43, 51, 52, 58, 59, 60, 61, 62, 68, 74, 81, 88, 99, 110, 112, 113, 117, 118, 119, 122, 131, 132, 133, 140, 144
bone 9, 10, 48, 49, 53, 70, 87, 99, 101, 102, 103, 104, 118, 123, 135, 142, 156
Borachio (Tourneur) 109, 110, 114, 118
Bosola (Webster) 136, 138, 139, 140, 141, 143
Bowers, Fredson 146, 147, 149
Boyd, Zacharie 25
Brachiano (Webster) 121, 122, 123, 126, 127, 128, 130
Braden, Gordon 19, 61, 149
Bradford, John 19
Broude, Ronald 1, 2, 19, 26, 27, 28, 29, 30, 38, 41, 45, 93, 145, 149
Browne, Thomas 8, 9, 21, 150
Buccola, Regina, 137, 150
Bucer, Martin 23
Burgess, Clive 3, 4, 5, 150

Calvin (Calvinism) 3, 5, 20, 21, 25, 89, 131, 139, 156
candle 79, 85
Cardinal, The 146, 147, 157
Cardinal (Webster) 134, 135, 136, 137, 138, 143, 144
Carlisle, Bishop of 8, 15, 17

Cartwright, Thomas 21, 22
Castile, Duke of (Kyd) 39, 40, 41, 152
Catholic (Roman) 1, 2, 4, 5, 6, 8, 9, 11, 13, 14, 15, 18, 19, 20, 21, 23, 26, 27, 28, 29, 30, 31, 35, 36, 37, 38, 41, 44, 45, 46, 48, 53, 60, 72, 73, 78, 79, 80, 84, 85, 88, 89, 90, 92, 93, 101, 103, 105, 108, 110, 111, 112, 115, 120, 122, 124, 126, 127, 128, 131, 132, 133, 134, 136, 137, 138, 139, 140, 142, 144, 145, 147, 149, 151, 152, 154, 156, 157
Chettle, Henry 146
Christian (Christianity) 3, 4, 5, 7, 14, 15, 16, 18, 20, 22, 23, 24, 25, 31, 32, 33, 40, 41, 45, 49, 52, 59, 60, 66, 68, 71, 94, 95, 98, 114, 115, 118, 123, 131, 133, 153, 156
church 1, 3, 4, 5, 6, 7, 11, 12, 14, 15, 16, 17, 20, 21, 23, 26, 31, 60, 75, 76, 77, 78, 79, 80, 84, 86, 93, 94, 95, 101, 114, 118, 120, 121, 122, 123, 124, 126, 131, 133, 134, 139, 142, 145
City Magistrates 77
Claire, Janet 14, 150
Claudius (Shakespeare) 60, 61, 63, 65, 67, 68, 70
Cole, James 25
Collinson, Patrick 8, 16, 150
comedy 9, 39, 67, 110
Commendatio Animae 127, 128
Cook, G.H. 79, 94, 95, 150
Cooper, W.R. 24, 150
Corinthians (Letter to) 3, 24
corpse 7, 8, 10, 13, 15, 16, 17, 31, 35, 36, 39, 51, 52, 54, 57, 63, 64, 71, 81, 83, 91, 99, 103, 104, 108, 112, 113, 118, 121, 125, 129, 130, 131, 136, 140, 157
Cox, John 14, 138, 150
Crawley, Robert 16
Cressy, David 4, 5, 6, 7, 8, 16, 19, 20, 25, 56, 150
Cripplegate 16
cross 8, 77, 85, 108, 132
Crossman, Robert 4

D'Amville (Tourneur) 109, 110, 111, 112, 114, 115, 116, 117, 118, 119, 120, 121
D'Avenant, William 146

Defense of Poesy, The 9, 25, 156
Delio (Webster) 142, 143, 144
devil 102, 114, 117, 121, 126, 127, 128, 138, 150
Devlin, Christopher 14, 150
D'Ewes, Simmonds 21
Diana 55, 108
Diehl, Huston 6, 13, 21, 40, 150
Dillon, Janette, 14, 15, 29, 37, 38, 40, 150
Directory for the Public Worship of God, The 15, 16, 17, 20, 26, 69, 107
dirge 6, 7, 37, 91, 95
Dolentis, O 110, 112
Döring, Tobias 19, 150
Douglas, Audrey 77, 150
Drabble, Margaret 110, 150
Drue, Thomas 146
Duchess of Malfi, The vii, 26, 97, 121–34, 150, 153, 154
Duchess (Webster) 134, 135, 136, 137, 138, 139, 140, 141, 142, 143
Duffy, Eamon 4, 5, 15, 85, 150
Duke (Middleton) 99, 100, 101, 102, 103, 105, 106
Dutton, Richard 14, 151

Earles, Bishop 78, 80
Echo (Webster) 142, 143
Edward VI (Edwardine) 4, 11, 21, 79, 85
Eliot, T. S. 62, 103, 130, 151
Elizabeth I (Elizabethan) 1, 2, 4, 5, 6, 7, 11, 14, 15, 16, 17, 21, 22, 27, 28, 29, 30, 35, 37, 44, 45, 55, 68, 79, 80, 85, 87, 94, 98, 107, 146, 149, 150, 151, 153, 154, 155
  accession of 6, 22
empty 61, 62, 72, 73, 98, 104, 138
Engel, William E. 5, 151
epitaph 8, 12, 85, 115, 125, 147, 156
Erasmus 23, 24
Erne, Lukas 30, 34, 41, 44, 47, 60, 151
Eucharist 3, 4, 44, 53, 60, 97, 116, 131, 132
excess 20, 21, 23, 24, 25, 42, 61, 65, 67, 68, 72, 75, 84, 95, 84, 95, 100, 101, 102, 111, 132, 141

feeling 11, 19, 31, 42, 56, 58, 59, 91, 111, 112, 130
Felton, John 80
Ferdinand (Webster) 134, 135, 136, 137, 138, 139, 140, 141, 143

Finnis, John and Patrick Martin 9, 151
Flamineo (Webster) 121, 122, 123, 126,
    129, 130, 131, 132, 133, 134
Fletcher, Beaumont and 146
Ford, John 12, 146, 147, 152
Fortinbras (Shakespeare) 74
Foxe, John 20, 21
Francisco (Webster) 121, 122,
    124, 125, 126, 129
Freud, Sigmund (Freudian) 18, 22, 61, 151
Frye, Roland Mushat 14, 151
funeral 4, 6, 7, 9, 10, 11, 12, 13, 15, 16,
    17, 19, 20, 22, 23, 30, 31, 32, 33,
    34, 36, 38, 39, 40, 45, 48, 49, 50,
    53, 54, 55, 56, 57, 62, 63, 68, 70,
    71, 73, 74, 82, 83, 86, 91, 92, 95,
    99, 100, 102, 106, 108, 110, 111,
    114, 116, 121, 123, 124, 125, 126,
    128, 130, 135, 144, 145, 146,
    147, 149, 151, 154, 155, 157

Gair, W. Reaveley 75, 76, 94, 151
Galloway, David 5, 151
Gardiner, Samuel 20
Gassner, John and William Green 37, 151
Gertrude (Shakespeare) 61,
    62, 63, 67, 68, 70
Geyl, Pieter 108, 151
ghost 14, 30, 31, 32, 34, 37, 41, 43, 60,
    67, 82, 86, 87, 89, 92, 102, 104,
    105, 107, 112, 113, 117, 118, 119,
    120, 125, 126, 130, 149, 151, 153
Gibbons, Brian 134, 137, 141, 144, 151
Giovanni (Webster) 124, 125, 134
Gittings, Clare 8, 15, 16, 17, 33,
    35, 115, 151, 153, 154
Globe, The 81
Goff, Thomas 146
Goodland, Katharine 19, 152
Gordon, Andrew 79, 152
Goth 44, 45, 46, 53, 55, 59, 149, 153, 154
Great Britans Mourning Garment 20, 149
Greenblatt, Stephen 7, 9, 11, 13, 14,
    33, 45, 60, 98, 115, 152
Grindal, Edmund 17
Guild, William, 6
Gurr, Andrew 10, 152,

Hadfield, Andrew 36, 152
Haigh, Christopher 1, 152
Hall, Edith 10, 145, 152

Hamlet (tragedy of) vii, 1, 10, 11, 13,
    14, 18, 25, 37, 31, 33, 38, 60–74,
    75, 76, 97, 98, 199, 111, 115,
    149, 150, 151, 152, 153, 155
Hamlet (Shakespeare) 10, 18, 60, 61
    62, 63, 64, 65, 66, 67, 68,
    69, 70, 71, 72, 73, 74
Hamlin, Hannibal 41, 152
Hammersmith, James P. 41, 152
Hammond, Martin 62, 152
handkerchief 34, 35, 36, 39, 40, 82, 162
Harris, Duncan 56, 152
Harrison, Robert Pogue 56, 152
Harvey, Robert 12, 147
Heaven 3, 5, 20, 22, 28, 33, 58, 61, 62,
    64, 66, 70, 73, 81, 82, 84, 87, 89,
    90, 91, 106, 107, 110, 111, 119,
    121, 127, 133, 137, 141, 142
Hector 31, 62
Hecuba 63, 64, 65, 67
Heinemann, Margot 145, 152
Hell 3, 5, 29, 31, 32, 33, 33, 52, 53, 89,
    98, 102, 103, 128, 132, 137, 139
1 Henry VI (Shakespeare) 9
Henry, Prince (Stuart) 20, 149
Henslowe, Philip 10, 155
Hieronimo (Kyd) 11, 27, 28, 29, 30, 31,
    35, 36, 37, 38, 39, 40, 41, 42,
    43, 44, 50, 64, 100, 125, 149
Hill, Eugene D. 27, 28, 29, 30, 39, 152
Hippolito (Middleton) 99, 100
Hodgkins, Christopher 5, 152
Homilies, Second Tome of 16, 17, 85
Hopkins, Lisa 137, 147, 150, 152
Horatio (Kyd) 30, 32, 34, 35, 36,
    37, 39, 40, 42, 43
Horatio (Shakespeare) 62, 63, 69, 71, 73
Horrox, Rosemary 33, 153
Houlbrooke, Ralph 18, 21, 153
Howe, John 76
Hurt, James R. 128, 153

idolatry 8, 12, 17, 21, 85, 147
*Institutes of the Christian Religion
    (Institutes)* 20, 21
irony 63, 90, 91, 92, 101, 107, 109, 110,
    114, 115, 116, 117, 118, 119, 120,
    126, 131, 132, 134, 141, 155
Isabella (Kyd) 28, 29, 36, 38, 39,
    42, 43, 44, 57, 71
Isabella (Webster) 121, 123, 124, 125, 126

Italy (Italian) 14, 81, 85, 86, 87, 94, 98, 101, 126, 134, 137, 142

Jackson, Macdonald P. 98, 153
James I (Jacobean) 2, 5, 12, 14, 21, 95, 127, 132, 150, 154
  accession of 2
Jenkins, Harold 18, 66, 67, 70, 153
Jensen, Ejner J. 34, 153
Johnson, S.F. 1, 38, 153
Jongh, Nicholas de 122, 150
Joseph, Miriam 14, 15, 153
Julio (Marston) 88, 89
Junior (Middleton) 99, 102, 104, 105

Kehler, Dorothea 44, 154
Kerrigan, John 11, 12, 30, 31, 33, 52, 153
Kilroy, Gerard 3, 13, 153
King of Spain (Kyd) 1, 39, 40
Klause, John 44, 45, 46, 153
Kliger, Samuel 45, 46, 153
Kyd, Thomas 1, 27, 28, 29, 30, 31, 32, 34, 35, 38, 39, 43, 44, 74, 75, 149, 151, 153, 155

Laertes (Shakespeare) 70, 71, 72, 73
Lake, Peter 2, 154
Last Battell of the Soul in Death, The 25
Latimer, Hugh 22, 23
Latin, 3, 14, 15, 23, 29, 37, 40, 54, 55, 76, 79, 82, 87, 110, 127, 133, 153
Lavinia (Shakespeare) 44, 49, 50, 51, 52, 53, 55, 56, 57, 58, 60
LeGoff, Jacques 32, 154
Lesko, Diane 108, 154
Libation Bearers, The 11, 31
liberties 77
Llewellyn, Nigel 20, 154
Lomax, Marion 34, 154
Loretto 136, 137
Loughrey, Bryan and Neil Taylor 98, 100, 154
Lucius (Shakespeare) 45, 46, 47, 48, 49, 50, 53, 54, 55, 56, 57, 58, 59, 60, 150
Luckyja, Christina 121, 127, 133, 154
Lucretius 107, 108, 156
Luke (Gospel of) 3
Luther (Lutheran) 3, 4

McAlindon, Tom 13, 154
MacDonald, Alan R. 132, 154
McLeod, Susan 127, 128, 154
Maltby, Judith 7, 154
Marcello (Webster) 121, 128, 129, 130, 131
Marshall, Peter 4, 5, 6, 19, 31, 32, 45, 87, 94, 150, 154
Marston, John 75, 76, 82, 89, 90, 92, 94, 95, 151, 156
martyr 9, 19, 44, 53, 56, 146, 147, 151, 153
Mary Tudor 4, 14, 15, 19, 79
Mary (Virgin) 127, 137, 150
Massinger, Thomas 12, 146, 147, 156
Matthews, R. and W.M. Atkins 78, 79, 154
Maus, Katharine Eisaman 28, 41, 56, 101, 142, 154
Mavericke, Radford 22, 23
Mayer, Jean-Christophe 13, 155
May, Thomas 12, 147
Meane in Mourning, The 19
Medici family 121
melodrama vii, 25, 27, 42, 62, 65, 73, 74, 97, 106, 116
memory (memorial, remembrance) vii, 2, 3, 4, 5, 6, 7, 9, 10, 11, 12, 13, 14, 15, 16, 17, 18, 19, 20, 21, 22, 23, 24, 25, 26, 27, 30, 31, 32, 33, 34, 35, 36, 37, 38, 39, 40, 41, 42, 43, 44, 47, 48, 49, 50, 51, 52, 53, 54, 55, 57, 58, 59, 60, 61, 62, 63, 64, 65, 66, 67, 68, 69, 70, 71, 72, 73, 74, 75, 76, 77, 78, 79, 80, 81, 82, 83, 84, 85, 86, 87, 89, 90, 91, 92, 93, 94, 95, 97, 98, 99, 100, 101, 102, 103, 104, 105, 106, 107, 109, 110, 111, 112, 113, 114, 116, 117, 118, 119, 120, 121, 122, 123, 124, 125, 126, 127, 128, 129, 130, 131, 133, 134, 135, 136, 137, 138, 139, 140, 141, 143, 144, 145, 146, 147, 150, 151, 153, 155, 156, 157
Merriam, Thomas 46, 154
Microcosmographie 78
Middleton, Thomas 75, 76, 82, 89, 90, 92, 94, 95, 151, 156
Midsummer Night's Dream, A 9, 10
Milward, Peter 154
mind 4, 12
moderate 5, 20, 21, 25, 73, 139
monastery 21, 44, 94, 95, 142, 151
Montferrers (Tourneur) 109, 110, 112, 113, 114, 115, 116, 117, 118, 120
Monticelso (Webster) 124

monument, 8, 20, 21, 36, 51, 52, 74, 76, 77, 78, 79, 80, 86, 87, 88, 94, 95, 98, 101, 103, 106, 115, 116, 118, 121, 125, 130, 138, 139, 140, 154
Morebath 4, 5, 11, 85, 151
Morgan, Philip 35, 154
Morris, Brian and Roma Gill 107, 109, 155
Mourning and Melancholia 18
Mousetrap, The 66, 67, 68
Muir, Edward 4, 41, 155
Mullaney, Stephen 98, 155
Mulryne, J.R. 27, 28, 29, 30, 36, 38, 39, 155

Nashe, Thomas 9, 10, 12
Neill, Michael 9, 18, 66, 68, 153, 155
Niobe 62, 67
Northern Rebellion 11
Nowell, Alexander 80

Of Death A True Description 25
Ophelia (Shakespeare) 38, 70, 71, 72
Order for the Burial of the Dead, The 15
Orlin, Lena Cowen 10, 155
Ostend, Seige of 2, 108, 109, 110, 113, 114, 115, 116
outrage vii, 25, 27, 29, 42, 43, 75, 125
Owens, Rebekah 42, 43, 155

pagan 18, 23, 31, 32, 66, 95
Pandulpho (Marston) 75, 82, 83, 84, 89, 90, 91, 92, 93, 94, 95
papist 2, 22, 27, 78, 93, 154
Parker, Archbishop Matthew 21, 23
parody vii, 11, 42, 44, 54, 90, 97, 104, 109, 114, 118, 120, 128, 129, 155
Paul's Cross 77
Paul IV, Pope 121
Paul's Theatre and Cathedral vii, 12, 26, 74, 75, 76, 77, 78, 79, 80, 81, 83, 85, 86, 87, 89, 91, 92, 93, 94, 95, 97, 116, 150, 151, 154
Pedringano (Kyd) 33
Percy, William 76
Phillippy, Patricia 22, 23, 132, 155
Phoebe 55
Phoenix and the Turtle, The 9
Piero (Marston) 75, 81, 82, 83, 84, 85, 88, 89, 90, 92, 93, 94, 95
Pigman, G. W. III 21, 22, 23, 24, 25, 98, 155
Pius V, Pope 80
Player (Shakespeare) 63, 64, 65, 66, 67, 68

Playfere, Thomas 19
politic 1, 2, 3, 5, 11, 12, 13, 14, 15, 23, 29, 36, 38, 40, 42, 44, 47, 65, 68, 79, 83, 89, 117, 147, 152, 153, 155
Polos 10, 11
popery 6, 7, 8, 15, 16, 22, 23, 47, 48, 79, 89, 145, 146
Prayer Book, 7, 14, 15, 16, 80, 154
Priest (Shakespeare) 70, 71, 72
Prosseur, Eleanor 14, 155
Protestant 1, 2, 3, 4, 5, 6, 8, 13, 14, 15, 16, 17, 18, 19, 20, 21, 24, 26, 28, 29, 40, 41, 45, 46, 73, 75, 79, 85, 93, 94, 95, 98, 108, 109, 115, 132, 142, 145, 146, 150, 154
Purgatory 4, 5, 6, 8, 13, 14, 30, 31, 32, 33, 60, 87, 93, 111, 115, 131, 132, 137, 138, 152, 152, 154
Puttenham, George 6, 12, 13, 25, 42, 43, 155
Pyrrhus 64

relic 11, 35, 71, 80, 85, 101, 134, 136, 139, 146, 147
religion 1, 2, 3, 4, 5, 6, 8, 11, 13, 14, 15, 16, 17, 18, 19, 21, 23, 24, 25, 26, 27, 35, 41, 44, 45, 46, 48, 52, 60, 66, 68, 76, 77, 79, 85, 90, 94, 98, 107, 108, 109, 114, 115, 118, 126, 131, 132, 134, 137, 145, 150, .152, 153, 154, 155, 156, 157
Repertories of the Court of Council 78
requiem 4, 9, 10, 37, 53, 72, 76, 94
Rerum Natura, De 107, 108, 120, 156
Revenger's Tragedy, The vii, 10, 26, 97–106, 153, 155
Richard III 10
rigour 21, 22, 23, 25, 26, 36, 40, 42
Rist, Thomas 13, 14, 27, 65, 155
rite (ritual) 4, 7, 9, 13, 15, 16, 17, 19, 20, 21, 22, 23, 25, 26, 30, 31, 32, 33, 35, 36 37, 38, 39, 40, 41, 47, 48, 49, 51, 52, 53, 55, 56, 59, 61, 63, 70, 71, 72, 73, 74, 75, 76, 77, 81, 82, 86, 88, 89, 92, 98, 107, 108, 112, 114, 121, 123, 124, 125, 127, 128, 129, 130, 131, 133, 134, 137, 140, 145, 146, 147, 150, 153, 155, 156, 157
Roman 3, 10, 12, 13, 23, 30, 41, 45, 46, 47, 48, 49, 50, 53, 54, 55, 56, 59, 60, 73, 147, 149, 152, 156
Roman Actor, The 12, 147, 156

rood 67, 68, 79, 85
Rosalind, Ann and Peter Stalybrass 82, 155
Rose, The 81
Rouse, W. H. D. 107, 156
Rowell, Geoffrey 15, 16, 20, 156
ruin 44, 51, 80, 94, 95, 118, 137, 140, 141, 142, 143, 146, 151

Sanbridge, William Lee 12, 147, 156
San Sebastian (church of) 3
Saturninus (Shakespeare) 47, 49, 55, 56, 57
Schiff, Gert, 108, 156
Schwyzer, Philip 10, 141, 156
Scodel, Joshua 12, 17, 85, 156
Scotland 132
Seneca 18, 29, 30, 61, 87, 149, 152
Shakespeare, William 1, 2, 9, 10, 12, 13, 14, 18, 27, 29, 34, 41, 44, 45, 46, 47, 52, 56, 57, 60, 62, 65, 66, 73, 74, 75, 78, 94, 98, 100, 142, 145, 149, 150, 151, 152, 153, 154, 155, 156, 157
Shell, Alison 1, 2, 20, 28, 121, 124, 145, 156
Shirley, James 146, 147, 157
Sidney, Sir Philip 9, 25, 42, 43, 156
skull, 10, 11, 69, 80, 87, 88, 99, 100, 101, 102, 103, 104, 107, 119, 120, 146
Snuff, Languebeau (Tourneur) 107, 108, 111, 112, 117, 118, 119, 120, 121
Soliman and Perseda 27, 28, 38, 39, 40
Soquette (Tourneur) 118
Southwell, Robert 35, 36, 45
Spain 1, 27, 28, 29, 30, 33, 39, 40, 43, 44, 71, 108
Spanish Tragedy, The vii, ix, 1, 16, 25, 27–44, 50, 55, 56, 57, 59, 62, 71, 74, 75, 88, 97, 125, 146, 149, 150, 152, 153, 155
stage-property 10, 104, 95, 155
St Mark's Church 75, 86, 89
Stow, John 8, 9, 16, 79, 150
Stymeist, David 75, 156
Summerville, C. John 63, 156
superstition 7, 8, 15, 16, 18, 20, 22, 23, 25, 37, 48, 79, 82, 85, 90, 107, 108, 109, 114, 118, 129, 130, 137
Survey of London 8
Survey of Popery, The 6
Swärdh, Anna 44, 45, 46, 52, 60, 156

tabula memoriae 4
Talbot (Shakespeare) 9, 10

Tamora (Shakespeare) 45, 48, 51, 52, 53, 54, 55, 56, 57, 122
tears 9, 10, 20, 29, 31, 34, 35, 36, 42, 45, 51, 52, 57, 58, 59, 62, 64, 65, 67, 72, 82, 83, 84, 86, 95, 105, 108, 109, 110, 112, 115, 116, 121, 123, 124, 126, 127, 129, 132, 140, 141
Theatre, The 81
theatricality 5, 13, 68, 76, 93, 145
Theseus, Duke (Shakespeare) 9
Thomas, Keith 23, 156
Titus Andronicus vii, 1, 25, 27, 44–60, 73, 75, 88, 107, 116, 122, 149, 150, 151, 153, 154
Titus (Shakespeare) 44, 45, 47, 48, 49, 50, 51, 53, 55, 56, 57, 58, 59
tomb 8, 9, 10, 11, 12, 31, 36, 39, 40, 48, 49, 52, 54, 55, 56, 76, 77, 79, 80, 84, 85, 86, 87, 88, 93, 99, 101, 102, 103, 106, 116, 117, 123, 126, 130, 135, 138, 152
Tourneur, Cyril 107, 108, 155
Travers, Walter 16
Tyacke, Nicholas 3, 89, 156
Tyndale, William 24, 25, 150

Veevers, Erica 11, 156
Verney, Sir Ralph 21
vestiary controversy, 16
Via Media 20, 25, 75, 89
Viceroy (Kyd) 33, 34, 39, 40
Vickers, Brian 46, 156
View of Popish Abuses 6, 7, 115
Vindice (Middleton) 10, 98, 99, 100, 101, 102, 103, 104, 105, 106
Virgil 29, 30, 31, 32, 33, 40, 152
Vittoria (Webster) 121, 122, 123, 124, 126, 128, 131, 132, 133
Voss, Paul 2, 156

Webster, John 103, 121, 122, 127, 128, 134, 137, 139, 146, 147, 150, 151, 153, 154
weeping 20, 23, 62, 83, 92, 109, 110
Wells, Stanley and Gary Taylor 60, 156
White Devil, The vii, 26, 97, 121–34, 150, 153, 154
Whitefriars, The 11, 81
Whitgift, Archbishop John 21, 22, 75
Wickham, Glynn 11, 157

widow 66, 67, 123, 134, 135, 136, 137, 139, 140
Wiggins, Martin 123, 141, 157
Wilson, Richard 2, 46, 73, 78, 157
Wilson, Thomas 22, 23, 24
Wisdom, Book of 17, 20
Woodward, Jennifer 19, 157
Wyclif, John 24

Yates, Frances 4, 5, 157
Yearling, E. M. 146, 157
Young, R. V. 2, 157

Zanche (Webster) 129, 131
Zimmerman, Susan 6, 13, 26, 157